MERGERS & ACQUISITIONS

SUBSCRIPTION NOTICE

This Wiley product is updated on a periodic basis with supplements to reflect important changes in the subject matter. If you purchased this product directly from John Wiley & Sons, Inc., we have already recorded your subscription for this update service.

If, however, you purchased this product from a bookstore and wish to receive (1) the current update at no additional charge, and (2) future updates and revised or related volumes billed separately with a 30-day examination review, please send your name, company name (if applicable), address, and the title of the product to:

Supplement Department
John Wiley & Sons, Inc.
One Wiley Drive
Somerset, NJ 08875
1-800-225-5945

For customers outside the United States, please contact the Wiley office nearest you:

Professional & Reference Division
John Wiley & Sons Canada, Ltd.
22 Worcester Road
Rexdale, Ontario M9W 1L1
CANADA
(416) 675-3580
1-800-567-4797
FAX (416) 675-6599

Jacaranda Wiley Ltd.
PRT Division
P.O. Box 174
North Ryde, NSW 2113
AUSTRALIA
(02) 805-1100
FAX (02) 805-1597

John Wiley & Sons, Ltd.
Baffins Lane
Chichester
West Sussex, PO19 1UD
UNITED KINGDOM
(44) (243) 779777

John Wiley & Sons (SEA) Pte. Ltd.
37 Jalan Pemimpin
Block B # 05-04
Union Industrial Building
SINGAPORE 2057
(65) 258-1157

MERGERS & ACQUISITIONS

Business Strategies
for Accountants

Joseph M. Morris, CPA
Scientific Software-Intercomp, Inc.

Contributing Authors

Mark A. Blackton, CPA
Thermo Companies

James N. Brendel, CPA
Hein + Associates LLP

James R. Krendl, JD
Krendl Horowitz & Krendl

E. Christopher Lang, JD
Hughes Clikeman and Associates

Robert J. Puls, CPA
Price Waterhouse LLP

Jeffrey D. Rudolph, CPA
Intelligent Electronics, Inc.

John Wiley & Sons, Inc.
New York • Chichester • Brisbane • Toronto • Singapore

Library of Congress Cataloging in Publication Data:
Morris, Joseph M., 1949–
    Mergers & acquisitions: business strategies for accountants / Joseph M. Morris ;
  contributing authors, Mark A. Blackton . . . [et al.].
        p.   cm.
    Includes index.
    ISBN 0-471-57017-6
    1. Consolidation and merger of corporations—Accounting.
  I. Blackton, Mark A.   II. Title.
  HF5686.C7M673   1994
  657'.96—dc20   94-29853

Printed in the United States of America

10 9 8 7 6 5 4

To you, Randi.

And you, Shane.

ABOUT THE AUTHOR

Joseph M. Morris is Vice President-Corporate Controller of Scientific Software-Intercomp, Inc., of Denver, Colorado, a provider of high-technology proprietary software and services to the petroleum and other industries. He was previously an FASB project manager. At the FASB, he was responsible for the project on consolidation policy and procedures, which included analysis study of alternate concepts and practices for accounting for acquisitions and consolidated financial statements. He previously worked on numerous acquisitions from a public accounting perspective as an audit manager with Coopers & Lybrand L.L.P. and from a private industry perspective with Lone Star Industries, Inc. Mr. Morris is the author of several other Wiley books, including *Software Industry Accounting*, which was named by the Association of American Publishers as its Accounting Practice Book of the Year for 1993.

ABOUT THE CONTRIBUTORS

Mark A. Blackton is controller of Thermo Companies of Denver, Colorado, a group of development companies with activities in the independent power, oil and gas, and commercial real estate industries. He was previously a senior tax manager with KPMG Peat Marwick LLP, where he primarily served the natural resources, manufacturing, and real estate industries. His experience includes extensive work in acquisitions and also partnership and corporate taxation.

James N. Brendel is a partner in the Denver-based accounting firm, Hein + Associates LLP. Previously, he was with Coopers & Lybrand L.L.P. Mr. Brendel specializes in SEC reporting, mergers and acquisitions, and consulting on other complex accounting transactions. He also provides litigation support services, including expert witness testimony.

James R. Krendl is a principal in the Denver law firm of Krendl Horowitz & Krendl. He received undergraduate and law degrees from Harvard University and has practiced commercial and corporate law for over 20 years. Mr. Krendl frequently writes and lectures on legal topics with particular emphasis on mergers and acquisitions.

E. Christopher Lang heads up the tax practice at Hughes Clikeman and Associates. Prior to that he was a tax specialist with KPMG Peat Marwick LLP and with the litigation bureau of the Massachusetts Department of Revenue.

Robert J. Puls is a partner in the Corporate Finance Group of Price Waterhouse LLP, where his activities include advising clients on achieving maximum benefits from the structuring of acquisitions, divestitures (including spin-offs and carve outs), and joint ventures. He also is active in managing preacquisition due diligence. Previously, he was a partner in Price Waterhouse's National Accounting Services Group where his activities included formulation of Price Waterhouse positions on accounting issues being addressed by the FASB, Emerging Issues Task Force (EITF), and other standard-setting organizations. Mr. Puls has authored numerous articles that have been published in technical accounting periodicals.

Jeffrey D. Rudolph is director of financial services for Intelligent Electronics, Inc., in Denver, Colorado. Previously, he was with Coopers & Lybrand L.L.P. for 11 years, specializing in the mergers, acquisitions, and financial advisory services, where he participated in numerous acquisitions. Mr. Rudolph has extensive experience in preacquisition reviews, due diligence work, business valuation, business divestitures, acquisition searches, and acquisition structure.

Acknowledgments

This book contains various references to, and brief quotations from, materials contained in pronouncements on accounting and auditing and other published materials, which are acknowledged as follows:

Copyright by Financial Accounting Standards Board
Statements of Financial Accounting Standards
FASB Interpretations
FASB Technical Bulletins
FASB Discussion Memorandums
EITF Abstracts

The references to, and quotations from, the above pronouncements are contained herein with the permission of the Financial Accounting Standards Board. Complete copies of the above are available from the Financial Accounting Standards Board, 401 Merritt 7, Norwalk, CT 06856.

Copyright by American Institute of Certified Public Accountants
Opinions of the Accounting Principles Board
Statements on Auditing Standards and Codification of
Statements on Auditing Standards

The references to, and quotations from, the above pronouncements are contained herein with the permission of the American Institute of Certified Public Accountants. Complete copies of the above are available from the American Institute of Certified Public Accountants, 1211 Avenue of the Americas, New York, NY 10036.

The *Checklist for Purchase of Corporate Assets and Assumption of Liabilities* included in Appendix 1-A is adopted with permission from *Colorado Methods of Practice*, by Cathy S. Krendl and James R. Krendl, copyright by West Publishing Company. Complete copies are available from West Publishing Company, 610 Opperman Drive, P.O. Box 64526, St. Paul, Minnesota.

The *Coopers & Lybrand Comprehensive Preacquisition Review Checklist* included in Appendix 2-A is adopted with permission from *Checking Into an Acquisition Candidate*, copyright by Coopers & Lybrand. Complete copies are available from Coopers & Lybrand, 1301 Avenue of the Americas, New York, NY 10019-6013.

Preface

Mergers and acquisitions is an important and demanding professional area for accountants. In addition to working with complex accounting requirements, accountants often find themselves in the middle of any number of business aspects of mergers and acquisitions. These include acquisition searches, preacquisition reviews and due diligence work, reviews of transaction structure and contracts, monitoring compliance with contract terms, planning for and complying with tax laws and regulations, SEC and regulatory compliance, auditing, postacquisition transition and integration, and so on.

While the central focus of this book is *accounting* for mergers and acquisitions, the authors have extended its scope to provide a resource to assist accountants in performing all their roles in the merger and acquisition environment. The book is intended to be useful to accountants in many roles—chief financial officers, controllers, accounting managers, business consultants, independent accountants, tax professionals, internal auditors, and others. Nonaccountants may also find some of the material in this book informative and useful.

The authors have many years of experience in merger and acquisition work. The professional adventures of the authors have resulted in the accumulation of considerable knowledge, perception, and experience in practical application. To the contributing authors, collaborating with you has been a rewarding professional experience. I would like to express my appreciation for your outstanding contribution. Also, many thanks to the fine publishing professionals at John Wiley & Sons, including Messrs. Jeffrey Brown and Sheck Cho, for their patience, support, and confidence.

JOSEPH M. MORRIS

Denver, Colorado
January 1995

Contents

CHAPTER ONE

Acquisitions—A Business and Legal Overview

James R. Krendl
Krendl, Horowitz & Krendl

1.1 INTRODUCTION

Determining whether to purchase another business, or to merge to form a larger and perhaps quite different company, is one of the most important decisions management is called upon to make. The right acquisition at the right time can be a shortcut to expansion, increased profitability, and a new direction for the business. With a single act, the acquiring company may accomplish growth which would have been impossible or which, at the very least, would otherwise have taken many years of investment and hard work.

However, a bad decision can be fatal, often stretching the acquirer's financial, managerial, and other resources beyond their capacity, causing the entire structure to fail.

An acquisition decision is, therefore, of extreme importance. Even if growth through acquisition or merger is a good idea, choosing the right acquisition candidate and completing the acquisition process are difficult and risky steps. Most successful acquirers evaluate numerous potential acquisition candidates for each transaction they actually consummate.

1.2 WHY COMPANIES BUY OR MERGE

(a) Faster Growth

The most common motive for making an acquisition is to accelerate the growth process and to expand the acquirer's business in a substantial way with one transaction. There are many potential benefits to such rapid growth. The acquirer may quickly increase its market share in an existing line of business. Growth may enable the acquiring company to realize substantial economies of scale, for example, by using the same management team, research and development organization, or sales force to service a much larger organization thus using existing overhead to produce more revenues. Rapid growth through acquisition has many other advantages such as allowing a company to increase its market share and recognition.

(b) Vertical Integration

Another goal in acquiring a new business may be to achieve vertical integration, for example, when a manufacturer acquires a key supplier or a major distributor. Reasons for vertical integration may include achieving a more stable market on the supply side, the marketing side, or both, providing for greater profits through elimination of the middle man. Similarly, through acquisition a manufacturer can assure a stable source of supply or obtain the security of a stable, controllable outlet for its products.

(c) Acquisition of Intangibles and Personnel

Purchasing an operating business is often a way to acquire specific assets, including intangible assets, which might not otherwise be available to the acquiring company. For example, the seller may have technology, a marketing network, contracts, or other resources which would be very difficult for the buyer to duplicate on its own, and which the buyer hopes to use more profitably than the seller. In many cases, these types of intangible assets are really nothing more than a group of individuals, sometimes the same individuals who own the acquired business—people who have knowledge, training, and experience which the acquirer needs. In these cases, the key to the acquisition is the ability to be sure that the target personnel can be acquired and retained. This is often accomplished by the use of employment contracts and noncompetition covenants, perhaps coupled with an earnout based on future profits or other incentives.

(d) Portfolio Investment

A company may want to invest excess cash at a higher rate of return than is available from cash accounts and other existing investments. In effect, the acquirer becomes a holding company with respect to the acquired business. It does not necessarily seek any particular synergism or operational benefit with regard to its existing business. Instead it looks for the prospect of controlling and profiting from a business which it believes will be a good long-term investment, in which case the operating expertise for the acquired company is often acquired with the business.

(e) Change in Industries

Another reason for an acquisition may be to gain entry into a totally new industry or industry segment, usually, but not always, an industry which appears to have some connection with the business of the acquiring company. The buyer may have determined that its own line of business is stagnant or in a decline, and thus chooses to use its resources to expand into an area with more potential. The purchase of an existing business is almost always a faster route to expansion than trying to develop a new operation with the buyer's existing resources, but this is especially true when the new industry is one with which the purchaser is totally unfamiliar.

(f) Marketability of Stock

If the acquiring company is publicly traded, it may wish to acquire a new or different line of business because of the potential beneficial effect on the acquirer's stock price. For example, the acquirer may want to enter a line of business which is seen in the marketplace as being more growth oriented or having a better future than the acquirer's existing business. Enhancement of market value may also exist if an acquiring company purchases an acquisition candidate with strong current and projected earnings. The stock of an established publicly traded corporation is likely to command a better price to earnings ratio than the stock of a smaller company. Therefore, the acquired company's earnings stream is worth more in terms of its effect on stock prices to the acquirer than to the acquired company. In some cases, the acquirer may be able to exchange its own publicly traded stock for the stock of the acquisition candidate, thus spending no cash, but receiving an immediate enhancement to its own earnings which in turn should cause its stock price to rise. Both sides benefit—the acquiring company from the overall improvement in its market value, and the acquired company's shareholders from the receipt of stock, which is likely to increase in value as a result of the acquisition.

1.3 THE ACQUISITION PROCESS

The remaining sections of this chapter discuss the acquisition process. In acquisitions, an efficient process is extremely important. One of the most common problems arising during the course of the acquisition process is that both sides tend to become distracted from other business opportunities. An inordinate amount of time, energy, and money can be spent and opportunity lost as the result of extended and inconclusive evaluation and negotiations. Knowing when to bring the process to an orderly conclusion, either by completing the purchase or by calling off the deal, is essential.

The discussion in the remainder of this chapter is divided into the following sections:

1.4   THE ACQUISITION TEAM

The acquirer needs a team of at least several individuals who will be involved with the purchase from start to finish. Continuity of participation is important. It is a mistake to realize at the last minute that someone is needed from, for example, your engineering or marketing department to evaluate the project, requiring that individual to scramble to catch up with the rest of the acquirer's team and the seller's team. Thus, at the beginning of the acquisition process, the acquirer should put together a team that includes substantially all the individuals needed to determine whether to make an acquisition, how to evaluate a particular acquisition candidate, and how to complete the transaction.

The acquisition team should have a clear leader, preferably someone in the acquiring company who is familiar with the needs of the company and who has enough experience in acquisitions to make sound decisions and to manage the process. Often the choice of a team leader is between a knowledgeable inside person who has little experience in acquisitions and an outsider who has strong acquisition experience. This can be a tough decision, but usually the better choice is to use an inside person who can learn what he needs to know about acquisitions. The more important thing may be for the team leader to know what the acquirer needs, as opposed to being an expert on acquisitions.

Other team members should include an attorney, one or more accountants (perhaps both an internal management accountant and an independent accountant), and at least one person who is highly qualified in the primary business of the company being considered for acquisition, such as an engineer, a marketing expert, or perhaps several individuals from different disciplines. The team also often includes someone who is an expert in financing, perhaps an investment banker, other outside financial expert, or an internal financial manager familiar with raising money. Most acquisitions involve the use of borrowed funds or new equity sources, and the financial expert must, therefore, be prepared to justify the price and the financing arrangements to lenders or investors.

Because of the importance of the acquisition process, the team leader should in many cases be the chief executive officer of the acquiring company. If this is not feasible, then the leader should be someone who has a good working relationship with the chief executive officer and who is able to make decisions on his behalf.

An acquisition team is sometimes only put together after the acquirer has already decided it intends to make an acquisition of a particular company. The better procedure is to organize the group as early as possible to allow the team to participate in the two preliminary, but fundamental, decisions: (a) whether to make an acquisition, and, if so; (b) who to acquire. Assuming, however, that these decisions have already been made, as is frequently the case, then the functions of the acquisition team include involvement in the following:

1. Evaluation of the candidate.

2. Review of regulatory and other legal problems that the acquisition may raise.

3. Financing issues, particularly how to raise enough money to pay for the acquisition. This often means being able to prepare a presentation that will be persuasive to a bank or other lender.

4. Tax aspects of the acquisition, including determination of structure, review of past tax liabilities, income tax effects of the acquisition, and transactional tax matters such as sales taxes.

5. Accounting for the acquisition and review of accounting principles, methods, and policies used by the acquisition candidate.

6. Perhaps most important, transition of operations and integration into the business of the acquirer.

Legal counsel with substantial acquisition experience should be involved in the team at the outset. While legal counsel may not, for scheduling and expense purposes, be involved in every step of the transaction, it is essential that legal counsel participate in the initial review and structuring discussions.

While many acquirers have in-house general counsel and legal staffs, buying a new business is an area in which the acquirer should be certain to be represented by an attorney highly experienced in the nuances of this type of transaction. This often means bringing in new legal counsel in addition to the existing corporate in-house staff or regular outside counsel. Legal matters that must be addressed at an early stage of the transaction include the following:

1. Legal structure, taking into account such matters as minority shareholder rights, tax treatment, and protection against contingent liabilities.

2. Compliance with regulatory and licensing laws.

3. Compliance with securities laws.

4. Review of contractual and other legal commitments of the acquisition candidate.

5. Review of special liability issues, such as environmental claims, affecting the acquisition candidate.

6. Negotiate legal documents, including the acquisition agreement.

The accounting specialists in the acquisition team will be particularly involved in the following areas:

1. Review and evaluate historical and projected earnings and cash flow of the acquisition candidate.

2. Assist in analysis of valuation issues.

3. Prepare loan or other financing proposals.

4. Review accounting systems and plan transition and setting up initial reporting functions for periodic operating results.

5. Evaluate systems and transition from a data processing standpoint.

6. Arrange for liaison for continuing matters requiring coordination with the seller's financial personnel.

7. Provide accounting for the acquisition.

Although not all of the team members need be involved in every step, all team members should be kept advised of all developments. It is often not possible to tell in advance what impact a problem in one area may have on other aspects of the acquisition. Therefore, everyone needs to be kept informed.

The procedures of the acquisition team may vary greatly from one situation to another, depending in part on the amount of experience in acquisitions that both the acquirer and the acquired entity or their owners have. Appendix 1-A to this chapter is a type of checklist a buyer might use to organize the process. Typically, the parties reach a preliminary agreement at a fairly early stage and they may then agree to a set of terms which is embodied in a letter of intent similar to that set forth in Appendix A at the end of this book. The execution of a letter of intent is often a suitable time for issuance of a press release or another announcement of the transaction. If there is no legal need (such as SEC rules) for a public announcement, then the letter of intent may be confidential and publicity may be delayed until closing. There should be both extended due diligence investigation of the acquisition candidate and, perhaps simultaneously, negotiation of the details of the deal, including possibly negotiating a purchase price or modifying a tentative purchase price which was set forth in the letter of intent.

If the process proceeds satisfactorily, the parties will eventually sign a formal acquisition agreement. The execution of the formal agreement sometimes occurs simultaneously with the actual closing, or it may be signed some weeks in advance of the closing. In the latter case, the agreement forms the basis for completing due diligence, submitting the proposed acquisition to shareholders and directors for approval, obtaining regulatory approval, and obtaining financing for the purchase. Legal counsel for both sides will normally handle the negotiations and contract drafting, but many business points are involved in these negotiations that require the attention of the entire team.

1.5 OVERALL ACQUISITION STRATEGY AND CRITERIA

(a) General

Acquisition strategies and procedures vary widely from company to company. For some, an acquisition may be an isolated event. For others, acquisitions are a regular part of their business. Companies in the latter category will undoubtedly have personnel and procedures in place to manage the process. The problems of organizing for an acquisition are more serious for companies that never or only rarely engage in acquisitions. However, even companies which regularly engage in acquisitions may have a false sense of security from doing things because "we always do it this way." The acquisition marketplace is one that is constantly changing, and last year's procedures are not always appropriate for this year's problems.

(b) Acquisition Criteria

At the beginning of this chapter, some of the reasons why a company may be motivated to make an acquisition were discussed. Without repeating that discussion, it is useful to remind the reader that there is no fundamental rule that acquisitions are a good idea for all companies or in all circumstances. Each company must make its own evaluation of the relative advantages and disadvantages of engaging in any acquisition. Assuming, however, that an affirmative decision to proceed with a purchase has been made, then, unless the target company is already identified, the next step is to search for and identify likely acquisition candidates. To accomplish this, the acquirer should start with a set of acquisition criteria. Useful guidelines include the following:

1. Characteristics and size of industry and company.

2. Size of market and expected market growth.

3. Share of market held by the candidate.

4. Barriers to entry by new competition.

5. State of the acquisition candidate's technology and ease with which it could be duplicated by the acquirer or by a competitor.

6. Competitive advantages of the acquisition candidate's product or service.

7. Amount of investment required by the acquirer and the projected return rates.

8. Existence of in-place management, technical personnel, and other key personnel.

9. Ability of the acquirer to acquire and retain the acquisition candidate's business. For example, is there a high degree of personal loyalty among customers that will evaporate once the acquisition candidate's owner is no longer on the scene?

10. Size and price range.

As noted, senior management often makes a decision to try to acquire a particular business before an acquisition team is even put together. Even when such a preliminary decision has been made, however, it is useful for the whole team to reevaluate the entire subject before allowing binding commitments to be made.

1.6   IDENTIFYING AN ACQUISITION CANDIDATE

Acquisition candidates may be identified from a wide variety of sources. Every community has a group of business brokers who solicit and list companies for sale. These brokers often have an inventory of companies that are actively looking for a buyer or that are at least willing to entertain an offer.

Other leads may come from lawyers, accountants, suppliers, sales representatives, or distributors who have contacts with a variety of businesses in a particular industry. The acquirer's own staff is, however, the most likely source of information about an acquisition candidate. Except in those fairly rare cases where the acquirer is looking for a business totally outside its own area of activity, the acquirer itself is likely to be knowledgeable about the companies it may be interested in acquiring, such as competitors, suppliers, distributors, or others who are engaged in a line of business similar to or complementary with that of the acquirer.

Prospective candidates may be contacted through a professional intermediary, such as an investment banker or broker. However, in acquisitions of medium and small businesses, the most effective approach is usually a direct contact: the chief executive officer of the acquirer calls the chief executive officer of the acquisition candidate and asks if his company would consider an offer to merge or be acquired. Many businesses consider it dangerous to advertise that they are looking for an opportunity to sell. This is often perceived as a sign of weakness, a weakness which will be seized upon by competitors who want to imply in the marketplace that the seller is going out of business or is in trouble. Therefore, a blind phone call to a likely candidate can have the surprising result of determining that the company is interested in being acquired but has not publicized that fact.

In identifying acquisition candidates, the acquirer should not, therefore, limit itself to those companies that it thinks are probably for sale. But it never hurts to consider those factors that are likely to make someone consider selling: (a) illiquidity of investment; (b) an older owner who has no logical successor in his present organization; (c) a company that needs to expand and lacks the capital resources to do so; or (d) a company that is suffering through internal problems, such as a dispute among co-owners. Another likely source of an acquisition candidate is a larger company that has a currently unprofitable operation or a division that does not fit into the structure and objectives of the entire operation.

Inevitably, throughout the search process, many contacts, investigations, and discussions take place, but few acquisitions are consummated. There is almost always much seemingly wasted effort in the process, which is one of the unavoidable disadvantages of becoming involved in the acquisition arena. Even if the candidate shows interest in being acquired, reasons for uncompleted acquisitions include: (a) disagreement about price or other basic terms; (b) incompatibility of personnel or procedures; (c) regulatory or other legal problems; and (d) inability to finance the purchase. Most importantly, even when there seems to be a good match on all issues, no acquisition candidate should be purchased until there has been a very thorough investigation, usually referred to as due diligence, by the acquirer. The purpose of due diligence is to find undisclosed problems that may make completing the acquisition undesirable. It is always discouraging when such problems are identified, but it can be catastrophic when the problems are not found, the acquisition is consummated, and then the problems emerge. Thorough due diligence eliminates many acquisition candidates, and the acquirer must realize that the time and expense of due diligence are essential to prevent acquisition disasters.

Due diligence usually occurs in two stages: (a) general review to determine whether the acquisition candidate is worth serious consideration (which is part of the initial evaluation); and (b) thorough verification of preliminary information which normally occurs after a preliminary agreement has been reached.

1.7 EVALUATING AN ACQUISITION CANDIDATE

The evaluation of an acquisition candidate usually starts with a review of the tangible assets and operations of the company. In many ways, this is the simplest step of the evaluation process. An examination of books and records, including earnings history over several years, usually the last five years or so, will tell a prospective buyer much about the operations, problems, and prospects of the business. A physical examination of real property, equipment, and other tangible assets by a knowledgeable purchaser will quickly disclose whether the acquisition candidate has obsolete or inadequate physical facilities or other serious problems.

Another very important step, which is sometimes neglected, is to examine the acquisition candidate's liabilities—not just a review of current liabilities and long-term debts, but an examination of problems that may not necessarily show up on a balance sheet, particularly among smaller companies that may have inadequate financial personnel or systems. For example, internally prepared financial statements often fail to disclose liabilities such as accrued employee benefits, future obligations relating to prepaid services, and product warranty obligations.

The acquirer should also evaluate the unrecorded intangible assets and problems of the business. Although many intangibles are not reflected on a balance sheet, most of them are fairly easy to identify. Personnel and information are two key intangibles. For example: (a) Does the acquisition candidate have unusual capabilities in areas such as engineering and design?; (b) What are its marketing capabilities?; (c) What patents, copyrights, trademarks, and other proprietary intangible property and information does the acquisition candidate have?; and (d) How secure is its customer base?

A review of intangibles frequently brings a buyer back to an identification of certain personnel who are key to the seller's business. These key people must either be acquired or neutralized. It does the acquirer little good to buy the building and equipment of a manufacturing company if the production manager, marketing vice-president, and chief engineer are all going to leave to work for a competitor. Under the best scenario, the buyer should recruit these key people and convince them that their best future lies with the acquirer. Their conversion to the acquirer's business can then be secured with long-term employment agreements, stock options, earnouts or other inducements to keep them committed. If the key personnel do not want to work for the acquirer, if, for example, they wish to retire, then the next best thing is to neutralize them with long-term noncompetition convenants to prevent them from becoming competitors.

Assuming that an acquisition candidate looks like a good potential business in the abstract, the next question is to decide whether it is a good fit with the acquirer. Many characteristics of a purchased business can be changed, but many cannot. For example, if the acquisition candidate has an accounting system or computer software that is incompatible with that of the acquirer, a certain amount of expense and time can solve the problem. Other differences are harder to accommodate. If there is a basic incompatibility in business styles or if the people in the acquired company and the acquiring company simply do not get along with each other, then there may be an irreconcilable difference that will kill the deal. A certain amount of social "getting to know each other" is, therefore, a useful ingredient in deciding whether the transaction should proceed.

A key problem to identify is the entrepreneurial seller who will never be a team player. If an acquisition candidate has a single primary owner and manager, watch out for his or her inability to fit into a larger organization. Most entrepreneurs are the kind of people who enjoy operating independently and making unilateral decisions. Their self-assurance and willingness to take risky actions on their own are often the characteristics that have made them successful. Unfortunately, in some cases they cannot or will not ever learn to consult with and listen to others. Therefore, they are unsuccessful when they are required to operate as subordinates or equals with other managers. If this is the kind of person who owns the acquisition candidate, the buyer may either have to decide that it can operate the business without the seller's future participation or the buyer may have to decide not to purchase the business at all.

1.8 STRUCTURING ACQUISITIONS

(a) General

There are three basic ways to acquire another company: (a) a purchase of assets, usually accompanied by an assumption of liabilities; (b) a stock purchase; or (c) a merger. There are advantages and disadvantages to each of the three structuring approaches.

(b) Assets Purchases

In the context of smaller businesses, the majority of acquisitions are assets purchases. In this sense, the term *purchase* is used broadly. For example, a purchase may involve the payment of cash, promissory notes or other debt instruments, or other consideration, including stock of the acquiring company. An assets acquisition only means that the buyer acquires the assets, not the corporate or other legal entity owned by the seller. Thus, the characterization of the transaction depends on what is being acquired, not what consideration is being given.

There are two principal advantages to an assets acquisition. First, in terms of tax treatment, most acquired companies have a basis in their assets that is lower than the fair market value of the assets, or at least lower than the fair market value of the operating business. If stock is acquired, the purchaser receives a carry over tax basis in the underlying assets (although a basis in the purchased stock equal to the purchase price). This means that for tax depreciation and amortization purposes, the buyer will continue to use the seller's old carry over tax basis in the assets. In effect, the buyer of stock typically spends more than it can deduct either as a current expense or as future depreciation or amortization, thus, substantially increasing the buyer's future tax liabilities.

The second reason why a buyer usually prefers an assets purchase is that the buyer may avoid many potential contingent liabilities of the acquired business. If the acquisition candidate is a party to a lawsuit, for example, the purchase of assets can probably be structured in such a way as to leave the litigation with the seller while delivering the assets to the buyer.

The foregoing analysis has many exceptions. For example, some environmental laws provide that liabilities, including the expense of future hazardous waste cleanups, attach to assets in addition to entities. Therefore, if a buyer acquires a piece of real property that is subject to environmental contamination, the buyer may also acquire the obligation to clean the property up at some point in the future. This is an extremely complex topic on which legal counsel should be consulted.

Other types of liabilities can also follow a purchased asset. For example, the traditional Uniform Commercial Code provisions applicable to what are known as *bulk transfers* provide that a purchaser may be subject to claims by creditors of the seller unless the purchaser has complied with the technical notice provisions contained in the Uniform Bulk Transfers Act. The Bulk Transfers Act has been repealed in some states, but this law still affects many transactions.

An assets purchase also lets the acquirer choose only those assets it wants, leaving others with the seller. This may be particularly useful where the seller is engaged in two or more lines of business, and the buyer does not want to purchase all of them.

A purchase of assets requires an allocation of purchase price to specific assets or classes of assets for tax purposes. There are strict tax rules applicable to this process that are beyond the scope of this chapter. However, the proper identification of types of assets and the determination of fair market values and useful lives of each category are crucial to the income tax effects on the parties. These issues also impact other tax issues, including sales and use taxes and real and personal property taxes.

(c) Stock Purchases

A stock acquisition usually entails the disadvantages of carrying forward a lower basis in assets, the possible inadvertent exposure to corporate liabilities, including undisclosed contingencies, and the need to deal with substantially all the assets and liabilities instead of being able to pick and choose those which the parties wish to transfer. An additional complication of a stock acquisition is that the buyer must deal with all of the shareholders of the selling corporation. If, for example, there is a single shareholder or group of shareholders who refuse to sell their stock, then the buyer must either accept the minority shareholders as future participants in the company or try to *squeeze out* the minority, a process which can be fraught with legal problems.

There are, however, advantages to a stock acquisition. First, it is mechanically easier. Instead of itemizing each and every asset and liability to be transferred and arranging for their assignment and assumption, a single stroke of the pen assigns the corporate stock and with it all the assets and liabilities of the seller's corporation, avoiding many potentially troublesome issues. For example, unless a lease, contract, or other agreement has a specific provision relating to transfers of stock, a stock sale automatically vests in the buyer all the seller's rights and obligations under the agreement. Most contractual agreements require a consent of the parties where there is an assignment of the contract to a new party and, therefore, if the seller transfers assets, it must usually obtain consents from its lessor, suppliers, and other contracting parties before being able to transfer its contractual rights. Similarly, lenders usually have veto power over asset sales unless they are paid off. These problems can, in many cases, be avoided in a stock transaction. Care must be taken, however, to review the acquired company's contractual and other agreements because those which are drafted carefully will often contain a provision that treats a stock transfer as if it were a sale of assets, requiring the consent of the other contracting party.

Another potentially significant advantage of a stock transaction is that it avoids sales and use taxes. In many states, such taxes are imposed on any transfer of assets, although various state statutes provide exemptions for inventory, intangible assets, and sometimes other assets. Nonetheless, the sales tax burden on purchases of furniture and equipment, for example, can be significant.

The most common reason for purchasing stock is because the seller insists on it. As a result of the 1986 Tax Reform Act, a corporate assets sale (unless the seller is an S corporation) usually results in two layers of income tax: (a) first the corporation pays taxes on its gain; and (b) then the corporation distributes cash or other consideration to its shareholders who pay tax again. While some tax planning opportunities exist, a corporate seller with a low basis in its assets and shareholders with a low stock basis will often try to insist on a stock sale, thus reducing the selling shareholders' tax costs.

Some stock transactions take the form of a *tender offer*, which may be either *friendly* or *hostile*. The tender offer is an offer made directly to the shareholders of a corporation as opposed to the management of the company. Some tender offers start with an offer to management and, after this offer is rejected, an appeal is made by the buyer over the heads of management to the shareholders. Hostile tender offers are obviously useful only if a majority of the stock is owned by parties other than the management team. The legal and financial problems associated with tender offers for publicly held corporations are too complex to discuss in detail in this chapter.

(d) Mergers

The term *merger* technically means the absorption of one corporation into another corporation, for example, if a selling corporation merges into a buying corporation. Usually, but not always, the selling corporation's shareholders receive stock in the buying corporation. The term merger is often used more loosely, for example, to include a consolidation which is technically the combination of two or more corporations to form a new corporation. Even more broadly, the term merger is sometimes applied to any tax-free reorganization as defined in § 368 of the Internal Revenue Code, which may include a swap of assets for stock, stock for stock, or the use of a third corporation, often a subsidiary of the acquiring company, to merge with the acquisition candidate.

Mergers can most easily be understood as being structurally similar to stock purchases. All of the corporate attributes of the merged corporation, including contractual rights, other intangibles, and liabilities, whether liquidated or contingent, are transferred into the acquirer (technically, the surviving corporation). In a true merger, this means that the acquirer becomes directly liable for all the liabilities of the acquired corporation, often an undesirable result. In a pure stock purchase, the acquired company can be kept as a separate subsidiary and, while its liabilities continue to exist, they do not become legal claims against the assets or earnings of the acquirer. However, for most purposes a special structure known as a triangular merger, where the acquirer sets up a subsidiary and then merges it with the acquired company, is little different from a stock purchase. Consideration is given to the selling corporation's shareholders, and, as a result, the selling corporation then becomes a partially or wholly owned subsidiary of the acquirer.

The more significant issue is often not whether the transaction is a merger or a stock acquisition, but whether it qualifies for tax-free treatment under § 368 of the Internal Revenue Code. A tax-free reorganization results in little or no tax to the selling shareholders and a carry over basis in the assets of the acquired company in the hands of the acquirer. The most important ingredient to qualify for tax-free qualification is that the acquisition be entirely or at least primarily for stock of the acquirer, so that there is *continuity of interest* by the acquired company's shareholders. Note that not all mergers are tax-free reorganizations. Under most state laws, a merger can be consummated for various combinations of stock, cash, and debt instruments of the acquirer. If the consideration is entirely or primarily nonstock or where the exchange otherwise fails to meet the Internal Revenue Code requirements, the transaction will be taxable even though it is a merger.

(e) Future Relationships

In consummating any type of transaction, a key issue should be the continuing relationship of the parties. In most small acquisitions and mergers, at least some of the selling shareholders and many of the key employees of the acquired business will work for the acquirer after the acquisition. Obviously, each side negotiates for the best possible terms and the least possible risk for itself. However, an acquiring company should bear in mind that it needs to maintain relationships with the acquired company's owners after the acquisition. Employment agreements, consulting agreements, noncompetition covenants, leases, long-term payouts, earnouts, and other legal as well as practical relationships will continue to exist. Thus, a totally adversarial approach to negotiating and structuring is usually an error. It is also a mistake to hide potential problems from the other side, only to have them be discovered after the acquisition with counterproductive results. Usually it is better to recognize the needs of both parties, disclose and deal with problems in a forthright manner, and try to carry out the transaction in a constructive manner which allows the parties room to work together comfortably in the postclosing structure. It is also wise to investigate the other party thoroughly on the assumption that it may not play the game according to the foregoing rules.

1.9   ESTABLISHING PRICE

(a) General

The single most important decision in making an acquisition (or completing a merger) is to set a price. In a classic merger, where the acquired company's shareholders exchange their stock for stock in the acquiring corporation, the negotiation of price is really a two-way discussion: (a) what is the seller's stock worth; and (b) what is the buyer's stock worth? Close on the heels of the question of total price are two ancillary but almost equally important issues: (a) what are the terms of payment (including how deferred payments are to be secured); and (b) what are the after-tax consequences to both parties? Thus, discussing price in the abstract is often misleading and the terms governing when and how the price is to be paid and its tax effects are also of much relevance to both parties.

The following discussion demonstrates several ways buyers and sellers try to determine price.

(b) Discounted Cash Flow

A common method of trying to value a company involves analyzing its cash flow, in effect trying to determine what return on investment the buyer will receive from the projected cash flow of the acquisition candidate. The term EBITDA is often used, meaning *earnings before interest, taxes, depreciation and amortization.* Computerized projections of such numbers are, of course, highly useful, but the parties should remember that the critical element in any projection is to guess how much the company will make next year as opposed to this year or last year. Elaborate computerized sets of numbers showing future cash flow are little more than impressive-looking guesses. Moreover, any projection that eliminates taxes, depreciation, and amortization is essentially a short-term projection. Eventually, the acquisition candidate's business will pay taxes, and it will have to replace depreciated tangible property and amortized intangible property.

(c) Price Earnings Multiples

In the public offering market, multiples of earnings are a fundamental guide to value. There are, of course, problems in trying to use historical earnings to project future earnings. Parties dealing with privately held businesses should also remember that any closely held corporation is likely to be subject to a much lower price-to-earnings ratio than a publicly held corporation because, among other things, the smaller business does not represent the same liquidity as an investment in public stock.

(d) Value of Assets

The underlying value of assets may be at least a floor to value. When purchasing an operating business, the buyer can reasonably assume that, at the very least, it can always liquidate the business and recover the knock down value. If this underlying value is at or close to the purchase price, then the purchase would seem to have very little risk.

(e) Restated Earnings

When buying a closely held business, the acquirer frequently decides that the selling corporation's book earnings have little relationship to its real level of profitability. For example, an owner may pay himself an unusually low salary (perhaps because he or she wants to retain more working capital in the company) or an unusually high salary (frequently because he or she does not want the corporation to pay nondeductible dividends). Fringe benefits and other questionable expenses for the owner's use may also reduce profitability. The parties may find it useful to adjust historical earnings to determine *real* earning levels.

(f) Market Value

If a corporation is publicly traded or has a limited private trading history, an established market value may give some comfort to a buyer. In many cases, however, this procedure is suspect. First, it implies that the market somehow has more knowledge of the business than the buyer, who has completed detailed due diligence and is presumably an expert on what he is investigating. Second, there is a considerable difference between the value of a share of stock in a thinly traded public market and the value applicable to a sale of all the stock of the same company.

(g) Combination Methods of Valuation

There are various other methods of valuing businesses. A knowledgeable purchaser can often make a good estimate of value based on gross revenues or other gross volume performance. A reliable measure of the value of a periodical or other publication, for instance, might be its total paid circulation. Various other generic methods of valuation are also common. A rule of thumb that the author has found helpful is to start with the liquidation value of tangible assets, the type of valuation which a bank would require in a form of an appraisal before lending against the assets. Then add to that number a going concern business value based on an average of about two years of estimated pretax earnings power. The total is often a good estimate of fair market value.

(h) Value to the Buyer

All of the above methods are merely suggestions as to how to approach the valuation question. As a series of confirmations of approximate value they are often very helpful. There are, however, really two questions involved in valuation: (a) what is the seller willing to sell for?; and (b) what is the buyer willing to pay? Sometimes the buyer is surprised to find that the second amount is significantly higher than the first, which it may very well be for a variety of intangible reasons, such as potential synergism or economies of scale available to the buyer.

1.10   FINANCING ACQUISITIONS

(a) General

It makes no sense for an acquirer to buy a company if the purchase price and terms stretch the resources of the acquirer so far that its existing business, as well as the acquired business, is jeopardized. Thus, the decision of how much to pay is often determined by the question of how much can the acquirer afford to pay?

(b) Use of Internal Assets

The easiest way to buy an acquisition candidate is to use the existing resources of the acquirer. If the fortunate acquirer has significant cash reserves or unencumbered assets that it can mortgage to secure future payments, then the acquisition is easy. If the acquisition candidate has stock, preferably publicly traded stock with an established market value, it may be able to trade its own stock for the seller's company or assets. This is even better, leaving the acquirer's cash and assets free for other purposes, although it does dilute the interests of the acquirer's existing shareholders. Acquisitions carried out completely with the internal resources of the acquirer are, however, not the general rule.

(c) Leveraged Transactions

Many acquisitions are leveraged in whole or in part. The hard assets of the acquisition candidate are appraised, the financial statements are recast showing a restructured company with assets at fair market value instead of book value, an EBITDA projection is prepared showing ability to service debt, and the transaction is financed with a bank, insurance company, or other institutional lender. In the *go–go* acquisition days of the 1970s and 1980s, we sometimes saw 100% leveraged transactions, often with management borrowing against the company's assets to buy stock from the outside shareholders. The subsequent collapse of many such leveraged buy outs (LBOs) has made such transactions rare in the current economy. However, the combination of a partially leveraged acquisition with some new capital being invested by the buyer is still the most common way of completing an acquisition.

There are various levels and types of debt financing. The simplest form of financing is borrowing as much as possible of the purchase price, encumbering all of the acquisition candidate's assets, and probably also encumbering all or some of the acquirer's assets with one mortgage. Note that borrowing against the acquisition candidate's assets almost certainly means paying off the candidate's existing debt because the new lender will want a senior encumbrance on all the assets.

After this simple scenario, there are many complex approaches. For example, a single lender might lend against the real property and equipment and other hard assets, and another lender or the same lender, under a separate loan agreement, might provide a revolving line of credit with receivables and inventory pledged as collateral. When arranging for such multilevel financing, it is useful to distinguish between acquisition financing (usually a term loan) and operating capital (usually a revolving line of credit). A line of credit is more or less permanent financing which funds ongoing operations and which should not require any outside collateral or guarantees. Acquisition debt is usually limited to a fixed payoff period and frequently requires additional collateral or guarantees until it is paid off.

Another lender, often referred to as a mezzanine lender, could make a further loan secured by a junior lien on the assets. Mezzanine financing is expensive, because it carries greater risk, which is customarily rewarded by providing stock warrants or other equity kickers to the lender as well as higher interest rates.

(d) Seller Financing

Another feature of many acquisitions is some amount of *carry back* by the seller. In a wholly leveraged transaction, the buyer may mortgage the assets of the acquisition candidate to finance a down payment and then persuade the seller to carryback a note for the balance of the purchase price. The seller's lien rights in such a case would be subordinate to those of the lender. This degree of cooperation from sellers is a little unusual these days. However, if the acquirer invests a significant amount in the acquisition, then it may be able to combine its own investment with the proceeds of a senior loan to make a very substantial down payment. In such cases the seller may be persuaded to carryback a promissory note secured by a junior secutiry interest in the assets which are being sold and probably further collateral-ized by a security interest in some or all of the assets of the acquirer. In these circumstances, projections of future cash flow become critical. Both the lenders and the seller must be convinced that there will be sufficient cash flow to satisfy all of their needs, with enough left to satisfy the ac-quired business's operational requirements.

1.11 TAX ISSUES

(a) General

As discussed above, an essential element in determining the purchase price includes ascertaining the after-tax consequences to both parties. From the seller's point of view, this analysis is fairly straightforward. If the seller is a Subchapter C corporation and if it sells assets and then distributes the sales proceeds to its shareholders, there are two steps to the tax computation. First, the corporation will pay income taxes to the extent that the total consideration received by it exceeds its adjusted tax basis in its assets. Second, the corporation will dissolve, all of the sales proceeds will be distributed to its shareholders, and the shareholders will pay taxes to the extent their total distributions exceed their cost basis in their stock. This two tier imposition of taxes is a severe detriment to most sellers, who often have very little basis in either the corporation's assets or their own stock. Therefore, sellers like to sell stock, not assets.

(b) Buyer's Tax Considerations

Buyers usually prefer to purchase assets because the acquired assets will then have a cost basis for tax purposes equal to their purchase price. In most cases, this increases the tax basis of the assets, therefore giving the buyer higher future tax deductions for depreciation and amortization. The tax analysis for buyers is, however, complicated. Tax treatment of buyers has changed substantially as a result of the Revenue Reconciliation Act of 1993. This Act, as discussed under § (d), Intangibles, below substantially alters the amortization of intangibles for tax purposes, although tax deductions for both tangible and intangible assets remain a primary objective for buyers.

(c) Miscellaneous Taxes

Federal income taxes are not the only tax issue in an acquisition. State and local sales and use taxes may be imposed upon some or all personal property sold. Some states and local governments also tax conveyances of real property. State income taxes may be significant factors for one or both parties. The allocation of purchase price to assets may affect future assessments for purposes of determining real and personal property taxes.

(d) Intangibles

Under prior tax law, there was considerable potential for flexibility in allocating purchase price among intangibles, often resulting in an allocation of significant amounts to intangible assets which could be amortized or otherwise written off over a relatively short period of time. Noncompetition covenants were particularly common in the small business environment, permitting a buyer to write off for tax purposes the amount reasonably allocated to a noncompetition covenant over the term of the covenant, which was usually five years or less.

However, § 13261 of the Revenue Reconciliation Act of 1993 (Internal Revenue Code § 197) has eliminated this flexibility. Under the new provision, the capitalized costs of *§ 197 intangibles* are ratably amortized over a 15 year period beginning with the month the intangibles are acquired. No other depreciation or amortization deductions are permitted with respect to these § 197 intangibles, which are defined to include:

(1) Goodwill.

(2) Going concern value.

(3) Certain items of intangible property relating to work force in place, know-how, customers, suppliers, and similar assets.

(4) Licenses, permits or other rights granted by a government agency.

(5) Covenants not to compete (and similar arrangements) entered into in connection with the acquisition of a trade or business.

(6) Franchises, trademarks, or trade names.

On the positive side, certain of these assets would have been classified as nonamortizable goodwill under the prior tax law and, therefore, could not have been written off for tax purposes. However, under prior law, many of the other items would normally have resulted in deductions over a useful life considerably less than the 15-year term allowed by IRC § 197. Generally speaking, therefore, the effect of the new law is likely to be to reduce the short term tax deductions permitted to a buyer.

See Chapter 8 for more detailed discussion of tax issues.

1.12 FORMALIZING THE DEAL AND DUE DILIGENCE

(a) Letter of Intent

For smaller transactions, particularly if the seller has never been involved in an acquisition, a letter of intent may be desirable. Some acquisition experts choose to bypass the letter of intent stage, arguing that it has no legal validity and that it simply slows down the transaction. A contrary view, however, is that there is great potential for misunderstanding leading to wasted effort and aborted deals unless there is a clear written understanding by the parties at the outset. Therefore, a letter of intent is recommended when dealing with an inexperienced buyer or seller.

An example of the structure and contents of a letter of intent is set forth in Appendix A. This skeleton form would probably be expanded in an actual deal to include terms specific to the particular transaction, such as compensation levels for consulting agreements, principal economic terms for real property leases, and the provision of information by the buyer if the buyer is trading its own stock or other securities as part of the consideration to the seller. The letter of intent usually expressly states that it is not legally binding, although specific provisions, such as the confidentiality clause, may be legally enforceable. Most letters of intent are based on incomplete preliminary information, and they cannot possibly contain all the final terms. The parties should, therefore, recognize that the letter is only an expression of intent and not a contract.

(b) Due Diligence

The term *due diligence* is used to describe a variety of actions that are taken to obtain or verify information about an acquisition candidate. The nature and extent of due diligence depends on many factors, including the size of the acquisition, the estimated potential for undisclosed liabilities or other problems, and the familiarity of the buyer with the seller's business.

To some extent due diligence duplicates or at least overlaps with the process involved in the discussion earlier in § 1.7 *Evaluating an Acquisition Candidate*. However, due diligence requires more investigation and verification than merely evaluating the information that is provided by the acquisition candidate. Due diligence is intended to ensure that the buyer is not deliberately or inadvertently misled by the seller, and the buyer must, therefore, independently investigate and confirm information. For example, due diligence should include such procedures as a review of public records to determine title to assets and the existence of liens or other encumbrances of record, inspection of internal documents such as corporate minutes, review of contract files including leases, loan documents, and other agreements, physical examination of tangible assets, and independent verification of financial information, such as the accuracy of records relating to accounts receivable and accounts payable. The buyer should also expect to perform a physical inventory as well as an audit of other financial information. In many cases, it is also necessary to investigate less obvious matters, such as liabilities for product warranties, actual or potential environmental problems, adequacy and stability of supplier relations, customer loyalty and problems, status of competition, and actual and potential value of technology and other intangibles.

In many larger acquisitions, most or all due diligence procedures are deferred until after a definitive purchase agreement has been signed. A purchase agreement may then establish procedures requiring cooperation on the part of the seller and permitting the buyer access to assets, records, and personnel. The completion of due diligence in this type of situation is often the primary action that occurs between the signing of the purchase agreement and the formal closing. At the other end of the spectrum, in transactions involving a relatively small seller, due diligence procedures sometimes occur prior to signing a contract, and the closing occurs simultaneously with execution of the acquisition agreement. In the latter cases, there is usually no formal written agreement regulating the due diligence procedures. Instead, there is a general understanding or perhaps a provision in a letter of intent that permits the buyer to conduct its investigation and review.

Obviously, the nature and extent of due diligence procedures vary significantly from one acquisition to another. It is, however, a mistake to take this process too lightly. An acquirer should not expect an acquisition contract, no matter how many warranties and indemnifications it contains, to be a substitute for due diligence actions. Adequate due diligence can disclose many problems that cannot possibly be covered by a contract, such as poor relations with employees or suppliers that might make the purchase undesirable but that would not amount to a violation of any normal contract provisions. Even the right to hold back future payments to the seller may not adequately protect a buyer in the event of unforeseen expensive litigation or liabilities, such as environmental contamination, which may involve potential liabilities to the buyer in excess of the purchase price.

It is impossible to provide a complete and specific checklist of due diligence procedures that will apply to all acquisitions. A good general approach, however, is to conduct the same type of financial review that would occur in the event of an independent audit of financial statements and the kind of internal business review that a wise businessperson would make of his or her own business, such as checking the morale of the work force, reviewing relationships with outside parties, examining the physical condition of equipment, buildings and other assets, and evaluating actual and potential competition. Section 1.7, *Evaluating an Acquisition Candidate* mentions some of the areas which due diligence procedures should explore in more depth. Section 7 of Appendix 1-A is also a short-form generic checklist for due diligence in an assets acquisition.

(c) Special Legal Issues

In addition to the general due diligence procedures relating to the operations of an acquisition candidate, there are several important legal issues that often affect acquisitions. Of these, one that is quite important at present is the identification and avoidance of environmental problems. Even apparently minor environmental violations can be very expensive.

Another important legal area is regulatory compliance. Many businesses are subject to some degree of licensing and supervision from local, state, and federal agencies. Trade association requirements can also be important. The buyer must confirm that it is not acquiring a business which is subject to some undisclosed disqualification or impairment which could interfere with future operations.

Labor law problems can also be a substantial factor in acquisitions, including labor union and collective bargaining issues, problems such as OSHA, COBRA, and discrimination against protected groups such as women, veterans, and the disabled. One of the most troublesome problems to acquire is a sex discrimination case. In the labor union area, buyers sometimes wrongly assume that they can buy assets, and thus terminate the existing collective bargaining obligations of the seller. To the contrary, there is a body of law that attaches the collective bargaining obligations of a seller to its underlying assets and operations, whether or not the corporation which is the party to the union agreement is acquired.

Other legal issues that can be important in an acquisition include examination of contracts and agreements which may or may not be assignable to a purchaser, the legal status of intangible rights such as trademarks and proprietary information, claims by minority shareholders, and potential antitrust claims.

1.13   CONSUMMATING THE ACQUISITION

If the parties have clearly agreed as to structure, price, payment terms, and other essential provisions, then the remaining process is to formally document these essential terms in a clear and precise way and to resolve and document the numerous details that are necessary for any acquisition.

(a) Drafting and Negotiating the Acquisition Agreement

Typically, the acquirer's legal counsel will draft a proposed acquisition agreement for submission to the acquisition candidate. The acquisition candidate's legal counsel will then review the agreement and respond with proposed changes. These suggested changes form much of the basis for final negotiations. Sometimes this process can be left in the hands of qualified legal counsel, although usually there are certain issues which arise during the course of the process that require face-to-face meetings among the respective clients for resolution. Legal counsel should narrow the range of issues as much as possible, define alternatives for the client, and assist in resolving such issues in an acceptable way.

Although many issues that arise in the final negotiating process may seem trivial and tedious relative to the whole transaction, the detailed issues can be extremely important. For example, the exact nature and extent of warranties made by a seller will determine whether a buyer has recourse against the seller in the event of certain future liabilities or losses incurred by the acquired business. Also, minor issues can mount up, and in the aggregate can form a basis for canceling or substantially changing a transaction. But as a practical matter, where well-motivated parties have agreed to substantive terms, a transaction rarely is terminated in the final drafting and negotiation stage. However, a party experienced in acquisitions knows that each side must be willing not only to compromise and try to make the deal work, but also to cancel the deal and walk away if the other side is too unreasonable. For example, the seller's unreasonableness in such areas as warranties as to contingent liabilities can signal some potential problem that due diligence procedures have not uncovered.

Attorneys are often accused of making acquisition agreements unnecessarily complex. An acquisition agreement is, however, by its nature, one document that should be thorough and detailed. The example stock purchase and assets purchase agreements set forth in Appendices B and C in this book are fairly minimal forms, provided to illustrate relatively simple and small transactions. Acquisition agreements can frequently be several times as long as these forms, depending on the size and complexity of the transaction.

An acquisition agreement serves two primary purposes. First, if there is a subsequent dispute over the terms of the deal, and if litigation or arbitration occurs, the agreement must set forth the acquirer's position with such precision that the acquirer can have a high level of confidence of being able to prevail. Second, and more important, the agreement is intended to flush out potential problems and avoid future disputes. If, as in the typical acquisition of a small business, a buyer is hiring or entering into consulting agreements with some or all of the sellers, then the last thing that either party needs is a lawsuit that will destroy their working relationship. Thus, the avoidance of conflict may be even more important than being able to win if there is a dispute.

Consider the following illustration of the sort of problem that can arise in this area. Assume that the seller is a distributing company that provides equipment and spare parts for office telephone systems. The buyer asks for a representation that none of the inventory to be purchased is *obsolete or slow moving*. The seller responds that it does carry on its books and records, at cost, an inventory of spare parts which are no longer manufactured, which may very well be considered to be obsolete or overstocked under some definitions. However, the seller further points out that one of the advantages it has in its business is that it maintains these older items in inventory and can make them available to customers who cannot buy them any place else. The overstock situation is actually desirable because the parts are no longer manufactured, and there would be no way to purchase replacements in the future. Having identified the potential problem through detailed drafting and negotiation, the acquirer and seller should be able to agree on a purchase price that might be less than the book value at which the old parts were listed, but which also recognizes that the parts have significant value to the ongoing business. Both sides should be satisfied, and no future disputes should occur. This is the type of problem which a detailed agreement and negotiations should resolve, thus avoiding future disputes.

(b) Other Closing Documents

In addition to the basic acquisition agreement, which may be a stock purchase agreement, an assets purchase agreement, or a merger agreement, the discussion below describes other important documents that may be involved in an acquisition.

(i) TITLE TRANSFER DOCUMENTS

Title transfer documents vary from transaction to transaction. In a stock sale, the transfer document is an endorsement or series of endorsements on stock certificates. In an assets acquisition, various documents are usually executed to effect the transfer of real property, equipment and furniture, contract rights and other intangible items. Frequently, in an assets acquisition, the parties use a general assignment and bill of sale with an attached schedule listing the miscellaneous smaller assets. In a merger agreement, an effective transfer occurs upon execution and filing of articles of merger with the appropriate state corporate authorities.

(ii) DEFERRED PAYMENTS

If deferred payments are to be made, there will be one or more promissory notes or other instruments evidencing these obligations.

(iii) SECURITY DOCUMENTS

Typical security documents might include a guarantee, a stock pledge, a security interest in personal property and a mortgage or deed of trust on real property. These documents secure the payment of notes or other deferred obligations.

(iv) PERSONNEL AGREEMENTS

Personnel agreements fall into three broad categories: (a) employment agreements with individuals who will continue to be full-time employees of the acquired business; (b) consulting agreements with parties who will provide part-time nonemployee services; and (c) noncompetition covenants with individuals who have agreed not to provide any services to competitors of the acquired business for an agreed length of time after closing.

(v) LEGAL OPINIONS

A legal opinion is a letter from counsel for one party, usually addressed to the other party, which gives opinions about certain legal aspects of the transaction. In a purchase of assets, for example, the buyer may require an opinion from the seller's legal counsel that all proper legal procedures were followed by the seller to authorize the sale of assets. Legal opinions assure each party that the opposing counsel believes formal procedural provisions of the agreement have been complied with. A legal opinion may sometimes also be issued by legal counsel to the attorney's own client. For example, where it is not practical to obtain a ruling from the Internal Revenue Service on the tax-free nature of a corporate reorganization, the client may ask its own legal counsel to give an opinion on that matter.

(vi) MISCELLANEOUS DOCUMENTS

Numerous other documents are executed in acquisitions. For example, real property may be leased rather than sold, and the lease document itself becomes an important document. Technology may be licensed rather than sold. The seller may have an earnout on future profits of the business, which may result in provisions which are incorporated into a license, employment agreement, or other document.

(c) Closing Procedures

The closing procedures for an acquisition or merger can be set forth in the acquisition agreement. See, for example, Article IX of Appendix B for such a list of closing steps. In a well-organized acquisition, these actions can be accomplished rather quickly.

Sometimes last minute problems or areas of disagreement arise at closing. One way this can occur is if the parties have agreed to make a final adjustment of the purchase price based on a closing financial statement that has been prepared immediately prior to the time of closing. Such issues may require last minute changes in documents and final negotiations and compromises among the parties. When such issues arise at closing, it is important for the parties to document any final compromises, modifications, or supplemental agreements.

(d) Closing File

An essential element in closing an acquisition is the preparation of a closing file by legal counsel for his or her own use and for his or her clients. The closing file should contain a closing memorandum describing the background of the transaction and any unusual problems or issues that arose. The closing file should further include the acquisition agreement and all supplemental documents, no matter how trivial. Finally, the closing file should include all disclosures and information on which the closing process was based. For example, if the selling corporation assigns a large number of contracts to the buyer, the closing file should clearly identify all of such contracts. Ideally, the file should include copies of the contracts. If this is not feasible, the documents should be identified by party and date.

One reason for the thoroughness of a closing file is that closing by no means completes the transaction. Many acquisitions include postclosing obligations and rights of the parties that extend for many years after closing. For example, an obligation of an acquirer to make noncompetition payments to a seller may be dependent on the accuracy of the representations and warranties made at the time of closing by the seller. By the time a potential difference of opinion surfaces, memories will have faded, some of the individuals involved may no longer be available, and it is essential that whoever must deal with the problem in the future has access to a clear explanation of what happened at the original closing.

1.14 POSTACQUISITION MATTERS

(a) General

The most important part of an acquisition occurs after it is concluded—does it work for both sides? Throughout the transaction the parties should, therefore, avoid thinking in terms of a closing which will solve everything and resolve all problems. Instead their negotiations and agreements should be directed at an ongoing relationship which will operate to their mutual satisfaction for many years.

Individual aspects of the acquisition agreement and specific documents should always be focused on this long-term relationship. For example, an employment agreement with a key employee of the seller should not be drafted simply to accommodate the immediate negotiating positions of the two parties—it should be consistent with the context of the whole transaction, encouraging the employee to participate and to make the contribution which the buyer needs from him in the future.

(b) Financial and Organizational Concerns

After consummation of the transaction, a new combined business entity comes into existence. From the accountant's standpoint, if the combination qualifies for accounting under the pooling of interests method, the existing balances of assets and liabilities are carried forward. If the combination does not satisfy all the conditions for a pooling of interests, the purchase accounting method is used. In that event, the assets and liabilities of the acquired entity are revalued to current market values. The accounting treatment is governed by different rules than the tax treatment. For example, purchase accounting may apply, even though the acquirer has a carryover basis for tax purposes. See Chapter 6. Systems and financial reporting methods must be reviewed and integrated with the acquirer's operations for processing of transactions and continued financial and operational reporting. These areas are covered in Chapters 2 and 3.

Checklist for Purchase of Corporate Assets and Assumption of Liabilities

Section One

PRELIMINARY MATTERS

(a) Identify parties.
    i. Owners of Seller's business, including inactive shareholders, warrant or option holders, etc.
    ii. Buyer, including partners or passive investors.
    iii. Organization of Buyer, *e.g.* C corporation, S corporation, limited or general partnership, proprietorship, limited liability company.
    iv. Other parties—lien holders, lenders, brokers or finders, etc.
(b) Exploratory discussions and negotiations.
(c) Preliminary authority to proceed from board of directors or other controlling group of both Buyer and Seller.
(d) Execute confidentiality agreement, probably two way agreement to protect both Buyer and Seller.
(e) Organize acquisition team (attorney, accountant, broker, lender, etc.)

---

*This material is adopted with permission from Krendl's Colorado Methods of Practice, Copyright 1989 by West Publishing Company, 610 Opperman Drive, P.O. Box 64526, St. Paul, Minnesota, 55164-0526; 1-800-328-9352.

(f)   Identify sources of financing.

Section Two

INITIAL REVIEW OF SELLER

(a)   Financial statements.
  i.   Usefulness will depend on whether statements are audited, reviewed, compiled or internal. Comparison of several years' statements is desirable.
  ii.   Consistency with Buyer's accounting procedures.
  iii. Earnings history and earnings adjustments, *e.g.*, excessive or under-payment of owner-manager.
  iv.   Review financial statement notes for major issues such as existence of loan agreements and liens.
(b)   Tax returns—Initial review focuses on consistency with financial disclosure and obvious potential tax problems.
(c)   Identify assets including assets not on the balance sheet.
  i.   Use financial statements and supporting documents such as depreciation schedules, receivables aging reports, and inventory lists.
  ii.   Leased assets, including equipment and real property.
  iii. Key personnel.
  iv.   Other intangible off book assets such as proprietary information, goodwill, contracts, and business relationships.
(d)   Liabilities including those not on balance sheet.
  i.   Start with financial statements and support documents such as list of payables.
  ii.   Contractual obligations.
  iii. Product warranties.
  iv.   Informal trade agreements such as supply agreements.
  v.   Contingencies such as litigation, threatened litigation, and government investigations.
(e)   Liens on assets.
(f)   Material contracts and agreements; identify major customers and suppliers.

Section Three

SPECIAL LEGAL ISSUES

(a) Securities problems.

(b) Antitrust problems, including possible Hart-Scott-Rodino notification.

(c) Specialized governmental regulations such as license requirements.

(d) Labor matters including existing or pending union.

(e) ERISA plans.

(f) Contractual problems.

(g) Finders fees.

(h) Litigation, actual, threatened, or possible.

(i) Proprietary information including patents, trademarks, and trade secrets.

(j) Tax problems.

(k) OSHA issues.

(l) Americans with Disabilities Act.

Section Four

STRUCTURAL PROBLEMS

(a) Tax planning.
  i. Review of Buyer's overall tax situation.
  ii. Tax and other characteristics of purchaser (S corporation, C corporation, existing or new corporation, limited liability company, partnership, proprietorship, etc.).
  iii. Financial and tax projections for Seller's business.
    (a) Probable allocation of purchase price.
    (b) Income projections.
    (c) Other tax planning, *e.g.*, effect of buying corporation's net operating loss carryforward.

(b) Buyer's authority, including corporate authority, if a corporation is the purchaser.

      i.   Requirement for directors and shareholders votes.

     ii.   Loan agreement or other restrictions.

(c)   Evaluate and research special legal problems relating to Seller.

(d)   Assess potential problems with transfers of assets such as "due on sale" clauses and requirements for third party consents to contract assignments.

(e)   Consider special problems relating to unexpected liabilities.

      i.   Bulk transfers.

     ii.   Tax liens or other statutory liens on assets.

    iii.   Ongoing obligations of Seller's business such as commitments to employees, warranty or service obligations to customers, etc.

    iv.   Environmental/hazardous waste exposure.

(f)   Evaluate government regulatory problems including requirements for licenses or other special permits.

Section Five

NEGOTIATIONS

(a)   Meeting of all parties including principals on both sides, attorneys, accountants, other acquisition team members.

(b)   Definition of major points of the transaction.

      i.   Identify specifically the assets and liabilities to be transferred.

     ii.   Preliminary consideration of purchase price.

    iii.   Payment terms and collateral.

    iv.   Requirements of other creditors, *e.g.*, subordination of obligations to Seller to Buyer's lender.

(c)   Related agreements.

      i.   Leases of real or personal property.

     ii.   Personnel agreements.

        (a) Consulting and employment agreements.

        (b) Noncompetition agreements.

    iii.   Earnout or other contingencies.

(d)   Other issues.

      i.   Timetable to closing.

     ii.   Public release of information.

    iii.   Additional confidentiality agreements.

    iv.   Procedures for investigation and exchange of information.

    v.   Possible basis for adjustment of purchase price (financial performance through closing, contingent liabilities, etc.)

    vi.   Conditions to closing (third-party approvals, verification of financial information, availability of financing, etc.)

(e)   Possible informal letter of intent.

(f)   Negotiation and revisions of letter of intent by parties.

Section Six

FINANCING FOR BUYER

(a)   Evaluate Buyer's financial resources.

(b)   Ability to borrow against assets of Seller's business.

(c)   Evaluate total financing needs of transaction.

    i.   Payment of purchase price.

        (a) Cash purchase price necessary at closing.

        (b) Carry back by Seller.

    ii.   Working capital necessary to operate and expand business.

    iii.   Cost of acquisition (legal fees, brokerage fees, accounting costs, etc.)

(d)   Possible equity investors (beware of securities problems).

(e)   Bank or other lenders.

    i.   Contact potential lenders.

    ii.   Possibility of multiple lenders or mezzanine financing.

    iii.   Negotiate commitment letter.

    iv.   Evaluate probable loan and effect of debt service on projections.

    v.   Determine effect of third-party loan on negotiations with Seller, *e.g.* probable need to subordinate Seller's collateral rights.

    vi.   Establish critical path for completing loan transaction.

    vii.   Negotiate subordination agreements with other creditors, including seller.

(f)   Evaluate possible ways of generating cash from the assets, *e.g.*, spinoff sale of some assets to third-party.

Section Seven

DUE DILIGENCE

(a) Assignment of responsibilities among members of acquisition team.

(b) Further legal research and evaluation of special concerns (see outline under Section 3 above).

(c) Financial statements and tax returns.
  i. Review for internal consistency and consistency with one another.
  ii. Verify payment of all taxes including sales taxes, property taxes, payroll withholding taxes.
    (a) Are any audits pending?
    (b) What years remain open for audit?
  iii. Review earnings history in greater detail, particularly with respect to possible adjustments.
  iv. Project cash flow.

(d) Corporate legal records: minutes, stock records, articles, and bylaws.
  i. Verify good standing and accuracy of documents against public records.
  ii. Determine what authority is necessary for approval of transaction.
  iii. Review minutes for unauthorized transactions and other problems.
  iv. Determine if there are shareholders agreements, voting trusts or other agreements which will affect authorization of the transaction.
  v. Use stock records and minutes to help determine presence or absence of adverse claims, options, warrants or other rights to acquire ownership.

(e) Real property.
  i. Title records and title insurance.
  ii. Survey and legal description.
  iii. Engineering report or other expert inspection.
  iv. Environmental audits.

(f) Other tangible assets.
    i.   Verify title, for example titles to motor vehicles.
    ii. Physical inspection of tangible property.

(g) Other assets.
    i.   Complete review of patents, trademark registrations and other legal title to intangibles.
    ii. Identify and review other intangible assets such as proprietary information.

(h) Liabilities and contingencies.
    i.   Financial statements.
    ii. Correspondence and other files indicating possible claims, especially attorney audit responses.
    iii. Standard warranty or other policies.
    iv. Consider representation and other language for final agreements to verify absence of liabilities.
    v. Statutory or common law sources of liability, *e.g.* improper disposal of waste products.

(i) Liens.
    i.   Review real estate, UCC records and other legal records (motor vehicle titles for example).
    ii. Review loan agreements and other files of Seller.

(j) Personnel relations.
    i.   Interview key employees; meet with all employees.
    ii. Review contracts, benefit plans and employee policies.
    iii. Evaluate importance of nonemployee personnel such as sales representatives, independent contractors, etc.
    iv. Evaluate importance of individual Seller to the business as it relates to consulting, noncompetition, and other arrangements.
    v. Review compliance with legal requirements such as the Employee Retirement Income Security Act of 1974 (ERISA) and Consolidated Omnibus Budget Reconciliation Act of 1986 (COBRA).

(k) Review all contracts and other agreements including verification of completeness and accuracy with third parties; obtain proof of non-default from third parties.
    i.   Contract files.
    ii. Course of dealing, customs in Seller's business.
    iii. Standard forms and procedures, especially warranty policies.

(l)   Identify and interview major suppliers, customers and other third parties on whom Seller is dependent. Interview material third parties.

(m)   Litigation.

    i.   Review all litigation files, including threatened or possible litigation matters.

    ii. Review attorney files and obtain assurances and opinions where appropriate from counsel.

    iii. Review court records.

    iv. Evaluate litigation.

        (a) Insurance coverage and third-party indemnification.

        (b) Legal fees and other projected costs.

        (c) Worst case damage assessment.

    v.   Identify threatened actions, investigations, conduct which may lead to future litigation.

(n)   Public records, *e.g.*, license and compliance files.

(o)   Review insurance coverage, cost, recent changes in premiums and coverage.

Section Eight

PRECLOSING ACTIONS

(a)   Take appropriate legal action for Buyer to approve transaction including votes by board of directors and shareholders if appropriate.

(b)   Verify that Seller has taken appropriate action for the approval of the transaction.

(c)   Determine whether bulk transfer compliance is appropriate. If so:

    i.   List of all creditors of Seller's business must be prepared and certified by Seller.

    ii. Notices typically must be mailed more than ten days prior to closing.

(d)   Obtain necessary regulatory approval, such as approval for transfer or reissuance of licenses.

(e) Resolve any special problems which may have been identified as a result of the evaluation under Section 3 above.

(f) Third party consents.
    i. Existing lenders and lien holders.
    ii. Equipment and real property lessors.
    iii. Other major contract parties, *e.g.*, franchisors, major suppliers, etc.

(g) Complete Buyer's arrangements for financing.

Section Nine

NEGOTIATING AND DRAFTING AGREEMENT

(a) Determine timetable and allocation of responsibilities.

(b) Draft purchase agreement including provisions for closing documents and exhibits.

(c) Draft ancillary agreements including noncompetition agreements, leases, bills of sale, etc.

(d) Prepare and review exhibits such as lists of assets and financial statements.
    i. Assign responsibility for preparation, *e.g.*, many will be prepared in-house by Seller.
    ii. Review all exhibits in advance of closing.

(e) Legal counsel negotiate and draft legal opinions.
    i. Legal research.
    ii. Verify factual information for opinions.
    iii. Implement necessary action to support opinion, *e.g.*, proper notice for corporate meetings.

(f) Define effective date for financial adjustments, if any.

(g) Exchange drafts and complete revisions.
    i. Lawyers narrow differences as much as possible.
    ii. Principals and others members of acquisition team meet with lawyers to resolve major issues.

Section Ten

CLOSING

(a) Complete Buyer's financing.

(b) Verify legal authority for transaction on both sides.

(c) Execute or verify prior execution of acquisition agreement.

(d) Release encumbrances by Seller's lender and other third parties.

(e) Provide proof of third-party approvals.

(f) Execute title transfer documents, including transfers of intangibles such as trade names.

(g) Execute ancillary documents, including employment agreements with Seller and key personnel.

(h) Close Buyer's loan, grant security rights, etc.

(i) Payment by Buyer.
   - i.   Cash purchase price, certified or cashier's check, or wire transfer of funds.
   - ii. Promissory note.
   - iii. Collateral and guarantees.

(j) Transfer existing insurance policies or obtain binders on new coverage.

(k) Identify any remaining issues, such as third-party approvals or adjustments of consideration and execute ancillary agreements necessary to provide for these.

(l) Pay finder's or broker's fees and receive release.

Section Eleven

POSTCLOSING MATTERS

(a) Record all security documents, including subordination agreements.

(b) Record transfers of title such as deeds and motor vehicle titles and security documents.

(c) Verify name change or other actions to be taken after closing by

Seller. File trade name or name change documents for Buyer. File change of registered agent for company to reflect new owner.

(d) Comply with Buyer's loan agreements.

(e) Compute postclosing adjustments, if any.
    i. Collection of doubtful accounts receivable.
    ii. Verification of inventory.
    iii. Adjustments in purchase price, if any.
    iv. Earnouts or other special considerations.

(f) Release of information.
    i. Press release.
    ii. Advise employees, contractors, etc.
    iii. Advise customers and suppliers.

(g) Prepare closing file.

(h) Provide directions to client concerning ongoing responsibilities.

(i) Pay sales taxes arising from transaction.

(j) Verify issuance of new licenses or any other governmental approval necessary for the transaction.

(k) File any required notices with Internal Revenue Service such as name changes and retirement plan amendments or terminations.

CHAPTER TWO

Preacquisition Reviews

Jeffrey D. Rudolph
Intelligent Electronics, Inc.

2.1 GENERAL

This chapter is written for financial professionals, referred to in the chapter as *accountants*, as the primary intended audience. However, it may be of interest to anyone working in a preacquisition environment, including general management personnel.

The preacquisition environment includes all activities taking place prior to the completion of an acquisition. Accountants usually participate in preacquisition activities, which can include searching for and screening acquisition candidates, evaluating acquisition candidates, and reviewing proposed acquisition structures, terms, and agreements. Working in these roles challenges accountants to think broadly in a general business sense—perhaps more so than when performing traditional accounting functions.

In a preacquisition environment, an accountant may participate extensively, or may only perform specific limited procedures. The more extensive level of involvement, often called *preacquisition reviews*, should enable an accountant to comment on all significant accounting and business matters that come to his or her attention from the perspective of an accounting, tax, and financial expert, and also someone with business insight and expertise in general. Indeed, an accountant can greatly enhance his or her credibility as part of a management team or as a valuable independent consultant by contributing a good general business idea or observation during preacquisition activities.

Failure of an acquisition can sometimes be attributed to a preacquisition team not carrying out sound and thorough preacquisition procedures. For example, the author observed an acquisition that failed 60 days after the documents were signed because the accountant responsible for the due diligence efforts was inexperienced at performing preacquisition reviews and more concerned with becoming the chief financial officer of the acquired company. It is important that the individuals performing preacquisition reviews have sufficient experience in this area and that their evaluation of an acquisition candidate be performed without a predetermined conclusion that the acquisition should be completed.

This chapter discusses procedures performed in a preacquisition environment, including:

(a) Searching for and screening of acquisition candidates;

(b) Reviewing an acquisition candidate's industry and business;

(c) Analyzing an acquisition candidate's financial statements; and

(d) Reviewing proposed acquisition structures, terms, and agreements.

The following sections discuss various preacquisition activities in each of the above areas. Appendix 2-A is a comprehensive preacquisition checklist developed by Coopers & Lybrand and included in this book with the permission of Coopers & Lybrand.

2.2 SEARCHING FOR AND SCREENING ACQUISITION CANDIDATES

(a) Corporate Objectives as the Basis for Acquisition Strategy and Criteria

Acquisition activities should start at a broad strategic level—the level of overall business planning. The board of directors and senior management, with assistance of company personnel and outside advisors, should carefully develop acquisition strategy and criteria based on their compatibility with the overall business objectives and plans of the company.

There have been cases in which acquisition teams have gone in the wrong direction because the overriding business objectives had not been translated into the acquisition strategy and criteria or because they had not been clearly communicated to or clearly understood by the acquisition team. For example, in one case a large regional health care provider began exploring acquisition ideas as a means for growth. The author was engaged by the controller of that company to assist in the search for an acquisition candidate. Many hours were expended gathering data about national health care companies in differing sectors of the health care industry. Upon completion of the possible target list and at the presentation to the company's president, it was learned that the board of directors had developed different objectives than originally understood by the controller.

(b) Identifying Acquisition Candidates

Searching for potential acquisition targets can be a time-consuming and tedious process. Methods of searching for and identifying acquisition candidates, which vary widely from company to company, often include establishing a network of business brokers, intermediaries, professionals, and the like, to find companies that could be acquisition opportunities in view of the defined strategy and criteria. This approach can tend to be somewhat random and unstructured, but does seem to lead to some acquisition opportunities.

A more structured approach is searching directly for acquisition candidates meeting specified criteria, which are usually designed to enable exploitation of an acquirer's strengths or offsetting its weaknesses. A list of potential targets can be developed based on defined criteria, such as standard industry codes, sales volume, profitability, geographical location, or number of employees, using available databases, such as Standard & Poor's, Compustat, which contain financial statement information, information reported to the SEC, and stock market information for many companies. Dun & Bradstreet provides extensive data base information and is useful for compiling information about privately owned companies. If information about a private company cannot be obtained from Dun & Bradstreet, then one normally will not be able to get the information without obtaining it directly from that company.

Exhibit 2.1 provides a list of sources to consider reviewing for company and industry information.

(c) Screening Potential Acquisition Targets

(i) FINANCIAL BENCHMARKS

In the initial screening phase, a preacquisition team will often focus on whether a potential acquisition target meets preset financial benchmarks. Financial benchmarks could include such characteristics as a low current stock price in relation to previous high stock prices and asset values, moderate financial leverage that would allow the acquisition candidate to obtain financing for future growth, and demonstrated growth in earnings over an extended period of time.

(ii) IDENTIFICATION OF RISK

A critical part of the initial screening process is identifying any apparent risks regarding a potential target. Many times, identifying a particular kind of risk can eliminate a potential candidate from consideration at an early stage, avoiding unnecessary expenditure of time in analyzing the potential candidate. Alternatively, a potential risk could be identified that requires further investigation for an acquisition candidate that is of continuing interest.

For example, a factor that might be identified as a risk at this stage could be possible market vulnerability if an acquisition candidate's business is

EXHIBIT 2.1 Sources of Information About Companies and Industries

Annual reports to shareholders
Shareholder proxy statements
Filings with the Securities and Exchange Commission
Trade and business periodicals
U.S. Industrial Outlook
Value Line Investment Survey
Standard & Poor's Industry Survey
Dun & Bradstreet

EXHIBIT 2.2 Illustration of Possible Financial Benchmarks for Analyzing Potential Acquisition Targets During the Search Phase

Price-earnings ratio equal to or less than 30% of the average high stock price during the last three years
Stock price equal to or less than 75% of the tangible book value per share
Stock market capitalization equal to or less than current assets less total liabilities
Ratio of current assets to current liabilities equal to or greater than 1.5 to 1
Ratio of total liabilities to stockholders' equity equal to or less than 4 to 1
Growth in income per share equal to or greater than 10% compounded annually over the last five years

with one or a limited number of customers. If a dominant customer is a governmental agency whose funding is uncertain, this could be a significant risk. A dependency on key employees with special technical expertise could lead to significant problems after an acquisition if such employees leave or if key employees leave along with vital customers who follow those employees. The potential for technological obsolescence through technological advances, creating a need to invest heavily in research and development, is an important consideration. Finally, the possible consequences of pending or threatened litigation matters can be significant.

2.3 REVIEWING AN ACQUISITION CANDIDATE'S INDUSTRY AND BUSINESS

(a) Industry Conditions and Competition

An understanding of the industry environment in which the potential acquisition candidate operates is important for properly carrying out a preacquisition review. Indeed, some level of understanding of the industry is essential before performing any of the procedures described in this chapter. If the potential acquisition candidate has significant operations in more than one industry or line of business, each should be reviewed and analyzed separately.

The acquirer should review the industries in which the potential acquisition candidate's principal customers and suppliers operate. Recent and expected future trends in the availability and cost of key materials and services are important. The overall stability and seasonal and cyclical aspects of the industry should be focused on. The acquirer should consider the extent to which government regulations, including environmental considerations, may influence the business.

The review should include identifying and analyzing the major competitors of the potential acquisition candidate. This is sometimes called a *SWOT* analysis—in which an acquirer reviews the strengths, weaknesses, opportunities, and threats of the potential acquisition candidate's competitors.

The relative financial, operational, and technological strengths of the companies in the industry should be compared, together with the relative acceptance and demand for each competitor's products or services. The possibility of customers or suppliers further integrating their operations, thereby increasing competition, should be evaluated. This may depend to some degree on the complexity of the industry's technology or the amount of investment required to enter the industry.

Trends and growth of the market with respect to the industry as a whole and the individual companies in the industry and the potential of the acquisition candidate to maintain or increase market share in light of the indicated trends can be important and indicative of the future potential of the acquisition candidate.

(b) Business and Organization of the Potential Acquisition Candidate

(i) ORGANIZATION AND PERSONNEL

Review and discussion of organization charts and procedure manuals can provide insight about the business and operations of the acquisition candidate and identify areas in which efficiency might be improved, reducing costs or otherwise improving operations after an acquisition. This type of information can assist an acquirer in measuring the profit potential in the future through better utilization of resources or the ability to reduce staff or other expenses.

The review of the organization of the potential acquisition candidate should include identifying key personnel in each area of expertise and reviewing the background and responsibilities of each. The potential acquisition candidate's management team should be considered in light of anticipated needs to provide continuity of competent management after the acquisition. If the successful management of the company is dependent on the abilities of one or a few individuals, that is a very key matter which should be identified and carefully evaluated.

The compensation of an acquisition candidate's personnel should be compared to compensation of personnel at comparable levels of responsibility in the acquirer's organization. Any employment contracts should be identified and reviewed. Sometimes, companies expecting to be acquired enter into employment contracts with key personnel, especially if such persons are also significant stockholders.

Employee benefit plans, particularly pension plans, should be carefully reviewed, including the funding status of pension funds. Review of this information can provide the acquirer with insight into important matters that should be negotiated in the terms of the purchase agreement in situations such as where the vested benefits under a pension plan exceed the balance of pension fund assets. Possible *hidden* liabilities related to employee benefit plans can be of great concern.

(ii) CORPORATE RECORDS AND ADMINISTRATION

Corporate Records. Corporate records of a potential acquisition candidate, such as minutes of board meetings, articles of incorporation, corporate by-laws, stockholder agreements, and listings of all legal and corporate entities controlled by or affiliated with the acquisition candidate should be reviewed.

Insurance Programs. This insurance program and policies of the acquisition candidate should be analyzed to determine major risks that are present as well as adequacy of coverage. Any self-insurance practices should be particularly noted. Even though self-insurance may be a prudent decision in the circumstances, the potential for financial exposure from self-insured losses from events both before and after the acquisition should be focused on by the acquirer. The review of product liability insurance policies can point out a product line that might be more susceptible to liability claims than the acquirer may consider acceptable. The acquirer may also be able to obtain reductions in premiums by combining insurance policies of the acquisition candidate with those of the acquirer.

(iii) ASSETS AND FACILITIES

Major plants, assets, facilities, and productive capacity in relation to actual capacity utilized should be identified, together with the remaining estimated useful lives of the assets and facilities. The preacquisition team needs to project future capital expenditure requirements based on replacement cost of assets that will need to be replaced and the growth rate of the acquisition candidate. Rapidly growing firms may require annual capital expenditures equal to more than annual depreciation expense, firms with average growth may require annual capital expenditures equal to annual depreciation expense, and firms in a declining industry may require little or no capital expenditures.

(iv) ASSESSING INTERNAL CONTROLS

Companies that grow at rates exceeding industry averages are primary candidates for acquisition. These companies typically report significant increase in market share, sales, number of employees, and earnings, to name a few. Often what does not develop at the same rate is the company's system of internal controls. Often, internal controls are put into place when a company is more mature, requires audited financial statements, or becomes an SEC reporting entity. Therefore, acquisition of a nonpublic company by a public company can sometimes run into practical difficulties because of inadequate financial reporting and internal control practices of an acquisition candidate.

For example, publicly held companies must comply with Form 8-K rules, which require that a current report be filed with the SEC within 15 days after an acquisition, with audited financial statements of the acquired business accompanying the report or provided in a Form 8 filing within 60 days thereafter. In one case, a Fortune 500 client of the author's firm stopped the negotiation of an acquisition of a privately owned company because the due diligence team reported that the internal controls and reporting process was so inadequate that the publicly held company could jeopardize its good standing with the SEC by possibly not being able to report timely financial results.

Internal controls and financial reporting procedures are also important to the acquirer's ability to rely on financial statements and financial data provided by the potential acquisition candidate and to the acquirer's operation of the acquired company after the acquisition.

(v) PRODUCTS AND INVENTORY

Product life cycle evaluation is important to the preacquisition review because it confirms information gathered about the industry and the competition. A company which is dealing with products that are early in the life cycle, but the industry is in a later stage, might indicate a higher degree of risk associated with the potential acquisition candidate. Most due diligence teams are careful to do an inventory count before closing an acquisition, but assuring a particular inventory level is not enough. The due diligence teams should also look for appropriate inventory reserve policies, write-downs, and inventory obsolescence, shrinkage, price changes, and damaged goods. The horror stories about inventory surprises after an acquisition are legion.

For example, the author is aware of a case in which the preacquisition team apparently did not ask enough questions about inventory of a hat manufacturer classified as seconds and overruns. Within six months after the acquisition, the acquirer suffered a $4,000,000 write-off of obsolete and excess inventory. In retrospect, the acquirer learned that this inventory was produced because the acquired company's sales agreements required the production of additional hats in the event the customer needed to order more hats. Over a five-year period, the acquired company had accumulated hats that were being sold in outlet and secondhand shops, and which were carried in inventory at full production cost. The preacquisition team did not investigate deeply enough to determine that these hats were being sold for less than the production costs.

(vi) TECHNOLOGY AND RESEARCH AND DEVELOPMENT

The company's activities and commitment to research and development activities should be noted, as well as the results of past efforts. In this area in particular, the accountant may not be qualified to evaluate the implications of research and development activities, but inquiries may provide additional information of interest to persons in the acquirer organization who are qualified to evaluate this area.

2.4 ANALYZING AN ACQUISITION CANDIDATE'S FINANCIAL STATEMENTS

(a) General

Assets acquired in an acquisition have value in terms of their production potential, the money they will generate over time, or their prices when liquidated. In addition, an acquired firm is expected to add to future profits and cash flows, and to have an effect on the future level of growth. An understanding of the financial characteristics assists in establishing the value of the firm. Annual financial statements show growth rates in sales and earnings over the years. These figures reveal a firm's ability to respond to the economic environment and management's ability to produce profits from sales. Financial information forms a basis for making estimates of future performance.

Financial analysis is a tool for interpreting financial statements. It can provide insight into two important areas of management: the return on investment earned and the soundness of the company's financial position. This technique compares certain related items in the statements to each other in a meaningful manner. The analyst evaluates results against the particular characteristics of the company and its industry.

(b) Statement of Cash Flows

Evaluating balance sheets and statements of operations of an acquisition candidate is important, but perhaps more important is evaluating the statement of cash flows. Through analyzing the statement of cash flow in conjunction with the other statements, the preacquisition team can determine if the entity is generating positive cash flow and whether it can continue to do so after the acquisition, before and after any debt service arising in the acquisition. In this analysis, the acquisition team should consider the following techniques of analyzing the cash flow of the acquisition candidate:

(1) Normalizing the cash flow by eliminating the effects of extraordinary and nonrecurring items. The analysis and review of historical financial data should include identifying any unusual or nonrecurring

items that distort reported earnings. Inquiry should be made regarding any significant adjustments made at year-ends that may give indication of the kinds of items that could cause distortion of current interim period data.

(2) Projected future capital expenditure requirements based on replacement cost of assets that will need to be replaced and the growth rate of the acquisition candidate. Rapidly growing firms may require annual capital expenditures equal to more than annual depreciation expense, firms with average growth may require annual capital expenditures equal to annual depreciation expense, and firms in a declining industry may require little or no capital expenditures.

(3) Eliminate intercompany, owner, manager, or employee benefit charges that are higher than costs that would be necessary after an acquisition.

(c) Financial Ratios

Financial ratios fall into four classes: (1) ratios appraising liquidity; (2) ratios measuring solvency; (3) ratios evaluating funds management; and (4) ratios measuring profitability. The categories indicate that different ratios may be more helpful than others for particular purposes. Therefore, rather than calculating ratios indiscriminately, the accountant precedes the ratio computations with some consideration of the kinds of insights he or she believes will be helpful in understanding the problem ahead. To get the most meaningful results, comparisons of these ratios against some standard should be made over a period of several years; in-depth, major variations from this standard are examined; and the various ratios are cross-checked against each other.

(i) LIQUIDITY

Liquidity ratios appraise a company's ability to meet its current obligations. These ratios compare current liabilities, which are the obligations falling due in the next 12 months, and current assets, which typically provide the funds to satisfy these obligations. The difference between current assets and current liabilities is called *net-working capital*.

(ii) SOLVENCY

Solvency ratios describe a company's ability to meet long-term debt payment schedules. There are a number of ratios that compare stockholders' equity to funds provided by creditors. All of these ratios are designed to give some measure of the extent to which ownership capital provides protection to the creditors should a company incur operating losses.

(iii) FUNDS MANAGEMENT

The financial situation of a company can be measured based on how its investment in accounts receivable, inventories, and fixed assets is managed. As the revenue of a business increases, it is not uncommon to find that the associated expansion of these three items is so great that, despite profitable operations, the company is short of cash. In such situations, the management of accounts payable becomes critical. It is a source of capital that should expand along with the increased sales.

(iv) PROFITABILITY

The accountant should look at profit in two ways: (1) as a percentage of sales; and (2) as a return on the funds invested in the business. Investors rate earnings-per-share amounts on a scale of high to low depending on their *quality*. Those companies with the highest quality earnings-per-share within their industry are usually given higher price-earnings ratios than those companies in the same industry category with the lowest quality earnings. In assessing the *quality* of a company's earnings, certain factors should be considered:

(a) Economic environmental influences, such as inflation and exchange rate changes.

(b) Recurring economic activities, such as normal sales of a company's products.

(c) Accounting policy changes, such as switching from straight-line to accelerated depreciation.

(d) One-time events, such as sale of an office building.

(e) Capital structure, such as the use of financial leverage.

(d) Signals of Financial Distress

Sometimes the stock market seems to anticipate the deterioration of a corporation's earning capacity and financial position before its actual publication by the company. One way investors are able to anticipate such situations is by identifying signals of financial distress in a company's financial statements. These are accounting signals that may suggest a worsening situation before it actually impacts the net income figure. Remember, these signals suggest further analysis should be undertaken. They do not necessarily mean that things are deteriorating, that management is trying to fool statement users, or that the accounting is inappropriate.

(i) DISCRETIONARY COSTS

Managed costs are those which can increase or decrease through management decisions. They include research and development expenses, maintenance, and advertising and promotion expenditures. Management is generally reluctant to reduce expenditures in these areas, since these expenditures are often vital to the company's success in future years. However, when companies get into trouble and management wants to keep up profits, management may cut the level of managed costs. So, decreases in the level of managed costs may be an indicator of a company with problems.

(ii) CHANGE IN ACCOUNTING POLICIES

Management prefers to reach its profit objectives without changing its accounting practices. Consequently, any company that has to resort to a change in accounting principles, a change in the way it applies its accounting principles, or a change in accounting estimates to improve its profits or balance sheet ratios is perhaps signaling that it cannot reach the desired goal without resorting to accounting games.

(iii) ACCOUNTS RECEIVABLE

When capital is expensive, business owners do not like to increase accounts receivable balances or let them get out of line with past experience any more than is absolutely necessary. So, increased accounts receivable balances, or a higher balance relative to sales, can many times be interpreted as a sign of trouble. The author, participating in a due diligence review of a company, noted that year to date sales were behind the company's budgeted annual sales. In order to increase year-end sales to improve profits, the company sold its customers unneeded products by granting generous credit terms. This transfer of goods was properly recorded as a sale, but what happened was a shift in the inventory from the seller's inventory to the customer's inventory. Sales projections for the current year were met, however, at the expense of future sales.

(iv) PROFITS RESULTING FROM NONOPERATING ACTIVITIES

Most management prefers not to use discretionary onetime generation opportunities to generate profits, such as the sale of an office building with a cost basis substantially below market price. Management enjoys the security of knowing that if profits need a sudden boost, the means are close at hand. However, they are often reluctant to use this profit source since they know that if the market discovers that one-shot gains were used to generate profits, their earnings quality may be rated lower. So, in many cases, management using one-time gains to produce profits usually do it because they have no other option.

(v) GROSS PROFIT

One key indicator of trouble is a decline in the gross profit margin as a percentage of sales. It may indicate an inability to raise prices, a cost-price squeeze, or a weakness in the market for the company's products.

(vi) CHARGING CURRENT OPERATIONS WITH PROVISIONS FOR FUTURE LOSSES

Finally, some companies have a bad year and management, looking ahead, sees nothing but future problems. The author again experienced a situation when management decided that since things were so bad currently, it wrote off a number of future losses to operations in the current period. This provided the company an easier road to reporting profits in the future. Management tried to explain this to the due diligence team as the setting up of reserves to solve the company's problems. Be cautious of such companies. The creation of the reserve is nothing more than an accounting entry and the fundamental business problems still exist with the company.

(e) Financial Leverage

There has been a long-term trend for corporations to use debt funding to finance growth and to maintain the return on stockholders' equity. However, overreliance on financial leverage is not thought to be prudent when business becomes more difficult and uncertain. A deterioration in such ratios, as described earlier, is used to pump up earnings-per-share and to compensate for the fact that the company is not self-financing. If a company has to utilize this approach more than its competitors or the industry leader, it probably did so because it was unable to make its profit goals through operations.

(f) Forecasted and Projected Financial Information

Forecasted and projected balance sheet, income statement, and cash flow data provided by the acquisition candidate should be reviewed and critically analyzed. A forecast refers to what is believed to be the most likely outcome based on the most probable future conditions, and may also include the effects of certain strategies planned by management. The assumptions on which the forecasted or projected data are based should be reviewed for reasonableness, and the accountant should consider to what extent the assumptions may be motivational or overly optimistic. If major assumptions have a significant effect, ranges should be computed to indicate the effects of possible variations of future outcomes that would be caused by different assumptions. Prior forecasts or projections should be compared with subsequent actual results to ascertain how accurate these have been in the past.

2.5 REVIEWING PROPOSED ACQUISITION STRUCTURES, TERMS, AND AGREEMENTS

(a) Reviewing Acquisition Agreements

A preacquisition review is not complete until a careful review is made of the proposed acquisition agreement is made to ensure that the procedures performed were consistent with the meaning and intent of all significant aspects of the proposed transaction. In addition, the review of the purchase contract will enable the accountant to make suggestions relating to financial covenants or how to better structure the transaction, or to provide advice on implications of tax accounting and generally accepted accounting principles.

(i) FINANCIAL COVENANTS

No matter how an acquisition is structured, most business combinations involve issuing debt or mandatory redeemable preferred stock. The financial members of the due diligence team should pay very close attention to the covenants drafted into the financing agreement. These covenants often do not receive enough attention because the borrowers are more interested in the availability of the funds and the timing and terms of the loan. Covenants that are often boilerplate and not specifically tailored to the transaction are often overlooked amidst standard representations, warranties, and other events of default.

The due diligence team should gain a complete understanding of the covenants by asking on what basis the covenants were developed, determine if the financial covenants have enough cushion and make sure that the definitions, stated and implied, are discussed carefully with the lender and borrower. Financial covenants must be developed so that the postacquisition entity can operate normally with respect to short-term financing, leasing, capital expenditures and routine operations. The financial covenants should allow the company to deviate slightly from plan.

In a recent transaction with an asset-based lender, the financial covenants were determined based upon the company's expected financial projections, which were then adjusted for a 10% decrease in the profit margin. The lender calculated the financial covenants—book net worth, debt-to-net worth, current ratio, and minimum debt service coverage—and then reduced the ratios by 10%. These allowed the company enough latitude to operate the business and provided the lender with reasonable financial covenants.

The lender should be questioned if definitions or statements are unclear or too complex to understand. If financial covenants are too complex to calculate and monitor, the due diligence team should offer alternatives if there is an easier measurement criteria. In the acquisition of a wholesale distributor of gasoline and propane, the loan documents defined *eligible inventory* as *canned oil and oil additives*. This definition was not an inventory definition the company was accustomed to using. In fact, the company referred to this type of inventory as *greases and oil*. After further investigation by the due diligence team, the loan documents were changed to use language that the company and the bank both agreed to include—greases and oil—which the company understood. In the same transaction, the definition of *affiliated parties* was too broad. The company was also able to get the lender to be more specific about who would be included as a related party.

(ii) ACCOUNTING FOR THE TRANSACTION

The accountant should carefully examine any sections that include terms dependent on accounting measurements. These types of terms can impact determination or adjustment of the purchase price, or representations made by the seller regarding the financial condition of the business being sold.

An area of particular concern for the accountant to focus on is the accounting basis on which the acquisition candidate's financial statements and data referred to in the purchase agreement are based. Frequently, *usual and customary accounting practices* will be mentioned and reference made to an attached set of financial statements. A typical passage from a purchase agreement could read "consistent with the company's usual and customary accounting practices used in preparing the attached financial statements in accordance with generally accepted accounting principles." A problem could develop in interpretation of the agreement at a later date if any of the accounting practices of the acquisition candidate are believed not to be in accordance with generally accepted accounting principles, and the accountant should be alert to any problems that could result from interpretation of such a definition. The possibility of a problem in this area can be reduced significantly if the financial statements have been audited and reported on by an outside Certified Public Accountant (CPA). However, differences of opinion on matters of generally accepted accounting principles can exist that cause one accountant to disagree with another as to the preferability or correctness of accounting principles and practices used in preparing financial statements.

(iii) IMPLICATIONS OF TAX AND GENERALLY ACCEPTED ACCOUNTING PRINCIPLES

A key area to be considered in reviewing a proposed transaction is to consider the desired tax and accounting effects. In particular, the accountant or a tax specialist should ascertain that if a tax-free transaction is desired, none of the terms of the agreement would prevent the transaction from being tax-free. Similar considerations would result in confirming that pooling of interests accounting will be applicable, if the parties so desire.

It may be appropriate, in reviewing the proposed transaction, to review or prepare pro forma financial statements on a historical and projected basis to provide a clear, forward-looking view of the impact of the transaction. Part of the evaluation of a proposed acquisition should include evaluating the expected financial impact on reported earnings after the acquisition. With the pooling of interests method, pro forma combination of data of the previously separate companies will be a more simple process than if a purchase acquisition is involved. Projecting the future earnings impact of a purchase acquisition will often require estimating higher depreciation charges from the written-up values of acquired fixed assets and the amortization of goodwill.

Furthermore, the initial period after an acquisition may include, in cost of sales, a higher charge for acquired inventories stated at a higher than normal amount. In view of the normal expectations of an acquirer that its accountants will provide advice on the accounting aspects of an acquisition, it is important that the accountant anticipate the postacquisition financial reporting implications of a proposed acquisition and that he or she advises the acquirer accordingly.

Coopers & Lybrand Comprehensive Preacquisition Review Checklist

Table Of Contents

INTRODUCTION

While few business activities are more complex or risky than making an acquisition, a thorough preacquisition review can help you gauge just how complex and risky the undertaking would be. The review gives you an important opportunity to assess values for negotiations and to anticipate some of the many business issues that generally emerge during the postacquisition period.

But since there's rarely enough time to gather all relevant information, an organized preacquisition approach is essential. This checklist works in several ways to help you organize this process.

First, it is divided into eight categories: "General Background," "Product Lines, Markets, Industry Conditions and Competition," "Operations," "Human Resources," "Financial Considerations," "Management Styles and Practices," "Research, Development and Engineering" and "Legal Matters." This breakdown allows you to assign the review by area, using the expertise of your various management groups, and to determine which areas require outside specialists.

Second, the checklist helps you decide in your own mind whether particular items of information are essential to proceeding, important in determining acquisition structure and price, relevant to representations, warranties and escrows or unimportant or inapplicable. Ranking questions this way will substantially enhance the efficiency and effectiveness of the preacquisition process—and will help you determine what role outside professionals should play. This publication serves only as a guideline for checking into an acquisition candidate and should not be considered a substitute for an in-depth review.

GENERAL BACKGROUND

How do you decide to commit your resources to reviewing a candidate in detail? Answers to the first eight questions in this section will help you determine if a company will make a worthwhile target for further study. In general, the more background information you gather in the first stage, the better position you are in to understand a proposed transaction, anticipate crucial issues and determine a candidate's willingness to negotiate.

	Yes	No	Notes
1. Have you obtained information or made a judgment about:			
a. The image of the company and its products and services compared to those of industry leaders?	☐	☐	
b. The reputation of present owners, directors, management and professional advisers?	☐	☐	
c. The trend of market share?	☐	☐	
d. Recent major developments among competitors?	☐	☐	
e. The extent of government regulation (including EPA and OSHA) under which the company operates?	☐	☐	
f. Other external factors affecting the company?	☐	☐	
g. New developments planned or in progress, including:			
• The realtionship of programs to the company's position in the industry?	☐	☐	
• The state of definition and discipline in specific plans?	☐	☐	
• Capital equipment commitments?	☐	☐	
h. Special skills and advantages, such as:			
• Technical position?	☐	☐	
• Established market?	☐	☐	
• New product success?	☐	☐	
• Survival from major setbacks?	☐	☐	
• Well-developed internal communications?	☐	☐	
i. Major litigation, pending or potential?	☐	☐	
j. Cyclical factors affecting the industry?	☐	☐	
k. Credit rating?	☐	☐	
l. Major operations discontinued in recent years or that may be discontinued in the near future?	☐	☐	
m. Contracts and leases nearing expiration?	☐	☐	
n. Labor negotiations pending?	☐	☐	
o. Trade association membership?	☐	☐	

2. Have the company's officers or directors been involved in criminal proceedings, regulatory commission violations or significant civil court litigation? ☐ ☐

3. Do you know the *real* reason the company is being offered for sale? ☐ ☐

4. Do you know how long the company has been for sale and if other transactions have fallen through? ☐ ☐

5. Have you considered whether management has done anything to make the company appear more attractive to a buyer, such as:

   a. Reducing discretionary expenditures for advertising, maintenance, research and development, new product introductions, capital improvements? ☐ ☐
   b. Deferring raises or bonuses? ☐ ☐

6. Are you aware of the aspects of the business that appear to be dominant in the industry (e.g., technology, product design, marketing, production)? Note what appear to be the key factors for success in the industry and how the company measures up in these areas. ☐ ☐

7. Do you know what factors make the company more attractive than other companies in the industry? Determine if the company can maintain its advantage, identify developments that could cause the company to lose that advantage and assess the likelihood of their occurring. ☐ ☐

8. Would the company provide a "bridgehead" to other desirable industry segments? Identify and evaluate the possibilities. ☐ ☐

9. Do you have the basic information you need about the company, including:

a. History of business, any predecessor companies and changes in capital structure, capitalizations or insolvency proceedings. ☐ ☐

b. Description of products, markets, principal customers, any subsidiaries and their lines of business? ☐ ☐

c. List of officers and directors, with their affiliations, ages and number of years in office? ☐ ☐

d. Number of people employed and their major areas of activity? ☐ ☐

e. Capitalization and stock distribution, including the number of shareholders and names of principal shareholders, rights of each class of stock and stockholders' agreements? ☐ ☐

f. Terms of outstanding warrants, options and convertible securities? Find out if these would have to be dealt with by issuing additional shares. ☐ ☐

g. If the stock is publicly traded, the exchanges on which it is traded or, if over the counter, the dealer making markets, the extent of public float, institutional holdings, trading volume and total market capitalization? Obtain any SEC filings and a shareholder list, if available. ☐ ☐

h. Organization chart? ☐ ☐

i. Names, addresses and contacts of company's professional advisers, including attorneys, auditors, principal bankers and investment bankers? ☐ ☐

j. Locations of company's financial and legal records? ☐ ☐

k. State of incorporation and date incorporated? ☐ ☐

10. Will a drastic change in the company's management or business approaches be necessary to meet your expectations? Determine if present employees or customers would be able to adjust to achieve your goals. ☐ ☐

11. Do you have this general data on the transaction:

    a. Terms of the acquisition?   ☐ ☐

    b. Accounting treatment?   ☐ ☐

    c. Arrangements that have been made with any brokers or finders representing either side of the transaction?   ☐ ☐

    d. If any subsidiaries are not wholly owned, the details of outside ownership? Consider completing a separate checklist for any major subsidiaries with significant minority interests.   ☐ ☐

    e. Other companies the company has a significant investment in, carried on the equity method? Consider completing a separate checklist for each investment.   ☐ ☐

    f. Details of any recent acquisition?   ☐ ☐

PRODUCT LINES, MARKETS, INDUSTRY CONDITIONS AND COMPETITION

A basic objective of many acquisitions is to expand product lines and markets, at a reasonable cost. The decision to pay a purchase price over that indicated by historical results—and how much over—is based on the type of information you gather here.

PRODUCT LINES

	Yes	No	Notes
1. Do you know how customers use the company's products?	☐	☐	
2. Are you aware of these basic buying considerations:			
a. Price?	☐	☐	
b. Quality?	☐	☐	
c. Service?	☐	☐	
d. Availability?	☐	☐	

e. Sales? ☐ ☐
f. Engineering? ☐ ☐
g. Credit terms? ☐ ☐
h. Right of return or consignment? ☐ ☐

3. Have you examined the past and prospective pattern of product changes in the industry? ☐ ☐

4. Do there appear to be new uses for the products? ☐ ☐

5. Are there related products or industry segments the company is not now serving? ☐ ☐

6. Have you looked into the warranty terms that are customarily offered and their cost? ☐ ☐

7. Does the product expose the company to significant product liability concerns? ☐ ☐

8. Is patent and trademark protection adequate?

MARKETS

1. Do you know if demand is:

a. Basic? ☐ ☐
b. Created? ☐ ☐

2. What type of customer buys these products:

a. Individual consumers? ☐ ☐
b. Railroads? ☐ ☐
c. Utilities? ☐ ☐
d. Industrial companies? ☐ ☐
e. Commercial or financial businesses? ☐ ☐
f. Federal, state or local governments? ☐ ☐

    g. Service businesses? ☐ ☐
    h. Construction contractors? ☐ ☐

3. Does the company operate in a "mature" market? ☐ ☐

4. Do you know the importance of domestic and export demand? ☐ ☐

5. Are you aware of the factors that affect demand:

    a. General business conditions? ☐ ☐
    b. Population changes? ☐ ☐
    c. New products, product changes or technological innovation? ☐ ☐
    d. Advertising or promotional pressure? ☐ ☐
    e. Governmental factors (e.g., fiscal policy, import-export controls, defense activity)? ☐ ☐
    f. Customer growth? ☐ ☐
    g. Energy availability? ☐ ☐
    h. Ecological considerations? ☐ ☐

6. Can the market be expanded by efforts of the company? ☐ ☐

7. Is the market segmented by:

    a. Type of customer? ☐ ☐
    b. Geographic location? ☐ ☐
    c. Product? ☐ ☐
    d. Channel of distribution? ☐ ☐
    e. Pricing policy? ☐ ☐
    f. Degree of integration? ☐ ☐

8. Do you know how the company has responded to market segmentation? ☐ ☐

9. Are there any seasonal sales patterns and shifts in established patterns? ☐ ☐

10. Do you have a 10-year record of product sales performance? Indicate the date the product was introduced and note any significant modifications. Relate trends to both external factors and company actions. Note the stages in the products' life cycles. ☐ ☐

11. Do you have a reasoned projection of growth or contraction trends for the product lines' industry or industries? ☐ ☐

12. Do you have a forecast of sales expectations and estimated share of market? Compare it to industry projections. ☐ ☐

13. Have you obtained an estimate of the industry's ability to supply present and anticipated demand? ☐ ☐

14. Have you reviewed sales backlog, accounts receivable, sales correspondence and customer continuity? ☐ ☐

15. Have you analyzed present and probable pricing policies for the product lines, considering:

    a. The sensitivity of both the industry and company to price changes? ☐ ☐
    b. Whether there is a price leader? ☐ ☐
    c. Whether there is good price discipline? ☐ ☐
    d. Any excess capacity in the industry that might tend to depress prices? ☐ ☐
    e. Whether the company has been able to pass along recent cost increases to customers? ☐ ☐

16. Have you analyzed present and potential domestic and export customers, including:

    a. The total number and major types of customers and the percentage of sales to each type? ☐ ☐
    b. Geographical locations and percentage of sales by location? ☐ ☐
    c. Names of principal customers, annual volume of sales and buying habits? ☐ ☐
    d. Any contractual relationships with customers? ☐ ☐
    e. The extent of government contracting subject to cost regulations or price redetermination? ☐ ☐

   f. A summary of special discounts and
      credit terms offered to significant
      customers?   ☐   ☐
   g. Possible loss of customers as a result of
      this acquisition?   ☐   ☐

17. Do you know the methods this and other
    companies in industry use to distribute and
    sell, including:

   a. The channels of distribution and their
      relative importance?   ☐   ☐
   b. If the company does not sell directly to
      end users, conditions in customers'
      markets?   ☐   ☐
   c. The nature and importance of the field
      sales effort?   ☐   ☐
   d. The manner of compensating sales
      personnel?   ☐   ☐
   e. Advertising and sales promotion prac-
      tices in this industry?   ☐   ☐
   f. Any changing patterns in the distribution
      process?   ☐   ☐
   g. Any trend among major customers to-
      ward integrating, purchasing substitute
      products or otherwise deviating from
      purchasing from the company?   ☐   ☐

18. Have you reviewed advertising appeals, me-
    dia and other sales promotion programs for
    cost and effectiveness?   ☐   ☐

19. Have you analyzed distribution and selling
    costs for the past few years to determine
    possible shifts in profitable customers and
    products? Describe any unusual marketing
    methods relating to foreign sales, including
    licensing arrangements and joint ventures.   ☐   ☐

20. Have you analyzed the trend of bidding suc-
    cess and costs, including:

   a. Invitations received?   ☐   ☐
   b. Bids submitted?   ☐   ☐

   c. Contracts awarded?   ☐ ☐

   d. Average contract size?   ☐ ☐

   e. Cost-per-contract award?   ☐ ☐

21. Have you reviewed trends in the major elements of marketing, including:

   a. Market forecasts compared to actuals?   ☐ ☐

   b. Sales cancellations and returns and the reasons for them?   ☐ ☐

   c. Departmental costs compared to budget?   ☐ ☐

   d. Sales and expenses per salesman?   ☐ ☐

   e. Customer service costs?   ☐ ☐

   f. Shift in product mix profitability?   ☐ ☐

   g. Order processing costs?   ☐ ☐

   h. Customer complaints and lost customers?   ☐ ☐

   i. Discount pattern by customer groupings?   ☐ ☐

   j. New accounts opened?   ☐ ☐

22. Do you know to what extent the company is overdependent on one or a few customers?   ☐ ☐

INDUSTRY CONDITIONS AND COMPETITION

1. Have you analyzed the industry's composition and, in particular, recent changes in that composition?   ☐ ☐

   a. Have you determined how many companies operate in this industry and whether that number has been declining or increasing?   ☐ ☐

   b. Have you reviewed the recent merger, acquisition and divestiture deals that have occurred in the industry?   ☐ ☐

   c. Have you analyzed the trends in the prices paid for these deals?   ☐ ☐

   d. Have there been recent plant closings or openings, or announcements of such?   ☐ ☐

   e. Have you examined the degree to which foreign companies are entering this market, possibly through joint ventures?   ☐ ☐

    f. Are the market leaders specialists in this industry or are they diversified into other businesses? ☐ ☐

2. Have you determined which factors are critical to success in this industry? ☐ ☐

    a. Have you determined who the industry leaders are and why? ☐ ☐
    b. What are the principal bases of competition: ☐ ☐
       • Price (low gross margin) ☐ ☐
       • Quality (high gross margin) ☐ ☐
       • Service (high margin to wholesalers) ☐ ☐
       • Innovation (high R&D expenses) ☐ ☐
    c. Does the market leader have a unique strategy? ☐ ☐
    d. Does this industry have a high rate of business failure? ☐ ☐
    e. Have you determined how important high production volume is to low cost? ☐ ☐
    f. Who holds the power in this industry and how did they get it? Do suppliers have more power than buyers or vice versa? ☐ ☐
    g. How reliant is the industry on exports and how vulnerable is it to imports? ☐ ☐

3. Have you obtained growth projections and other industry analyses from hard-copy and electronic information sources? ☐ ☐

    a. What growth trends is the industry, including its companies and trade organizations, projecting? ☐ ☐
    b. What trends are industry outsiders, including consultants, economists and security analysts, projecting? ☐ ☐
    c. Have financial, investment or industry analysts reported adverse conditions? ☐ ☐

4. Have you determined the extent to which external factors influence the industry's health? ☐ ☐

a. Will existing or pending litigation affect the production of or demand for the industry's products? ☐ ☐

b. Do governmental regulations affect the industry? ☐ ☐

c. Do any environmental issues affect the industry? Have any new studies been released that would increase the industry's liability? ☐ ☐

d. Are there any potentially adverse political, social or economic conditions (e.g. trade restrictions, high interest rates, probability of nationalization or expropriation, currency revaluations)? ☐ ☐

e. Is the industry vulnerable to any external forces cutting off supply? ☐ ☐

OPERATIONS

It is critical to evaluate operations in the areas of plant and facilities, production, purchasing and inventories. For example, the failure to uncover the need to replace technically obsolete or worn-out equipment will significantly reduce the chances of a successful acquisition.

PLANT AND FACILITIES

	Yes	No	Notes

1. Have you obtained information on:

a. Location and description of plant or plants and property? ☐ ☐

b. Proximity to transportation facilities, materials sources and labor supply? ☐ ☐

c. Description of the area, including climate and natural hazards? ☐ ☐

d. Restrictions imposed by building codes and zoning laws? ☐ ☐

e. Utilities, including availability, usage and rates? ☐ ☐

    f. Real estate taxes and other fixed costs? □ □
    g. Title to realty and title insurance policy? □ □
    h. The adequacy of insurance coverage? □ □
    i. Any liens or actual or potential condem-
       nation proceedings? □ □

2. Have you obtained land information,
   including:

    a. Acreage? □ □
    b. Cost? □ □
    c. Assessed value and fair market (ap-
       praised) value? □ □
    d. Current and possible future use and
       value? □ □

3. Do you have adequate building information,
   including:

    a. Description, pictures and current use? □ □
    b. Cost, accumulated depreciation and de-
       preciation rates and policies (or lease
       terms)? □ □
    c. Assessed and fair market (appraised)
       value? □ □

4. Do you have all machinery and equipment
   information needed, including:

    a. A list of principal machinery and equip-
       ment showing cost, age and condition,
       accumulated depreciation, location and
       departmental use? □ □
    b. Depreciation rates and policies (or lease
       terms)? □ □
    c. Additions during last five years, by
       categories? □ □
    d. Fair market (appraised) value? □ □
    e. Technological obsolescence? □ □
    f. Health and safety considerations? Find
       out if the plant complies with OSHA and
       EPA regulations. □ □

g. What level of maintenance has been performed? Review what major repairs or betterments will be required. □ □

5. Do you have a list of any surplus and idle buildings and equipment? □ □

6. Have you analyzed estimated future plant, machinery and equipment requirements? □ □

7. Have you evaluated maintenance and "housekeeping" controls? □ □

8. Do you know capitalization vs. expense policies for repairs and maintenance? □ □

9. Have you made an industrial engineering assessment of the adequacy of auxiliary equipment—tools, patterns, material handling equipment? □ □

PRODUCTION

1. Do you know the nature of the manufacturing process (e.g., assembly, machine shop, extraction, metal forming)? □ □

2. Have you identified the important elements in the manufacturing process (e.g., capital investment, know-how, design of plant, skilled labor, pool of available labor)? □ □

3. Have you evaluated:

   a. The organization and departmentalization of manufacturing? □ □
   b. The basis for and adherence to the production schedule? □ □
   c. The use of economic production order quantities, bills of material, time and motion studies, formal machine scheduling routines based on capacities and speed and similar techniques? □ □

    d. Production methods, efficiency and
       layout?   ☐ ☐
    e. Safety and security measures?   ☐ ☐
    f. Storage and inventory requirements and
       warehousing facilities?   ☐ ☐
    g. Major and critical raw materials, their
       availability and price prospects?   ☐ ☐
    h. Make or buy practices, purchasing and
       inventory controls and subcontracting
       done by others?   ☐ ☐
    i. Critical lead times for materials or tool-
      ing and significant current problems?   ☐ ☐
    j. Materials handling methods employed—
      pallets, conveyors, vacuum pipe, mag-
      netic lifts, forklifts, trucks?   ☐ ☐
    k. Quality control?   ☐ ☐
    l. Industrial engineering?   ☐ ☐

4. Do you know the general elements of production costs (materials, direct labor, indirect
   labor, manufacturing expenses) and the proportion of each to the whole? Relate these to
   industry norms.   ☐ ☐

5. Have you determined the relationship between fixed and variable costs, the break-
   even point and the relation of volume to the
   break-even level? What are the effects of
   non-cash costs and cost accounting for idle
   capacity and volume variances on analysis of
   production costs?   ☐ ☐

6. Do you have a recent schedule of manufacturing overhead? Review it for any significant trends.   ☐ ☐

7. Have you reviewed the trend over the past
   three years in these elements of
   manufacturing:

    a. Defective production?   ☐ ☐
    b. Idle time—stoppage, delays, improper
      materials, etc.?   ☐ ☐
    c. Labor efficiency?   ☐ ☐

d. Waste and scrap? ☐ ☐

e. Absenteeism, accidents, grievances and overtime? ☐ ☐

f. Coordination of production planning with sales forecasts—partial or short runs, peaks and lulls? ☐ ☐

g. Goods manufactured for others whose needs may change? ☐ ☐

h. Labor turnover? ☐ ☐

i. Excess production times and the reasons for them? ☐ ☐

j. Delays in delivery time? ☐ ☐

k. Returned goods? ☐ ☐

l. Downtimes and the reasons for them? ☐ ☐

m. Preventive and emergency maintenance costs? ☐ ☐

n. Engineering change notices? ☐ ☐

8. Have you reviewed the trend in the number of days it takes a customer's order to go through the plant? ☐ ☐

9. Could possible changes in production methods make the manufacturing process obsolete? ☐ ☐

10. Have you evaluated the efficiency of the company's production process in relation to the industry? ☐ ☐

11. Have you determined what factors might lead to an increase in production costs? ☐ ☐

PURCHASING

1. In the purchasing function, have you looked into:

   a. The relationship of raw materials to goods bought for resale? ☐ ☐

   b. The percentage relation of material costs to sales over the last five years? ☐ ☐

2. Have you identified principal raw materials or products required, commenting on future price trends, market conditions, raw materials supply, competitors' activity and general economic conditions in suppliers' industries? ☐ ☐

3. Have you evaluated all principal suppliers, locations and materials or products supplied? ☐ ☐

4. Are there multiple sources of supply for critical materials? Note any monopoly suppliers. ☐ ☐

5. Have you determined the extent of reciprocal buying, if any? ☐ ☐

6. Do you know the company's policy on carrying inventories of regularly used materials or supplies? Determine the existence of inventory limits such as min-max levels and number of months' supply. ☐ ☐

7. Have you considered the effect on the purchasing function of technological or product-line changes? ☐ ☐

8. Have you determined the degree of centralization/decentralization and autonomy of the procurement function? ☐ ☐

9. Do you know how the department is organized (e.g., by commodity, division, function)? ☐ ☐

10. Do you understand the relationship between production and procurement functions for short- and long-term planning? ☐ ☐

11. Have you studied the procurement procedures that are followed—authorized requisitions, inquiry, priced purchase orders, receiving and supplier payment? ☐ ☐

12. Do you know which of these preferred practices are used:

    a. A formal purchasing manual? ☐ ☐
    b. Formal use of economic order quantities? ☐ ☐

   c. Up-to-date vendor evaluation files (containing delivery and performance reliability records)? ☐ ☐

   d. A formal program of reviewing purchased materials (value analysis)? ☐ ☐

   e. A program to standardize materials and supplies throughout the company? ☐ ☐

   f. Competitive bidding procedures? ☐ ☐

   g. Minimal use of vendors "suggested" by operating (as opposed to procurement) personnel? ☐ ☐

   h. Lead times established by product and vendor? Determine the extent to which operating personnel consider these lead times in requisitioning materials and the percentage of "Rush," "Emergency" and "As Soon As Possible" orders placed. ☐ ☐

   i. Formalized make-or-buy analyses? ☐ ☐

   j. A small purchase system? ☐ ☐

   k. Commodity specifications? ☐ ☐

   l. Price standards and variance accounting? ☐ ☐

   m. Use of inventory and usage records as purchasing guides? ☐ ☐

13. Do you know how much vendors are relied on for unit prices? ☐ ☐

14. Is there undue concentration of purchases of any items from individual vendors? ☐ ☐

15. Have you reviewed operating information and trends for the purchasing department, including:

   a. Trend of cash discounts earned? ☐ ☐

   b. Operating costs compared to budget? ☐ ☐

   c. Waste, scrap and salvage disposals? ☐ ☐

   d. Rejection of material on incoming inspection? ☐ ☐

INVENTORIES AND COSTING

1. Do you have information on:

   a. Trends in inventory levels by reporting category (e.g., raw materials, work in process, finished goods)? ☐ ☐

   b. Stratification into value by fast-moving, slow-moving, excess and obsolete inventory? ☐ ☐

   c. Seasonal inventory fluctuations? ☐ ☐

   d. Inventory turnover (ratio of average inventory to cost of sales) by product line, line of business, division of subsidiary? ☐ ☐

   e. Basis of valuation (FIFO, LIFO, average costs), any recent changes to it and their effect on reported performance? ☐ ☐

   f. Trends in customer service levels— stockouts, substitutes, back orders? ☐ ☐

   g. Sales and write-offs of obsolete stock over the past few years? ☐ ☐

   h. Maintenance and plant equipment parts inventories? ☐ ☐

   i. Returnable packages, sacks, containers? ☐ ☐

   j. Arrangements for and experience with inventory held by others, whether under consignment or otherwise? ☐ ☐

   k. Extent of any "field warehousing" financing activity? ☐ ☐

2. For cost accounting procedures, have you determined:

   a. Whether the cost system is job cost or process cost? ☐ ☐

   b. What costs are included in overhead? ☐ ☐

   c. Whether idle plant costs offset inventory unit costs? ☐ ☐

   d. How overhead is distributed? ☐ ☐

   e. If standard costs are used, how under- and overabsorbed costs are allocated to inventory and cost of sales? ☐ ☐

   f. In ascertaining lower of cost or market, how market is determined (i.e., on a unit basis, by class or product or on the inventory as a whole)? ☐ ☐

g. If LIFO is used, what the approximate difference between LIFO and current cost is? ☐ ☐

h. The treatment of intercompany profit in inventory and its effect on ratio analysis by line of business? ☐ ☐

3. Do you have enough information on long-term contracts, including:

a. Contracts entered into, noting products, types of customer, price terms, payment schedules, extent of subcontracting and dollar volume? ☐ ☐

b. The method of recording income and provision for losses? ☐ ☐

c. Cost-estimating procedures and an analysis of cost overruns or underruns? ☐ ☐

d. Bidding procedures and strategy? ☐ ☐

e. If contracts are with the U.S. government, adherence to its cost accounting requirements? ☐ ☐

f. Any disputes or litigation with customers or subcontractors? ☐ ☐

4. Have you reviewed trends of important controllable elements, including:

a. The frequency and adequacy of physical counts and extent of adjustments required? ☐ ☐

b. The accuracy and quality of perpetual inventory records? ☐ ☐

c. Management reports—turnover, discontinued lines, asset percentage? ☐ ☐

d. Inventory security and insurance coverage? ☐ ☐

HUMAN RESOURCES

It's important to determine whether employee costs will remain reasonably stable. A substandard wage scale, a weak incentive system, employee dissatisfaction or labor shortages can all lead to growing labor problems and costs. In addition, you have to investigate whether a candidate's personnel policies—benefits, overtime, wage structure and the like—are compatible with yours and, if not, how long will it take to make them so. And, finally, you need to decide how you are going to retain an acquired company's key employees during the transition.

	Yes	No	Notes
1. Do you know the number of employees by sex and age, grouped into production, sales, purchasing, engineering and administration and approximate total wage or salary cost of each category?	☐	☐	
2. Have you examined all union affiliations and contracts for significant agreements?	☐	☐	
3. Have you determined average pay scale and fringe benefits for production employees?	☐	☐	
4. Have you reviewed strike history for the past five years—dates, duration, issues and settlement terms?	☐	☐	
5. Are there any formal charges pending before federal or state labor agencies? Determine how similar cases have been resolved in the past.	☐	☐	
6. Do you know what labor unions are represented in the industry and the general area? Find out if there is any special organizing effort going on in the area.	☐	☐	
7. Have you looked into the incentive system, average rates (incentive and hourly), date they were established and date of the last updating of standards?	☐	☐	
8. Have you reviewed:			
a. Labor morale and the handling of labor relations?	☐	☐	
b. Working conditions, statistics on turnover and reasons for it?	☐	☐	

   c. Employment, recruiting and personnel
      policies and procedures? □ □
   d. Accident frequency and safety inspection
      reports? □ □
   e. Medical problems and sick leave
      frequency? □ □
   f. The wage and salary administration
      system? □ □
   g. Training programs and apprenticeship
      systems—their effectiveness and costs? □ □
   h. The productivity of the labor force? □ □
   i. Any unfilled positions? □ □
   j. The cost and effectiveness of the person-
      nel department? □ □

9. Have you looked into the general labor market, including:

   a. The types of skills available in the area? □ □
   b. Current pay rates and personnel prac-
      tices, of the industry and of other com-
      panies operating in the immediate area? □ □
   c. Area transportation, community recrea-
      tion facilities, housing and schools? □ □
   d. The overall labor situation? □ □
   e. What union demands were made in the
      last bargaining process and what de-
      mands will likely be made in the next? □ □

10. Do you have this information on management personnel:

   a. The organization of management func-
      tions and responsibilities? □ □
   b. Management and key employees, includ-
      ing position, career path, age, compensa-
      tion, retention outlook and management
      training received? □ □
   c. Any employment agreements or unwrit-
      ten understandings? □ □
   d. Any replacement candidates for present
      management? □ □

    e. Recent key personnel losses to
       competitors? □ □

    f. The character and attitude of key
      personnel? □ □

11. In evaluating employee benefit programs,
    have you reviewed:

    a. The details and costs of pensions, profit
       sharing, life insurance, disability insur-
       ance, medical benefits, travel, accident,
       bonus, deferred compensation and sever-
       ance plans? □ □

    b. The funding status of plans and the per-
       formance of fund managers? □ □

    c. Benefits and salary levels compared to
       those of the acquirer? Determine if either
       company would need to upgrade its ben-
       efit programs or salaries as a result of
       the acquisition. If so, estimate the cost. □ □

    d. Vacation and sick pay policies? □ □

    e. The number of company-provided cars? □ □

    f. Any stock option or stock bonus plans
      and the number of outstanding options?
      Look into how the plans would integrate
      with the buyer's plans or otherwise be
      treated. Estimate the resulting costs. □ □

FINANCIAL CONSIDERATIONS

Financial analysis may be essential to identifying operating problems. Moreover, competent financial analysis will contribute importantly to structuring and valuing the transaction. The choice of equity or debt and loan repayment schedules for financing the acquisition will be directly related to information derived from financial data.

The scope of your study, of course, will depend on the information available. If the basic financial statements can be supplemented by detailed breakdowns, analyses and statistics of the type included in internal operating statements, more extensive comparisons are possible.

The candidate's internal accounting controls are important for similar reasons. In this area, the advice of your independent accounts can be invaluable.

FINANCIAL DATA

	Yes	No	Notes

1. Have you obtained:

    a. Audited financial statements, preferably on Form 10-K if the company is publicly held? ☐ ☐

    b. Recent registration statements? ☐ ☐

    c. Comparative financial results by major division? ☐ ☐

    d. The most recent unaudited financial statements? ☐ ☐

    e. Tax returns for the last five years, IRS reports, schedule of unused loss and investment credit carryforwards? ☐ ☐

    f. Projected operating and financial statements? ☐ ☐

    g. The chart of accounts and a description of accounting practices? ☐ ☐

    h. Sales backlog information? ☐ ☐

2. Have you examined operating results, analyzing:

    a. Trends in sales, net income, earnings per share, dividends and return on stockholders' equity? Determine compound growth rates. ☐ ☐

    b. The effects of acquisitions, dispositions and changes in accounting presentation (either discretionary or from changes in generally accepted accounting principles)? ☐ ☐

    c. The cost of goods sold, selling expenses and general and administrative expenses? Review these for significant trends, especially in controllable costs such as advertising, travel and entertainment and repairs. ☐ ☐

d. All extraordinary and nonrecurring expenses for the period reviewed? Schedule significant items in other income and expenses. ☐ ☐

e. Annual interest expense and other fixed charges? ☐ ☐

f. Compensation paid to officers and key personnel? ☐ ☐

g. Legal retainers, consultants' fees and similar arrangements? ☐ ☐

h. The terms of the following agreements, where applicable, and of any other pertinent contracts or agreements affecting income (excerpting if possible):

- Bonus or profit-sharing plans? ☐ ☐
- Royalty agreements? ☐ ☐
- Union contracts and employment contracts? ☐ ☐
- Long-term leases? ☐ ☐
- Sales contracts and dealership agreements? ☐ ☐

3. For financial ratios, have you compared:

a. Current assets to current debt? ☐ ☐

b. Net profits to net sales, tangible net worth and net working capital? ☐ ☐

c. Net sales to tangible net worth, net working capital and inventory? ☐ ☐

d. Collection period (number of days' sales in accounts receivable)? ☐ ☐

e. Fixed assets, current debt and total debt to tangible net worth? ☐ ☐

f. Inventory to net working capital? ☐ ☐

4. For cost of doing business percentages, have you compared sales or revenue to:

a. Cost of goods sold? ☐ ☐

b. Selected operating expenses:
- Compensation of officers? ☐ ☐
- Rent paid on business property? ☐ ☐

- Repairs? ☐ ☐
- Bad debts? ☐ ☐
- Interest paid? ☐ ☐
- Taxes paid? ☐ ☐
- Amortization, depreciation and depletion? ☐ ☐
- Advertising? ☐ ☐
- Pension and other employee benefit plans? ☐ ☐

5. Have you checked industry sources for pertinent data on:

    a. Market trend? ☐ ☐
    b. Economics of the industry? ☐ ☐
    c. Accounting and auditing implications? ☐ ☐
    d. Taxes? ☐ ☐
    e. Management technology? ☐ ☐
    f. Employment benefit plans? ☐ ☐

BALANCE SHEET REVIEW

1. Have you reviewed cash position, present and projected, including:

    a. Listing banks where the company maintains accounts and related balances at balance sheet date? ☐ ☐
    b. Analyzing total cash by function of account? ☐ ☐
    c. Reviewing monthly cash balances and inquiring about unusual fluctuations? ☐ ☐
    d. Determining whether idle cash balances are promptly invested? ☐ ☐
    e. Determining whether seasonal bank borrowings are required? ☐ ☐
    f. Evaluating the company's cash management techniques? ☐ ☐

2. For accounts receivable, have you:

a. Obtained an analysis of the total receivable balance for amounts due from customers, officers, employees and others? ☐ ☐

b. Obtained "aged" trial balances of the receivable accounts above? Compare them to aging percentages for previous years and note any trends. ☐ ☐

c. Inquired about customer receivables, including:
   - Terms of sales? ☐ ☐
   - The number of customers? ☐ ☐
   - The names of large customers and volume of annual sales to each by product line? Find out if there are any unusual arrangements with any of these customers. ☐ ☐
   - Turnover? ☐ ☐
   - Credit policies? ☐ ☐
   - The amount of unfilled orders? ☐ ☐
   - The effectiveness of the credit department? ☐ ☐
   - The real significance of credit limits? ☐ ☐

d. Scheduled the ratio of returns and allowances to sales by month for the last six months of the year and inquired about fluctuations? Indicate any evidence of dissatisfaction with the company's products. ☐ ☐

e. Determined whether customers' receivables are discounted to finance operations? The amount, if any, should be noted. ☐ ☐

f. Ascertained the purpose and repayment terms of loans (other than minor amounts) to officers and employees? ☐ ☐

g. Inquired about the collectibility of receivables and adequacy of reserves? ☐ ☐

h. Determined how the company establishes credit terms? ☐ ☐

i. Evaluated the collection efforts? ☐ ☐

3. For prepaid expenses, deferred charges and other assets, have you:

   a. Obtained a listing of securities and investments held by the company, showing the cost, carrying value and market value of each item? ☐ ☐

   b. If the company carries any investments on the equity method, obtained details of the origin of the investments, their cost, market value (if available) and earnings and dividend history? ☐ ☐

   c. Obtained details of patents owned by the company? ☐ ☐

   d. Determined the amortization policy for any prepaid expenses or deferred charges? ☐ ☐

   e. Determined how any goodwill or other intangibles arose and how they are being amortized? ☐ ☐

   f. Investigated the nature of any other assets? ☐ ☐

4. For accounts payable and accrued expenses, have you:

   a. Obtained an analysis of the type (vendors, taxes, payroll, payables on reimbursable contracts, etc.) and described payment practices for each? ☐ ☐

   b. Compared the balances in the various accounts with those at the end of the previous month, quarter and year? ☐ ☐

   c. Determined whether the company takes appropriate advantage of discounts for prompt payment? ☐ ☐

   d. Obtained a list of the company's principal suppliers, together with the approximate annual amounts purchased? Note all delinquencies in settlement of vendors' and suppliers' accounts. ☐ ☐

    e. Asked about the amounts of outstanding purchase commitments? □ □

    f. Asked about any other nonfinancial current liabilities? □ □

    g. Described the company's policy on vacation and sick pay accruals? □ □

5. For contingent liabilities, have you inquired about:

    a. Contracts and agreements to which the company is a party? □ □

    b. Price redetermination or renegotiation? □ □

    c. Sales subject to warranty and service guarantee? □ □

    d. Product liability? □ □

    e. Unfunded past service costs of pension plans? □ □

    f. Antitrust matters? □ □

    g. Any possible equal opportunity employment problems? □ □

6. Concerning environmental regulations, do you know:

    a. Whether the facility has received a waste treatment, storage and disposal permit under Sections 3004 and 3005 of the Resource Conservation and Recovery Act (RCRA)? □ □

      If so:

      • The financial liability of the site? □ □

      • Whether there have been any notices of violations or warnings? Make sure you have copies. □ □

    b. Whether the facility discharges wastewater into something other than a public owned treatment works (POTW)? □ □

      If so:

      • Have you obtained a copy of the discharge permit? □ □

      • Have there been any notices of violation? □ □

- Are there any "treatment facility changes" required? Note any costs involved. ☐ ☐
c. If the facility does use a POTW:
  - Whether "pretreatment" is required by the POTW? ☐ ☐
  - If so, its estimated costs? ☐ ☐
d. Whether the plan has generated hazardous wastes, as defined in Section 3002 of RCRA? ☐ ☐
  If so:
  - Where these wastes have been stored or disposed? ☐ ☐
  - What volume of waste was/is generated in a year? ☐ ☐
  - The plant's EPA/ID number (from manifest form)? ☐ ☐
e. Where there have been environmental disclosures in the 10-K? Make sure you have copies. ☐ ☐

7. Have you determined the purpose of any reserves, obtained an analysis of activity and determined the extent to which reserves are discretionary? ☐ ☐

8. Have you inquired about any other liabilities? ☐ ☐

FINANCING AND CAPITAL STRUCTURE

1. For borrowings (short- and long-term), have you:

   a. Listed the amounts of all financial liabilities and determined the general terms of notes, bonds and mortgages payable (e.g., lender, payment schedules, interest rates, seniority, personal guarantees and other pertinent information)? ☐ ☐
   b. Noted the nature and exact amount of assets pledged as collateral? ☐ ☐

   c. Noted aggregate payments due? □ □

   d. If any amounts are due to officers or stockholders, discovered the nature of the advances and repayment terms? □ □

   e. Determined the terms of indentures and ascertained that all covenants have been complied with? □ □

   f. Determined whether there are any restrictions in the indentures that would interfere with the acquisition? □ □

   g. Obtained credit reports from Dun & Bradstreet? □ □

   h. If debt is publicly held, obtained bond ratings? □ □

   i. Obtained the terms of capitalized leases and long-term noncapitalized leases? Determine the nature of property subject to the leases and what renewal or purchase rights exist. □ □

   j. Inquired into any quasi-financing agreements (take or pay contracts, etc.) and guarantees of debt of other entities? □ □

   k. Obtained information on any established lines of credit, terms and unused amounts available? □ □

2. Have you obtained details of any preferred stock outstanding and determined if the terms of the stock specify treatment in an acquisition or merger? □ □

3. For common stockholders' equity, have you:

   a. Obtained a shareholders' list? □ □

   b. If there is more than one class of common stock, determined the rights of each class? □ □

   c. Reviewed any treasury stock acquisitions, determined whether any treasury stock is "tainted" for purposes of pooling interests and ascertained that none is carried as an asset? □ □

    d. Determined whether the company has any obligations to issue or repurchase shares? ☐ ☐

    e. Inquired about the company's past dividend policy? ☐ ☐

    f. Inquired about any unusual capital accounts (donated capital, appraisal surplus, etc.)? ☐ ☐

4. Have you determined the percentages of the company's capitalization represented by the various types of long- and short-term obligations? ☐ ☐

5. Have you determined interest and fixed charge coverages for the last five years? ☐ ☐

6. Have you received the source and use of funds statements for the last few years? ☐ ☐

7. Have you determined the extent to which the company's growth has been (or could have been, ignoring nonrecurring transactions) financed by internally generated cash? Analyze the implications for the combined enterprise. ☐ ☐

8. Have you inquired about the company's policy on financial needs? ☐ ☐

9. Have you inquired about capital budgeting procedures? ☐ ☐

10. Have you evaluated the company's relationship with banks, lenders and the financial community in general? ☐ ☐

11. Have you reviewed the capital budget and planned sources of funds? ☐ ☐

12. Have you determined whether the existing debt repayment schedule can be met from operating cash flow? If refinancing will be

necessary, determine the effect of current interest rates. ☐ ☐

FORECASTS

1. Have you obtained available projections of earnings and cash flow? If possible, obtain the worst, best and most probable results. ☐ ☐

2. Did you subject the projections to the same ratio analysis applied to historical results and determine that relationships are consistent? ☐ ☐

3. Have you determined and evaluated the reasonableness of the assumptions used? ☐ ☐

4. Are projections consistent with industry and overall business expectations? ☐ ☐

5. If no projections are available, have you developed forecasts based on continuing historical growth trends, industry conditions and known factors? ☐ ☐

6. Did you adjust the projections for any items resulting from the acquisition? ☐ ☐

7. Have you reviewed cash flow projections (or developed them if unavailable) to determine that investment in working capital, new plant and equipment and scheduled debt maturities is appropriately provided? Determine the net cash flow that would be available to the buyer (preferably a range of minimum and maximum cash flows). ☐ ☐

8. Did you relate the cash flows developed to the proposed purchase price, using net present value or similar techniques? ☐ ☐

FINANCIAL MANAGEMENT

1. Have you formed an opinion about the overall credibility and reliability of the account-

ing and reporting of the company? Consider
the effects of private vs. public ownership,
tax-oriented accounting and the attitudes of
senior management.   ☐   ☐

2. Do you know to what extent the company's
   earnings have been "managed?"   ☐   ☐

3. Is the company audited by an independent
   accounting firm? If so, investigate the firm's
   reputation.   ☐   ☐

4. Have the accountants for the buyer reviewed
   the working papers of the company's auditors to note the adequacy of auditing work,
   the adjustments proposed by the auditors,
   problem areas and any differences of opinion
   between the company and its auditors?   ☐   ☐

5. Have you reviewed the adequacy and sophistication of the internal auditing department?
   Find out what its major recent findings were,
   if "operational audits" have been conducted
   and what those findings were.   ☐   ☐

6. Have you assessed the adequacy of internal
   accounting controls and the company's atti-
   tude toward strong controls?   ☐   ☐

7. Are you alert to any practices adopted to
   make the company appear more attractive,
   including:

   a. Adoption of less conservative accounting
      policies?   ☐   ☐
   b. Cutbacks in discretionary expenses, such
      as advertising, personnel development
      and maintenance?   ☐   ☐
   c. Unconservative accounting judgments,
      such as inappropriate provisions for sales
      returns, obsolete inventories or contin-
      gent liabilities?   ☐   ☐
   d. Company expenses being paid by stock-
      holders, directly or through bargain pric-
      ing (e.g., lease arrangements)?   ☐   ☐

    e. Whether stockholder-managers are draw-
       ing inadequate compensation?   □   □

8. Have you assessed the strength of the financial management and controllership function? □   □

9. Have you determined:

    a. How often internal reports are issued
      (monthly, quarterly or not at all)?   □   □
    b. How soon after the end of the period the
      reports are available and if they are
      used?   □   □
    c. Whether the internal reporting timetable
      and content are consistent with your
      monthly closing requirements?   □   □
    d. What changes may be needed and what
      their cost and training implications are?   □   □

10. Have you reviewed:

    a. How centralized the accounting function
      is?   □   □
    b. Whether subsidiaries have autonomous
      accounting departments that may not be
      functioning uniformly and, if so, how
      overall control is exercised?   □   □

11. Do you know how accurate interim reports
  are?   □   □

12. Have you investigated?

    a. If interim reports are prepared on a con-
      solidated basis or only by autonomous
      entities?   □   □
    b. How foreign subsidiaries or branches
      report?   □   □

13. Do you know how management information
  reporting is integrated with financial accounting? Find out if management reports compare results to budget and prior years.   □   □

14. Are controllable and uncontrollable costs separated in departmental reporting? □ □

15. Does management reporting provide the right information, the right amount and a sufficient base to take corrective action as needed? □ □

16. Have you considered how exception reporting is used? □ □

ELECTRONIC DATA PROCESSING

1. Have you listed all significant accounting and operational functions currently on computer? Find out if the company plans to computerize others. □ □

2. Have you assessed the sophistication of the EDP installation and the extent to which various needs are integrated? □ □

3. Is the EDP function centralized? □ □

4. Have you obtained a list of hardware used by the company and indicated lease terms, if any? Find out if the equipment is up-to-date. □ □

5. Do you know what the company's short- and long-term hardware plans are? □ □

6. Are any EDP functions being performed by service bureaus? □ □

7. Have you investigated how the EDP function would integrate with that of the buyer? □ □

8. Is there any intangible software value? □ □

RISK MANAGEMENT

1. What insurance is currently in effect? □ □

2. To what extent is the company assuming large deductibles or self-insured retentions? ☐ ☐

3. What unusual risks or products or events has the company been unable to insure? (Example, hazardous waste disposal, pharmaceutical products, satellite launching.) ☐ ☐

4. Will the company be able to obtain necessary insurance in the future? ☐ ☐

5. What insurance coverage is written on a "claims made" basis? Have the rights to purchase extended discovery period coverage been exercised? ☐ ☐

6. What liabilities have been assumed or transferred through contractual arrangements? ☐ ☐

7. What financial techniques are being utilized? Find out about premium financing, deferalls, use of captives, etc. ☐ ☐

8. Have you reviewed any loss experience for insured and uninsured claims? Have you reviewed reporting and reserving practices? ☐ ☐

9. Have any insurance policy aggregates been penetrated or exhausted? ☐ ☐

10. Are there any unusual circumstances which may give rise to claims in the future which are as yet unreported? ☐ ☐

11. Are there any recent or outstanding OSHA violations, citations or recommendations? ☐ ☐

12. Has the decision been made whether the buyer or seller is to assume liability for all prior acts? Will the company assuming liability for prior acts be financially sound enough to back up its indemnifications? ☐ ☐

13. Is there potential for cancellation of coverage such as Director's and Officer's liability insurance due to the sale or potential bonding problems due to highly leveraged condition? ☐ ☐

14. Are there any special service agreements that have to be maintained or renegotiated? ☐ ☐

15. Are there any outstanding premium adjustments (audits, retros, etc.) and will the buyer or seller receive credits or charges for them? ☐ ☐

16. Have you reviewed the methods by which accruals and tax deductions for premiums are handled? ☐ ☐

17. Does the company have an internal risk management/insurance department? Assess the management of the function. ☐ ☐

TAXES

1. Have you reviewed the principal taxes to which the company is subject and the amounts paid for the past three to five years? ☐ ☐

2. Have you obtained detailed reconciliations of the company's effective tax rate for the past three to five years? ☐ ☐

3. Have you considered recent changes in the tax law that would affect the company? ☐ ☐

4. Are deferred taxes provided on a comprehensive basis? Find out if the company has provided for unremitted earnings of subsidiaries. ☐ ☐

5. For federal taxes on income, have you reviewed:

   a. What years are still open? ☐ ☐
   b. What adjustments the company was required to make as a result of the most recent revenue agent's examination? ☐ ☐
   c. If the balance sheet accrual for open years has been adjusted to give effect to the agent's adjustments for years already examined? ☐ ☐

d. If there are any examinations currently in progress? Find out whether there have been any preliminary findings or matters under appeal. ☐ ☐

e. A schedule reconciling book income to taxable income (Schedule M of Form 1120) for the last three to five years? Determine that treatment has been proper. ☐ ☐

f. Amounts and expirations of any carry-overs of net operating or capital losses, investment tax credits foreign tax credits, *and other tax credit carryovers*? Consider how the acquisition will affect the status of these carryovers. ☐ ☐

g. What is the tax basis of the company's assets? Determine the effect on purchase price allocation under the residual method. ☐ ☐

6. For other taxes, have you examined:

a. In what state is the company domiciled and in what states the company has locations from which it accepts orders and/ or does business? Find out if it is required to file income, franchise, *intangible* or other business tax returns in those states and, if so, whether they have been filed and taxes have been paid. ☐ ☐

b. If all state and local taxes have been accrued and paid currently? Determine if any of these taxes are in dispute. ☐ ☐

c. What percentage of federal taxable income is being reported to all states in which the company files returns (i.e., what is the sum of all state *apportionment* factors)? Consider whether the company could owe taxes in states where it is not currently filing. ☐ ☐

d. If there are or have been any state tax audits? ☐ ☐

    e. If adjustments to federal taxable income
made by revenue agents' examinations
have been reported to the states affected? ☐ ☐

    f. If the state tax returns have been
amended to reflect Internal Revenue Service adjustment? ☐ ☐

    g. If the company is collecting and remitting all required sales *and/or use taxes*? ☐ ☐

    h. If all payroll taxes *have been* withheld
from employees *and* deposited promptly
in our authorized depository? ☐ ☐

    i. Any problems with other taxes to which
the company is subject (e.g., *real* property tax, *intangible tax*, excise tax)? ☐ ☐

7. Does the company have any significant foreign taxes or any significant U.S. tax problems relating to its foreign operations, such
as:

    a. Subpart F income? ☐ ☐

    b. Exposure to denial of foreign tax credits
because of potential allocation of expenses to foreign source income? ☐ ☐

    c. Intercompany pricing and reallocation of
income or expenses between related
entities? ☐ ☐

    d. FSC qualification? ☐ ☐

    e. Any transfers of intengible property to a
foreign corporation? ☐ ☐

8. Have you assessed all other areas of potential tax exposure or savings? ☐ ☐

9. Has the company tracked "earnings and profits" for tax purposes? Determine dividend
paying potential. ☐ ☐

10. Has the company obtained any private letter
rulings or determination letters? ☐ ☐

11. For the internal tax function, do you know:

a. If the company has a tax department?
   Find out how many people are employed
   and what functions are performed.   □ □
b. To what extent the company relies on
   outside attorneys or accountants for tax
   planning and return preparation?   □ □
c. If the tax function has technical expertise
   or merely serves compliance functions?   □ □
d. How oriented the company is to tax
   savings?   □ □
e. If the company maintains good tax records of items such as the tax basis of
   depreciable assets, basis of subsidiaries,
   accumulated earnings and profits and deferred taxes?   □ □

MANAGEMENT STYLES AND PRACTICES

Reviewing the candidate's management is one of the most sensitive and critical aspects of your analysis. You need to understand the roles in the organization of all key individuals and their effectiveness, centers of strength and weakness, unclear lines of communication, overlapping of responsibilities, the degree of delegation, morale and any other factors that will affect continuing operations.

MANAGEMENT APPROACH

Yes   No   Notes

1. Do you know what the basic approach of
   management is—entrepreneurial, authoritative, management-by-objectives? Determine
   the extent of centralization or decentraliza-
   tion of authority.   □ □

2. Have you assessed how the company's management approach will fit with that of the
   buyer?   □ □

3. Have you reviewed to what extent management would be integrated or permitted to operate autonomously? Decide if there are any areas in which functions of the company could be fully integrated. Then figure the cost savings that would result and weigh these against the advantages of allowing the company to be fully autonomous (preserving entrepreneurial spirit, integration costs). ☐ ☐

4. Have you considered to what extent existing management will stay on? Consider whether the buyer will need to provide management expertise in any areas. ☐ ☐

5. Does the company have management or operating expertise that complements any weaknesses in the buyer? ☐ ☐

6. Have you considered the record of the management team as a whole, including:

   a. The success of the company relative to the industry? ☐ ☐
   b. Whether the success of the company can be attributed to good management or a good market and industry? ☐ ☐
   c. The strategies management is using to increase market share and profitability? ☐ ☐
   d. The intelligence demonstrated in taking advantage of anticipated changes in the marketplace and the environment? ☐ ☐
   e. The work environment management has created in the company? Determine if people are working together. ☐ ☐
   f. Whether the management is as small in scale and as low in cost as posslbe? See if the company makes any effort to measure the ratio of administrative managers to total personnel and otherwise reduce administrative overhead. ☐ ☐

g. Whether management seems to work as a smooth integrated whole or is constantly dealing with crises and emergencies? ☐ ☐

h. The problem-solving and decision-making process? Are the right decisions being made at the right level of management? Find out if executives are spending most of their time preventing problems from arising, or if they are using their time to solve the same problems over and over. ☐ ☐

7. Have you determined the extent and effectiveness of basic concepts and tools of good management, including:

a. Documented objectives? ☐ ☐
b. Strategic and tactical plans? ☐ ☐
c. Responsive organizational structure and controls? ☐ ☐
d. Effective policies and procedures? ☐ ☐
e. Adequate management information systems? ☐ ☐
f. Budgetary control and responsibility accounting? ☐ ☐
g. Standards of performance and control? ☐ ☐
h. Management and manpower development? ☐ ☐

PLANNING

1. Do you know:

a. What the company's attitude is toward the planning process, long-range as well as annual? ☐ ☐
b. If plans are well thought out? ☐ ☐
c. If the plans and budget are real management tools? ☐ ☐

2. Have you determined who in the organization is responsible for long-range plans? ☐ ☐

3. Are the plans documented and communicated to the people responsible for implementing them? ☐ ☐

4. In the budgeting process, are sales forecasts
   based on real assessments of the market,
   rather than on percentage increases? Find out
   how costs are estimated and how far down
   into the company the budgeting process
   extends. ☐ ☐

5. Do budgets embody realistic assumptions of
   the availability of manpower, productive capacity and working capital? ☐ ☐

6. Are long-range plans integrated with capital
   budgeting and financial planning? ☐ ☐

7. Do long-range plans reflect competitive
   reactions? ☐ ☐

8. Do plans include alternative strategies? Determine if they are sufficiently flexible in relation to the operating environment. ☐ ☐

9. Are objectives described so achievement can
   be monitored? ☐ ☐

10. Does senior management judge whether op-
    erating personnel are working toward and
    achieving specified objectives? ☐ ☐

11. Has the company a history of meeting its
    goals? ☐ ☐

12. Are the budgeting and internal accounting
    functions integrated so that actual perfor-
    mance is reported on the same basis and un-
    der the same assumptions as budgets were
    prepared? ☐ ☐

13. Is actual compared to budget, and is there a
    formal procedure for documenting variances? ☐ ☐

14. Is the budget regularly updated? ☐ ☐

15. Do you know what procedures are used to monitor the marketplace, such as:

    a. Market share? ☐ ☐
    b. Activities of competition? ☐ ☐
    c. Attitudes of customers? ☐ ☐

INTERNAL CONTROLS

1. Do you know the company's attitude toward controls? ☐ ☐

2. Have you found out to what extent these basic elements of control operate:

    a. Are the duties and responsibilities within the company organized to provide segregation of duties? ☐ ☐
    b. If the company is too small for adequate segregation of duties, are other elements of control substituted? ☐ ☐
    c. Are the authority and responsibility of each function and person clearly defined and understood? ☐ ☐
    d. Is there an adequate accounting system that provides control over all assets and transactions? ☐ ☐
    e. Are there documented statements of policies and procedures? ☐ ☐

3. Are there any cost reduction or profit improvement programs? ☐ ☐

RESEARCH, DEVELOPMENT, AND ENGINEERING

Occasionally, a company that is looking to be acquired will eliminate costs that represent a drain on current earnings but are essential to long-term product development. It is not enough to depend on a candidate's past record of success in this area, instead, you must look closely at its current research and engineering capabilities to make sure it is being maintained at the same high level.

	Yes	No	Notes
1. Do you know the quality of product, process and market research in the company? Compare it to that in the industry as a whole.	☐	☐	
2. Are you familiar with the industry's basic source of effective research?	☐	☐	
3. Have you reviewed industry expenditures for research and how the company's research expenditures compare?	☐	☐	
4. Do you know what the company's policy has been on research and development? Review the percentage of sales it has been spending on research and development, any significant new products under development and the known R&D activities of competitors.	☐	☐	
5. Have you evaluated the company's technical activities and services by classification (e.g., contract, services, customer services, company R&D, manufacturing engineering, tool design, product engineering)?	☐	☐	
6. Have you reviewed the current and proposed staffing and personnel requirements for each activity?	☐	☐	
7. Do you know the methods of authorization, funding and reporting for product engineering and company R&D, related to overall research plans and market requirements?	☐	☐	
8. Have you assessed the caliber of the research staff? Find out if the staff has dealt with long-term research as well as day-to-day product engineering.	☐	☐	
9. Has the research program actually produced any new products during the past five years?	☐	☐	

10. For contract engineering, are you familiar with the programs, their tie-in to products and their follow-on prospects? □ □

11. Do you know the relationship of customer services to market activity, product sales and profitability? □ □

12. Have you assessed the type, condition and adequacy of engineering space and laboratories? □ □

13. Are proprietary rights on all products under development adequately secured to the company? □ □

14. Are you aware of any patents and trade-marks held or that have been applied for? □ □

15. Is the company protected in foreign as well as U.S. markets? □ □

16. Do agreements exist under which the company is licensee or licensor? Find out what the estimated royalties are. □ □

17. Are any key patents held by shareholders, management or other individuals? Find out if the company's rights to these patents are satisfactory. □ □

18. Are any infringement suits or claims outstanding? □ □

LEGAL MATTERS

In researching a company, be sure to identify any pending or threatened litigation and obtain counsel's opinion on the outcome. The consequences of any error can be severe, and, typically, escrow accounts or warranties are not sufficient. By using professional, independent help, you avoid some of the pitfalls.

	Yes	No	Notes
1. Are any charges pending against the company by any federal or state agency?	□	□	

2. Would this acquisition raise any antitrust problems? ☐ ☐

3. Does the company have in-house counsel? Assess whether it would be more effective to use outside attorneys. ☐ ☐

4. Have you obtained a copy of the most recent legal representation letters sent to the company's auditors? ☐ ☐

5. Is the company in compliance with environmental, equal opportunity employment and OSHA requirements? If not, find out what compliance will cost. ☐ ☐

6. Have you obtained legal opinions that stock is validly issued, fully paid and nonassessable and that the corporation is in good standing in the state of its incorporation and all states in which it is doing business? ☐ ☐

7. What outstanding legal matters should be dealt with in the acquisition agreement? ☐ ☐

8. What legal problems have competitors experienced? Find out if they will eventually confront the company. ☐ ☐

Overview Preacquisition Review Checklist

The following checklist summarizes major areas to address in a preacquisition review. This checklist does not provide procedures within each area in as much detail as the checklist provided in Appendix 2-A. Someone performing a preacquisition review may find both, either, or a combination of the two checklists to be useful.

GENERAL BUSINESS AND INDUSTRY MATTERS

1. Develop an understanding of the major business factors in the industry or industries in which the potential acquisition candidate operates.
   (a) Identify the major companies, market share, and distinctive features and way of doing business (production, marketing, etc.) of the potential acquisition candidate and major competitors. Determine if there are features that make the potential acquisition candidate more attractive than its competitors.
   (b) Determine trends in market share, revenues, unit quantities and volumes, and profitability for the acquisition candidate and major competitors.
   (c) Determine what the important technological aspects of the industry are and if there have been any significant recent developments and how this appears to influence the business of the potential acquisition candidate.
   (d) Evaluate the significance of government regulation and regulatory requirements, including new or proposed regulatory requirements that may not have yet affected the potential acquisition candidate's reported results.
   (e) Determine how difficult it is for a new competitor to enter the industry and to what extent competitors or suppliers might try to integrate their operations, resulting in additional competiton.
2. Analyze the major materials and resources used in producing and providing the potential acquisition candidate's products or services and the status of relationships with major vendors and suppliers, including information of recent years' volumes and prices for purchases from the vendors and suppliers.
3. Review listings of major customers and ascertain the amounts and types of business done with each. Consider the risk factors present if a significant percentage of the potential acquisition candidate's business is done with one or a few customers.
4. Determine to what extent the business of the potential acquisition candidate is seasonal and how this impacts the compatibility of the potential acquisition candidate's trends with the trends of the acquirer's existing operations.
5. Evaluate the labor relations in the industry, including the extent to which the labor force of the industry and of the potential acquisition candidate

are unionized. If the labor force of the potential acquisition candidate is not unionized, evaluate the likelihood that this could become a concern in the future and evaluate the additional costs that could result.

BUSINESS AND ORGANIZATIONAL INFORMATION

1. Obtain the history and background of the potential acquisition candidate from the time it was founded to the present.
2. Obtain details of the current capital and debt structures of the potential acquisition candidate, including any contingently issuable stock.
3. Review organization charts, procedures manuals, and information about key personnel, including compensation, age, position, and background. Review management compensation for several preceding years.
4. Review all current contracts. Note all important aspects, including transferability clauses. Ensure that the following kinds of contracts have been reviewed:
   (a) Employment contracts.
   (b) Stockholder agreements.
   (c) Sales and purchase agreements.
   (d) Union agreements.
   (e) Pension and other employee benefit plans and agreements.
   (f) Leases.
   (g) Loan and banking arrangements.
5. Identify all related parties and analyze the details of all intercompany transactions, including transactions with unconsolidated related parties.
6. Review procedures for preventing illegal acts or payments.
7. If the potential acquisition candidate is a subsidiary, consider what services provided by the parent may need to be replaced after the acquisition.
8. Obtain and review credit reports on the potential acquisition candidate.
9. Read minutes of board of directors and stockholder meetings for the last few years, articles of incorporation, corporate bylaws, and all other documents related to the corporate activities of the potential acquisition candidate.
10. Obtain geographical information on location of markets, facilities, and employees.
11. Obtain a listing of all employee benefit plans. Review pension plan

financial statements, the status of pension funding related to prior service and vested benefits, and compliance with ERISA and IRS requirements.

12. Obtain copies of all insurance policies and analyze major coverages and exposures, including any self-insurance practices, and details of any major insurance claims in the last few years.

13. Obtain an understanding of the potential acquisition candidate's research and development activities, including an analysis of funds and resources committed and results of past activities.

14. Review the acquisition candidate's major assets and operational facilities and estimate their remaining useful lives and productive capacity in relation to capacity utilized in recent years.

15. Evaluate adequacy of the system of internal control.

REVIEW OF PROPOSED TRANSACTION

1. Ascertain the following:
   (a) The reason the potential acquisition candidate is for sale.
   (b) Whether any previous proposed acquisitions have been terminated by the prospective acquirers and, if so, why.
   (c) Whether any cosmetic actions have been taken by the seller to make the potential acquisition candidate look more attractive then it really is.

2. Review the purchase agreement and any other documents related to the acquisition.

3. If applicable, review the prospectus or offering memorandum and related correspondence.

4. Evaluate alternative structures for tax purposes and the accounting method to be used (purchase or pooling of interests) and determine if the terms of the transaction are consistent with the desired effects.

5. Consider any filings with the SEC or other regulatory authorities that may be required.

6. Ascertain and consider the role of any intermediaries and other professionals associated with the transaction and inquire about the amount of fees payable to each.

7. Consider whether any possible antitrust issues could exist and whether any related pretransaction filings or approvals are necessary.

ACCOUNTING AND FINANCIAL

1. Develop an understanding of significant industry and company accounting practices and policies.
2. Review financial statements, annual reports, and SEC registration statements for several preceding years and also the most recent interim financial data available.
3. Review income statement, balance sheet, and cash flow forecasts for current and future periods, including product line and line of business breakdowns.
4. Determine carrying values of major facilities owned and identify any assets pledged as collateral or that are subject to liens.
5. Review copies of recent years' tax returns, information on status of tax examinations for open years, and copies of any reports on tax examinations.
6. Ascertain details of any pending or threatened litigation.
7. Review auditors' letters of recommendation and, if possible, review auditors' workpapers.
8. Review current backlog information by product line and line of business and compare to backlog levels of prior periods.
9. Review detailed accounting records to the extent considered appropriate in the circumstances, comparing details to trial balances used in preparing financial statements. Be alert for adjustments made late or in consolidation for judgmental items.
10. Perform any direct verifications considered necessary, such as physical inventories and inspection of facilities and assets.

CHAPTER THREE

Postacquisition Transition and Integration

3.1 GENERAL

After an acquisition has been completed, the critical process of transition and integration begins. A well-managed acquisition team will prepare for this before the closing of the acquisition. Overall responsibility for coordinating the accounting and systems transition is often assigned to someone in the acquirer's accounting department, who is assisted by specialists in accounting, data processing, and other areas.

The transition team should develop a priority list of the most critical areas to have under immediate control. Generally, it is critical to ensure that systems are in place to handle processing of transactions with minimum slowing down or loss of control over the ongoing flow of business. Some primary areas of concern are payroll, billing, collection, purchasing, and cash disbursements. If an acquired company has its own data processing capability, the continuation of processing transactions may be relatively simple. However, if the acquired company has been a remote location with processing done on a central system, the transition may be more difficult. In an extreme sense, one could imagine a seller *pulling the plug* that connects the remote location to the central system, bringing processing to a halt.

Typically, arrangements are made with the seller to continue to process transactions and produce essential output until an acquirer can establish independent systems for the acquired operation or complete the connection of systems of the acquired operation to a central system of the acquirer. Sometimes, temporary procedures must be put in place to handle parts of some systems on a manual basis until long-term data processing capability can be put in place.

An acquirer should establish procedures for regular monthly closings and operational and financial reporting by the acquired company, including establishing monthly closing schedules, procedures, and formats for providing balance sheets, income statements, and other data to the acquirer for consolidation. In addition, the acquirer should consider establishing procedures for periodic written reports analyzing and commenting on operating results by management of the acquired company. General management individuals of the acquirer who are responsible for the acquired company should be asked to describe the information they would like to be provided with to monitor the performance of the acquired company.

Accounting personnel should be assigned responsibility for handling the acquisition accounting, for reviewing internal control, and for reviewing accounting policies and procedures of the acquired company for compatibility with those of the acquirer and ensuring that any required reclassifications or adjustments are properly made in consolidation.

Personnel aspects of transition and integration are important. In some cases, an acquirer should consider transferring one or more supervisory or management individuals from the acquirer to the acquired company. An alternative is to assign someone from the acquirer organization as liaison to the newly acquired company to assist with understanding and implementing the acquirer's policies and procedures, as appropriate. This provides the acquired company ready access to someone familiar with the acquirer's systems, procedures, and accepted ways of operating. It also gives the acquirer comfort to know that one of its own management personnel is *minding the store* at its newly acquired operation.

Selected aspects of postacquisition transition and integration are discussed in the following sections.

3.2 PERSONNEL MATTERS

Personnel matters in accounting, financial, and systems departments are critical after an acquisition. If an acquisition is in progress or has already happened, uncertainty about possible organizational and personnel changes can cause great concern to employees about job security. If these concerns are not addressed by an acquirer, there can be losses of key employees that reduce the ability of the acquirer to carry forward the benefits of an existing and trained work force of an acquired company. While management is working out the details of an acquisition, attempts should be made to obtain permission to visit the potential acquiree's financial and systems management personnel. In initial meetings, it is advisable to recognize the existing chain of command because there will be in-place staff relationships and operating styles that often should be left intact at this point.

In an acquisition environment, morale and productivity may decline, partly because of distraction due to uncertainty about the future. There might even be negative feelings because employees may believe they have worked hard to gain recognition and credibility and now face the task of proving themselves all over again to a new management group. Effective communication is usually the best way to address this issue. In some cases, something as simple as a written communication from an officer of the acquirer company to all the employees of the acquired company, welcoming them to the acquirer organization, can provide much comfort to employees.

Employees at all levels will have questions that are important to them about future operations of the acquired company. Some of them may be difficult to answer. It is advisable to limit the first few meetings to discussions of general matters. Management of the acquirer should accept all questions, however, and be prepared for pointed ones. The employees of an acquired company will seek, and deserve, professional treatment.

Despite its best efforts, an acquirer should usually expect to lose some employees of an acquired company. A positive aspect of this is that the remaining employees may see more potential for security and career opportunity. Also, the acquirer can bring in some new employees who will not have prior allegiances.

It is essential to understand the levels of professional expertise in each department. All key employees should be evaluated. A good starting point is a review of personnel files to obtain familiarity with the backgrounds, talents, career progress, and problems, if any, of the employees of an acquired company. Difficulty or even failure in integrating an acquired company can result from an acquirer not properly assessing the level of personnel skills and resources needed to operate and control an acquired company in accordance with the acquirer's expectations.

A key issue is whether to place managerial personnel from an acquirer organization in the lead roles of an acquired company's accounting and systems departments. Although some acquirers do this as a matter of policy, it is sometimes more effective to have existing management continue if their qualifications, performance, and willingness to cooperate with the acquirer are sufficient.

3.3 ACCOUNTING AND REPORTING

(a) General

Starting the accounting and reporting process of an acquired company involves an array of technical and administrative matters. It is relatively easy if an acquirer can simply use the financial and operating reports that were previously used by the acquired company, but this is rarely the case.

Chapters 4 through 7 discuss accounting for acquisitions from the perspective of readily available information. In practice, more time is often spent trying to locate, assemble, and evaluate the facts and circumstances related to an acquisition than in applying the technical accounting principles and procedures. It is important that someone qualified in acquisition accounting be assigned responsibility for accounting for the acquisition—someone with enough experience to develop information about the acquisition in addition to applying the technical accounting principles and procedures.

(b) Recording the Acquired Balance Sheet

This discussion relates primarily to purchase method acquisitions of corporations. If the pooling of interests method has been used, historical amounts are carried forward and the postacquisition accounting and financial reporting process is much simpler. If the acquisition is a purchase of assets, the acquisition accounting allocations will be recorded in the primary books of account.

An acquirer will need to include an acquired company in its consolidated balance sheet as a consolidated subsidiary in its accounting close for the month in which the acquisition occurs. This is often done using estimates because the process of compiling and analyzing information with which to complete the acquisition accounting may have only begun. Intensified efforts to develop more precise acquisition accounting data should be made for year-end balance sheets or for financial data released to the public, such as at the end of a quarter.

As each month after an acquisition passes, an acquirer becomes aware of more information that affect the balance of an acquired company at the acquisition date. The kinds of information that an acquirer should be alert for include:

(a) Liabilities for expenses properly allocable to prior periods. These should be recorded as liabilities in the acquired balance sheet unless the purchase agreement enables recovery from the seller, in which case they would be reductions of the purchase price.

(b) Assets that do not have the values originally estimated. This can include uncollectible receivables, obsolete or damaged inventory that must be written off or sold at a loss, and equipment or other fixed assets that do not have the usefulness or fair market value originally estimated.

(c) Extraordinary repair and maintenance costs required to put machinery and equipment into adequate operating condition.

(d) Employee termination or severance costs.

(e) Rentals on facilities to be abandoned or otherwise not used.

Some of these items are resolutions of preacquisition contingencies for which adjustment to the purchase price allocation is *required* during an *allocation period* usually expected to last up to one year after the date of acquisition.

Although it is acceptable to continually adjust the opening balance sheet as additional information arises, it may not be sensible to change an estimated opening balance sheet every month during the year following an acquisition. An acquirer should consider revising the purchase price allocation in the accounting records only when sufficient information has arisen to finalize the allocation, unless a significant change has occurred. At some point, it makes sense to *freeze* the allocation and recognize any minor subsequent variations as income or expense items in the postacquisition income statement.

(c) Reporting Profit and Loss of an Acquiree

In the initial months following an acquisition, there may not be enough time to complete *pushing down* opening balance sheet adjustments and accounting practices of an acquirer into the records and reporting procedures of an acquired company. During this period, the basis of accounting and financial reporting by the acquired company may be the same as before the acquisition. If so, the acquired company's financial results must be adjusted for estimated acquisition accounting adjustments and accounting policy adjustments prior to consolidation or in consolidation.

Typical adjustments required to results of operations for inclusion in consolidation are:

(a) Recording goodwill amortization

(b) Adjusting depreciation expense to reflect cost allocated in the purchase accounting and changes in estimated useful lives.

(c) Reversing from profit and loss any items included as assets or liabilities in the purchase accounting balance sheet, if such items were included as income or expense in the acquired company's historical books in the postacquisition period

(d) Adjusting income and expense items to conform to accounting policies of an acquirer

(d) Keeping the Books of an Acquired Company

Push down accounting is a procedure in which acquisition accounting adjustments are reflected in the separate financial statements of an acquired company. This can be done either by worksheet adjustments to the acquired company's historical general ledger balances in preparing the financial statements or by recording the adjustments directly into the acquired company's general ledger.

The more current values that result from the push down procedure are usually more relevant than historical cost amounts for future review of financial condition and operating performance of an acquired company. However, there is a practical question of whether the primary books of an acquired company should be adjusted or whether they should continue to be kept using historical amounts. This decision should be made after considering the extent to which historical accounting data will be needed in the future. Typical reasons why historical data is needed are:

(a) Tax returns of the acquired company. Even if an acquired company is included in the consolidated return of an acquirer, historical tax information must be included in the tax return if the acquisition was tax-free or if it was a taxable transaction and the inside basis of the acquired company was not stepped up.

(b) The existence of a minority interest requires continuing data on an historical basis for accounting for the minority interest share.

Acquisition accounting adjustments may be made by the accounting staff of an acquired company before providing data to the acquirer for consolidation. If the acquisition accounting adjustments include sensitive or confidential information, it may be advisable for the acquirer to receive financial data from an acquiree on an historical basis and for the acquirer to make the acquisition accounting adjustments prior to or in consolidation.

3.4 TRANSITION OF SPECIFIC SYSTEMS

(a) General

A team consisting of accounting, data processing, and user department personnel should be established to evaluate the extent of systems changes required, to develop timetables and procedures, and to carry out the transition of specific systems.

An organized approach should be used to develop an action plan for transition of each system, considering the following:

(a) Ensuring that ongoing transactions are processed

(b) Ensuring that adequate controls are in place and that data will be properly summarized through transaction listings or general ledgers to enable monthly closings and operational reporting

(c) Establishing temporary procedures for screening all transactions over specified amounts for review for proper cutoff and possible claim to the seller

(d) Developing plans for transition to the systems and procedures that will be used on a medium- and long-term basis

Circumstances can range from situations in which most systems can be continued as before to situations in which substantial modification or even complete replacement of systems is required. Initially, a determination should be made of the extent to which each system will be retained, modified, or replaced.

Critical short-range planning is necessary if the acquired company's systems have relied on computer processing capability of a central location of the seller organization. A seller in this situation is typically not agreeable to continuing to process data for a long time for a company it has sold. Furthermore, to do so for a long time is not advisable for an acquirer for many reasons. If temporary dependence on a seller's remote data processing capability is necessary, an acquirer should plan to have its systems personnel quickly install and establish independent capability either at the acquired company or by use of the acquirer's central data processing capability.

Sometimes a seller is not willing or able to provide continuing data processing support, and hastily designed and implemented systems are necessary for use while more permanent systems are being arranged and installed.

An immediate item to address is whether any new forms, such as invoices, purchase orders, checks, and the like, must be ordered. Outside printers and job shoppers will require some advance notice, even in an expedited mode at a premium price, to manufacture and deliver preprinted forms.

The following sections discuss some transitional aspects of specific systems after an acquisition. There may be other systems that are unique to a particular acquired company that have important transition considerations.

(b) Payroll

Continuing the processing and payment of salaries and wages is a primary concern. If new bank accounts must be opened, this should be done immediately to enable meeting the first payroll processing cycle. If new forms, such as payroll checks, cannot be obtained in time, temporary measures can be taken, such as using blank check stock of a printing shop, which can print new bank account numbers on the checks.

The date of acquisition may occur in the middle of a pay period. If so, it is best to have the seller run the payroll to the end of the pay period or for the acquirer to pay the employees for the entire period and have one reimburse the other for a pro rata portion of the payroll.

In transitioning payroll systems, the following should be considered:

(a) The existence of proper payroll controls prior to printing the payroll checks

(b) That payroll reports satisfy all payroll department needs in addition to tax withholdings, such as credit union reporting, savings bonds, union reports, and other miscellaneous withholdings

(c) That payroll is processed in a secure location and with security precautions in place for signing plates

(d) If there is a practice of producing computer payroll files for the IRS, that continuation of these procedures is arranged

(e) Validation that every printed payroll check is received by an active employee

(f) If manual checks are written for vacation, termination, or other special payments, that procedures exist for updating year-to-date payroll information

(g) That check numbers are recorded and tracked and that all voided checks are recorded in the system

(c) Purchasing and Disbursements

Plans should be made immediately to ensure a proper cutoff of purchasing activity if a seller is responsible for all transactions prior to the acquisition date. This can include taking meter readings for utilities, cutoff and transfer of telephone services, and ensuring continuation of services without interruption. All purchase transactions and invoices received over a specified amount should be reviewed for several months after the acquisition to determine if they are the responsibility of the seller. Communications should be sent to vendors to inform them of the change in ownership and possibly to request that any billings for transactions prior to the acquisition be sent to the seller.

(d) Billing and Accounts Receivable

An acquirer's credit and collection personnel should immediately review the credit and collection policies and practices of the acquired company. The acquirer should review all overdue accounts and ensure that adequate collection actions are being taken and should also consider possible recoveries from the seller.

As with vendors, in some cases it is advisable to communicate with customers to inform them of the new ownership and any changes in practices that will be implemented.

If necessary, new lockboxes for cash receipts should be opened.

(e) Fixed Assets

Maintenance of fixed asset records after an acquisition can be a difficult task. If assets have been revalued to fair market value in the purchase accounting, accountability is often needed for both the historical basis and depreciation, and also the related amounts adjusted for the acquisition accounting.

Sometimes only one set of detailed fixed asset records is maintained that reflects the historical amounts. When an amount is needed for a particular asset with adjustment for the acquisition accounting, individual computations are made to allocate a portion of acquisition accounting adjustments to the particular asset. This need arises if, for example, an asset is sold after the acquisition.

Sometimes, a fixed asset ledger is established that reflects the purchase accounting adjusted amounts. If the value assigned to fixed assets is the total appraised value, then the appraised value of each asset can be used. If less than their total appraised value is allocated to fixed assets, then a pro rata amount of appraised value may be assigned to each asset. If a formal appraisal has been performed by an independent appraiser, a detailed report is usually provided that lists each significant asset and its appraised value.

Depreciation accounting and record keeping is another area of concern. Depreciation for consolidated purposes is computed using estimated useful lives from the date of acquisition. These remaining useful lives, as well as the depreciation method, may not be the same as those used for historical accounting purposes. An acquirer will need to decide whether to establish a complete set of acquisition accounting adjusted fixed asset and depreciation records or whether to compute summary adjustments to post in consolidation as acquisition accounting adjustments.

Depending on the circumstances, it may be advisable to take a physical inventory of all fixed assets and compare them to the detailed fixed asset records.

(f) Personnel Information Reporting

Increasing requirements to provide statistical information on hiring and employment practices to private and government agencies has led to companies installing systems to help satisfy these requirements. Some acquired companies have installed up-to-date systems of this type and others have old ones or none. It may be more efficient to install a new system for personnel information reporting than to try to continue with an old one.

(g) Computer Systems Transition

A computer systems specialist should be included on the transition team. The acquirer should review all available information and contracts related to data processing equipment and take a complete inventory of the equipment. The acquirer should also review maintenance contracts and records of periodic maintenance and repairs. It is particularly important to identify if there are any equipment leases or maintenance contracts that contain automatic renewal clauses if the vendor is not informed about a customer's desire to cancel.

The extent to which an acquired company's computer systems should be examined and evaluated will depend on the specific circumstances. Some or all of the following additional activities may be appropriate:

(a) Review of all hardware contracts, including manufacturers' hardware contracts, leasing or purchase contracts, telephone lease line agreements, modem rental agreements, and computer operating software contracts

(b) Review of capacity utilization and systems adequacy, including paper and data entry volumes, computer system efficiency, and hardware capacity

(c) Reviewing and evaluating code, program listings, and program documentation

(d) Discussions with user departments to ascertain their views about the effectiveness of the data processing function and quality of information provided

Checklist for Transition and Integration

GENERAL

(a) Review the purchase agreement and prepare a list of all areas requiring accounting or systems follow-up and ensure procedures are in place to address those areas.

(b) Review all forms and documents used in conducting the acquired company's business and determine if modifications must be made or new forms must be obtained.

(c) Determine if an outside appraisal will be necessary to assign fair market values.

(d) Arrange for any new permits, licenses, or registrations that may be required.

(e) Evaluate management personnel in the acquired company and determine if any changes should be made and if any personnel from the acquirer organization should be transferred to the acquired company.

(f) Arrange for training and orientation of staff in procedures and policies of the acquirer.

(g) Review contracts and leases for any required notifications to lessors and other parties.

ACCOUNTING AND REPORTING

(a) Assign a qualified accountant to handle accounting for the acquisition and for preparing acquisition accounting adjustments.

(b) Review accounting policies of the acquired company and arrange to conform to those of the acquirer if necessary.

(c) Prepare the opening balance sheet of the acquired company, giving effect to acquisition accounting adjustments.

(d) Prepare a list of preacquisition contingencies and ensure procedures are in place to monitor their resolution and to reflect such in the acquisition accounting.

(e) Develop a long-range plan for record keeping for acquisition accounting adjustments.

(f) Ensure that records will be maintained that provide all necessary information for federal, state, and local tax returns.

(g) Review the general ledger system and chart of accounts and make any changes that are required.

TAX COMPLIANCE

(a) Ensure that any required short period tax returns are prepared and filed.

(b) Ensure that sales and use tax requirements are met, including filing of proper returns and payment of any sales taxes due as a result of the acquisition.

(c) Review payroll tax implications of the acquisition, including whether FICA, FUTA, and SUTA tax limits must start over or if certain successor employer rules apply.

SYSTEMS

(a) Determine if the acquired company's systems are autonomous or dependent on a central data processing capability of the seller.

(b) Determine if any data processing capability will disappear as a result of the acquisition and evaluate need for replacement of such capability.

(c) Evaluate and arrange to continue any outside service bureaus as appropriate (e.g., payroll processing services).

(d) Ensure that adequate backup procedures are in place.

(e) Conduct a complete physical inventory of all computer hardware.

(f) Review maintenance contracts and records.

(g)   Determine to what extent computer capacity is being utilized and how much growth the existing system can absorb before system expansion is required.

(h)   Determine what languages the computer programs are written in and evaluate the quality of code.

(i)   Determine the extent to which the systems provide users with what they need.

(j)   Review and ensure adequacy of systems documentation.

PERSONNEL AND PAYROLL

(a)   Arrange for payroll processing for the period in which the acquisition occurs.

(b)   Arrange for proper filing of payroll taxes.

(c)   Evaluate human resource reporting system.

(d)   Review IRS reporting requirements.

(e)   Obtain any necessary new payroll deduction authorizations.

FIXED ASSETS

(a)   Develop a plan for record keeping for re-evaluations of fixed assets.

(b)   Develop a plan for record keeping for depreciation of revalued amounts and changes in useful lives.

BILLING AND ACCOUNTS RECEIVABLE

(a)   Set up procedures for allocation of cash receipts to any receivables that have been retained by seller.

(b)   Ensure that proper credit procedures are in place.

(c)   Ensure that overdue accounts are identified and are being pursued.

CASH

(a) Arrange to open new general, disbursing, and payroll bank accounts as necessary.
(b) Change authorized signers on bank accounts.
(c) Open new lockboxes for customer remittances.

CHAPTER FOUR

Accounting for Business Combinations—Overview

4.1 THE PURCHASE METHOD AND POOLING OF INTERESTS METHOD

(a) General

The primary accounting standard on accounting for business combinations is Accounting Principles Board (APB) Opinion No. 16, *Business Combinations*, which was issued in 1970. Although there have been numerous interpretations of and amendments to it, Opinion 16 is still the primary standard on accounting for business combinations. FASB Statement No. 109, *Accounting for Income Taxes*, which was issued in 1992, made significant changes to accounting for differences in book and tax bases of assets acquired and liabilities assumed in purchase acquisitions, for deferred taxes at acquisition date, for goodwill and negative goodwill, and for acquired net operating loss and tax credit carryforwards.

Under Opinion 16, there are two methods of accounting for business combinations: (a) the pooling of interests method and (b) the purchase method. Opinion 16 describes 12 conditions which, if met, *require* the use of the pooling of interests method. If any of the conditions are not met, then the purchase method *must* be used.

(b) Pooling of Interests Method

A pooling of interests business combination is accounted for as a combining of stockholder interests, and the historical values of assets, liabilities, and stockholders' equities of the pooling companies are combined as of the date of the business combination. Because assets are not adjusted to fair value, the historical asset values carried forward usually result in lower future depreciation and amortization expenses than would have resulted from the purchase method. Also, goodwill is not established and there is no future goodwill amortization in a pooling of interests.

Prior income statements are restated to combine the operations of the pooled companies as if the combination had always been in effect. An incentive to some to use the pooling of interests method has been to have higher reported earnings in future periods and higher reported returns on equity as a result of lower depreciation and amortization expense.

(c) Purchase Method

Under the purchase method, one company is viewed as having acquired the net assets and business of another. The acquirer records the assets acquired and liabilities assumed based on their fair values at the date of acquisition. Any excess of total acquisition cost over the fair value of identifiable assets and liabilities is assigned to goodwill, which is amortized to expense in future periods.

4.2   DETERMINING WHICH METHOD TO USE

If a business combination meets all 12 conditions specified in Opinion 16, the pooling of interests method must be used. If any of the conditions are not met, the purchase method must be used. *The pooling of interests method and purchase method are not alternatives to choose from in accounting for a business combination.*

Most business combinations are accounted for by the purchase method because they do not meet one or more of the conditions for use of the pooling of interests method.

Prior to the issuance of Opinion 16 in 1970, accounting for business combinations was not well defined. Some believed there was inappropriate use of the pooling of interests method for business combinations completed with exchanges of stock that were really purchase acquisitions. Some business combinations were paid for partly in cash and partly in stock and were accounted for as part purchase and part pooling, a procedure effectively done away with by Opinion 16.

4.3   THE FASB CONSOLIDATIONS PROJECT

(a) General

Since the early 1980s, the FASB has been evaluating alternate approaches to consolidation policy and procedures in its project on consolidations and related matters. While there are many parts to this broad project, a central group of issues about consolidation policy and procedures has important implications to many other parts of the project. These fall into two major categories: (a) those related to how to determine when one entity becomes a subsidiary of another—or said in another way, how to determine when an acquisition has occurred and (b) those related to how to account for a parent-subsidiary relationship in consolidated financial statements, including accounting for the acquisition.

In September 1991, after years of work by its board members, staff, and task force members, the FASB published a Discussion Memorandum (DM), *Consolidation Policy and Procedures*. While serving on the FASB staff from 1988 to 1990, the author was the project manager responsible for this project and worked extensively on developing materials for the DM, including the DM's illustrative examples of alternate approaches to acquisition accounting.

In August 1994, the FASB issued a Preliminary Views (PV), *Consolidation Policy*. PV's are issued for public comment, after which the FASB redeliberates the issues before preparing an exposure draft of an FASB Statement. In the PV, all FASB board members, except one, support control (as defined in the PV) as the basis for consolidation policy—regardless of whether the controlling party holds an equity interest in the controlled party.

As a result of the project, it is likely that the FASB will issue one or more Statements that will change present acquisition accounting principles and practices—possibly significant changes, in how to determine when an acquisition has occurred, in how acquisition accounting is done, or in both. The following sections discuss the aspects of the September 1991 DM and the August 1994 PV that are relevant to acquisition accounting.

(b) Consolidation Policy

(i) BASIS FOR CONSOLIDATION POLICY

Consolidation policy is the basis for determining if there is a parent-subsidiary relationship that requires inclusion of the subsidiary in the parent's consolidated financial statements. Ownership of a majority voting interest is the basis for consolidation policy under generally accepted accounting principles in the U.S., as provided in FASB Statement No. 94, *Consolidation of All Majority-Owned Subsidiaries*.

In recent years, with development of increasingly sophisticated business structures and ways of doing business, it has become apparent that if one entity controls another, it can realize significant benefits from that control. The FASB identified and studied many circumstances in which one entity can control another without majority ownership.

At one extreme, control can be achieved without any equity ownership, in which case some believe consolidation is appropriate despite the absence of any equity interest. Others are not comfortable with consolidation in that situation and believe that for consolidation there should be ownership of some equity interest. That view leads to what is sometimes called the *slippery slope* dilemma, which is struggling with how it could be theoretically sound to almost arbitrarily require consolidation if control exists with 40% equity ownership but not if there is only 39%, or to require consolidation at 30% but not at 29%, and so on. At the other end of the spectrum, some believe that control should be present for consolidation but that there should also be ownership of a majority equity interest.

Control advocates and ownership advocates seem to generally agree that present consolidation policy based on ownership of a majority voting interest leaves out some situations that probably should be consolidated. It has been quite difficult for the FASB to decide what approach (control, ownership, or a combination of the two) should be the basis for consolidation policy.

After extensive work and deliberation, the FASB arrived at the following preliminary view on consolidation policy and definition of control, which are included in the PV document:

> "A controlling entity (parent) shall consolidate all entities that it controls (subsidiaries) unless control is temporary at the time that entity becomes a subsidiary. For purposes of this requirement, control of an entity is power over its assets—power to use or direct the use of the individual assets of that entity to achieve the objectives of the controlling entity." [paragraph 7]

The PV document distinguishes between two types of control—legal control and effective control.

(ii) LEGAL CONTROL

Legal control is usually attained by a controlling entity having majority voting rights. As a result, there is no possibility of other stockholders aggregating enough votes to overrule the controlling entity in electing or appointing a majority of the board of directors or other governing board. Legal control by having majority voting rights can be achieved in a multiple-tier subsidiary structure, sometimes called a *pyramid*, by having each corporation in the structure hold at least a majority voting interest in the corporation one sequential tier below it. The parent may own a small equity interest in the lower-tier corporations, yet have legal control over them. Another way to attain legal control is through ownership of a class of voting stock with disporportionate voting rights. Yet another way is through the use of voting trusts.

(iii) EFFECTIVE CONTROL

Effective control exists if one entity controls another even though it does not own a majority voting interest or otherwise have legal control. Effective control is most often achieved by ownership of a large minority interest where there are no other concentrated blocks of voting stock that could enable other stockholders to overrule the holder of the large minority interest in electing or appointing a majority of the board of directors or other governing board. Effective control is presumed if a party owns a minority voting interest of approximately 40% or more and no other party or organized group of parties owns approximately 20% or more.

Under the approach of the PV document, effective control is presumed if a party has demonstrated recent ability to dominate the nomination of candidates for another entity's governing board and has been able to itself cast a majority of votes cast or has been able to otherwise dominate the voting process in electing members of the other entity's governing board. Effective control is also presumed if one entity has a unilateral ability to *obtain* a majority voting interest without incurring significant additional cash cost, such as by ownership of convertible securities. Effective control also exists if control is predetermined through such devices as provisions in a corporation's charter that limit its activities to those intended to provide cash flows or other benefits to a specified entity.

Effective control may also exist even if circumstances leading to a presumption of effective control are not present. The PV document discusses an array of circumstances that indicate that an entity may have effective control over another.

Under the PV document, an entity's management would be responsible for determining whether that entity controls another entity.

(c) Acquisition Accounting Procedures

(i) GENERAL

Consolidation procedures deal with accounting for an acquisition of a subsidiary and subsequent accounting for the subsidiary's assets, liabilities, revenues, expenses, gains, and losses in the parent's consolidated financial statements. Major project issues related to acquisition accounting include how to account for:

(a) An acquiree's identifiable assets and liabilities and goodwill at the acquisition date,

(b) Step acquisitions, and

(c) Acquisition of additional interests in a subsidiary after the initial acquisition

Exhaustive study and further development of theories about consolidation policy and procedures led to three prevailing concepts of consolidated financial statements: (a) the economic unit concept, (b) the parent company concept, and (c) the proportionate consolidation concept.

There is a theoretical linkage between the accounting procedures for acquisitions that would be used under each concept and the way one would set consolidation policy, or determining when an acquisition has occurred. Those strongly in favor of a concept-based approach believe that it would be incorrect to use consolidation policy associated with one concept and acquisition accounting procedures associated with another. Others are more flexible and seem willing to mingle policy and procedures of two or more concepts in ways that in their view provide the best information for financial statement users, despite what some would call a lack of theoretical consistency.

(ii) THE ECONOMIC UNIT CONCEPT

The economic unit concept views consolidated financial statements as those of a group of legal entities operating as a single unit under common control. When control of an entity is attained, an acquisition has occurred, regardless of whether majority equity ownership or, for that matter, any equity ownership is acquired.

Stockholders' equity includes the ownership interests of all parties, divided into a controlling interest and a noncontrolling interest, all of which are included in equity in the balance sheet. Acquisition, or the attaining of control, would result in acquisition accounting that includes all of the acquiree's assets and liabilities in the consolidated statements at fair value at date of acquisition—even for interests not owned by the acquirer. This contrasts with the current practice of accounting for minority interests on an historical basis. Under a *full goodwill interpretation* of the economic unit concept, an acquirer would record goodwill to the extent of all interests in the acquired entity and under a *purchased goodwill interpretation*, an acquirer would record only the portion of goodwill related to the acquirer's interest.

Step acquisitions are accounted for by valuing an acquiree's assets and liabilities at fair value at the date control is attained. Holding gains or losses are recognized if previously purchased interests cost less than fair value at the date control is attained. This would be a significant change from present practice.

Subsequent transactions in a subsidiary's stock (additional purchases or sales by the parent) are accounted for as treasury stock transactions—investments by or distributions to owners. This would be a change from current practice of a parent using purchase accounting for acquisitions of additional interests in a subsidiary or recognizing gain or loss on sales of stock of a subsidiary.

The economic unit concept is based on consistent logic that leads to consolidation policy and procedures for a consolidated entity operating as a unit. Its foundation was in a traditional theory of consolidated financial statements known as the *entity* theory. In the project, the FASB staff developed the economic unit concept as a further evolution of the entity theory.

(iii) THE PARENT COMPANY CONCEPT

The parent company concept views consolidated statements as reporting on the beneficial interests (the right to share in profits, receive dividends, and recover one's investment through stock sale or asset liquidation) of the parent company's stockholders, including their partial interests in subsidiaries if they are not wholly-owned. The parent company concept does not specify what level of beneficial interest should require consolidation and views on that point differ. To consolidate, control must be present along with an adequate beneficial interest.

A minority interest is not considered to be part of stockholders' equity. The familiar procedures of purchase accounting are applied to the equity interest of a subsidiary that is acquired and any minority interest is accounted for on an historical basis. Step acquisitions are accounted for by purchase accounting allocations of the cost of each purchase, with separate determinations of goodwill for each or partial interest purchased, or *layer*. Acquisitions of additional interests in a subsidiary are accounted for as purchases, with separate determination of fair values and goodwill for the additional partial interests acquired. Sales of stock, whether by direct sale of a portion of the parent's holdings or by additional issuance of stock by the subsidiary, are accounted for as dispositions with recognition of gain or loss.

The parent company concept is the most similar of the three concepts to current practice using the purchase method.

(iv) THE PROPORTIONATE CONSOLIDATION CONCEPT

The proportionate (or pro rata) consolidation concept is a variation of the parent company concept. The basis for consolidation and accounting for the parent's beneficial interest in a subsidiary is essentially the same as under the parent company concept. The distinctions are that ownership is given even more importance in consolidation policy. A minority interest's shares of assets, liabilities, revenues, expenses, gains, and losses are not included in the consolidated financial statements—only the parent's share is included.

4.4 SUMMARY

At present, Opinion 16, Statement 109, and various APB and FASB Interpretations and EITF consensuses govern accounting for acquisitions.

The following three chapters have been prepared to provide explanations and illustrations of current acquisition accounting procedures and practices. Chapter 5 addresses the pooling of interests method, Chapter 6 addresses the purchase accounting method, and Chapter 7 addresses special accounting requirements for leveraged acquisitions.

APPENDIX 4-A

Accounting Standards on Business Combinations

Following is a list of primary accounting standards for accounting for business combinations. This list is not an all-inclusive index of accounting standards and published guidance on accounting for business combinations.

APB OPINIONS

No.	Description
15	Earnings Per Share (effects on earnings per share of mergers and acquisitions)
16	Business Combinations (the comprehensive professional standard on accounting for business combinations)
17	Intangible Assets (accounting for goodwill and other purchased intangibles)
21	Interest on Receivables and Payables (discounting to present value)

AICPA ACCOUNTING INTERPRETATIONS

No.	Title and Description
N/A	Unofficial Accounting Interpretations of Opinion 16 (contains 39 interpretations issued between December 1970 and March 1973)

N/A   Unofficial Accounting Interpretations of Opinion 17 (goodwill in a step acquisition)

FASB STATEMENTS

No.	Title and Description
38	Accounting for Preacquisition Contingencies of Purchased Enterprises
79	Elimination of Certain Disclosures for Business Combinations by Nonpublic Enterprises (exempts nonpublic enterprises from Opinion 16 requirements for pro forma disclosures)
94	Consolidation of All Majority-Owned Subsidiaries
109	Accounting for Income Taxes (deferred taxes, goodwill, and accounting for net operating loss and other carryforwards)

FASB INTERPRETATIONS

No.	Description
4	Applicability of FASB Statement No. 2 to Business Combinations Accounted for by the Purchase Method (accounting for assets from research and development acquired in a purchase method acquisition)
21	Accounting for Leases in a Business Combination

FASB TECHNICAL BULLETINS

No.	Description
85-5	Issues Related to Accounting for Business Combinations

CHAPTER FIVE

The Pooling of Interests Method

5.1 CONDITIONS FOR USE OF THE POOLING OF INTERESTS METHOD

In Opinion 16, the conditions that require use of the pooling of interests method are organized into the following three categories:

1. Attributes of the combining companies (Opinion 16, paragraphs 46a and 46b).

2. Manner of combining interests (Opinion 16, paragraphs 47a through 47g).

3. Absence of planned transactions (Opinion 16, paragraphs 48a through 48c).

These conditions are discussed in the following sections.

5.2 ATTRIBUTES OF THE COMBINING COMPANIES

(a) Autonomy (Opinion 16, paragraph 46a)

Condition
Each of the combining companies is autonomous and has not been a subsidiary or division of another corporation within two years before the plan of a combination is initiated.

A wholly-owned subsidiary that distributes voting common stock of its parent qualifies if the parent would have met all the conditions for a pooling if it had issued its own stock. If a parent owns substantially all the voting common stock of a subsidiary, that subsidiary is wholly-owned for this test. Less than 90% is not considered substantially all and generally the percentage is expected to be higher.

The two-year autonomy requirement does not apply to a company newly incorporated within two years prior to initiation of the business combination or to a portion of a company that was acquired in a purchase method business combination during the two-year period preceding initiation. An established company may not *spin-off* a subsidiary or a portion of its business or assets into a newly formed corporation to escape the two-year autonomy rule. However, a subsidiary or a new company that acquires assets divested as a result of a regulatory or judicial decree is considered autonomous. Personal holding companies and sole proprietorships are normally exempt from the autonomy requirement.

The *date of initiation* of a plan occurs when an issuing corporation has made an offer and is obligated to consummate the combination if it is accepted or any other specified conditions are met. The obligation may be subject to required approvals from regulatory authorities, stockholders, or others. For a business combination negotiated by the combining companies, the date of initiation is the date on which the major terms of a plan have been announced. For a business combination effected by a tender offer, the date of initiation is the date the stockholders of a combining company are notified in writing of an offer. The ratio of exchange upon which the exchange of voting common stock is to be based must be announced as part of the initiation of the plan.

(b) Independence (Opinion 16, paragraph 46b)

Condition
Each of the combining companies is independent of the other combining companies.

The combining companies may hold as intercorporate investments no more than 10% of the outstanding stock of any combining company.

5.3 MANNER OF COMBINING INTERESTS

(a) Complete Transaction (Opinion 16, paragraph 47a)

Condition
The combination is effected in a single transaction or is completed in accordance with a specific plan within one year after the plan is initiated.

The *consummation date* is the date on which assets have been transferred to the issuing company and ownership of the issuing company's stock has been transferred to the stockholders of the other combining company. Consummation must occur within one year after the date of initiation, unless there are delays beyond the control of the combining companies such as those caused by deliberations by regulatory agencies that must approve the transaction or certain kinds of litigation such as antitrust litigation.

Changes to terms of an exchange of stock results in termination of a plan of combination and the initiation of a new plan. If earlier exchanges of stock are adjusted to the new terms, the one-year period permitted for completion remains the same as under the original plan. If earlier exchanges of stock are not adjusted to the new terms, they are intercorporate investments at the date of initiation of the new plan. If a plan is formally terminated and a new plan initiated at a later date, any shares exchanged under the previous plan are intercorporate investments at the date of initiation of the new plan, even if the new plan is identical to the previous one.

Initiation of a plan occurs if an option has been issued that requires unilateral performance by one party or bilateral performance by both parties. Granting of a right of first refusal does not result in initiation. Payment of cash or other consideration for a right of first refusal would preclude pooling of interests accounting.

(b) Exchange of Voting Common Stock (Opinion 16, paragraph 47b)

Condition
A corporation offers and issues only common stock with rights identical to those of the majority of its outstanding voting common stock in exchange for substantially all the voting common stock interest of another company at the date the plan of combination is consummated.

An issuing company must exchange shares of its own voting common stock for at least 90% of the other combining company's outstanding voting common stock at the date of consummation. Shares held as intercorporate investments at the date a plan is initiated, shares acquired other than in exchange for voting common stock of an issuing company, and shares of an other combining company that remain outstanding after consummation of the plan are excluded from the computation of shares exchanged at the consummation date.

In determining if the 90% test is met, intercorporate investments are included in the number of shares outstanding and excluded from the number of shares exchanged. If an intercorporate investment in common stock of an issuing company is held by another combining company, either acquired before or after initiation of the plan, an adjustment must be made to reduce the number of shares exchanged for the 90% test. That adjustment is computed by reducing the number of shares of the other combining company exchanged by an equivalent number of shares of the issuing company held based on the ratio of exchange. This is required because some of the stock being issued by the issuing company is essentially a reacquisition of some of its own shares and not an exchange for independent interests held by stockholders of the other combining company.

To illustrate, in Exhibit 5.1 assume that Company A and Company B engage in a business combination effected by a ratio of exchange of one share of Company A stock per three shares of Company B stock. Company B has 100,000 shares outstanding. Company A exchanges 32,000 shares of stock for 96,000 shares of Company B stock. Company B holds an intercorporate investment of 1,000 shares of Company A stock. The following illustrates the 90% test.

EXHIBIT 5.1. Illustration of 90% Test if the Other Combining Company Holds an Intercorporate Investment in the Issuing Company

Outstanding shares of Company B voting common stock at date of consummation	100,000
Shares of Company B received by Company A	96,000
Less, intercorporate investment of Company B in Company A, expressed in equivalent shares of Company B (1,000 × 3)	(3,000)
Shares of Company B exchanged for 90% test	93,000
Percentage of Company B shares exchanged	93%

In Exhibit 5.1, the 90% test is met. However, if Company B held an intercorporate investment of 3,000 shares of Company A stock, the adjustment for intercorporate investments would have been 9,000 shares, decreasing the number of shares exchanged to 87,000, or 87% of Company B's outstanding voting common stock. The 90% test would not be met and the pooling of interests method would not apply to the business combination.

If an issuing company receives at least 90% of the voting common stock of an other combining company, any additional receipt of voting common stock of the other combining company in exchange for cash, debt securities, warrants, or *tainted* treasury stock (see § 10.6(b)(ii)) does not disqualify the use of the pooling of interests method.

A business combination accounted for by the pooling of interests method may be structured by the formation of a new corporation to issue stock to effect the combination of two or more other companies. To use the pooling of interests method in that transaction structure, the 90% test must be met by each of the combining companies in the exchange of stock with the new corporation and, furthermore, it is necessary that the 90% test would have been met giving consideration to intercorporate investments if any one of the combining companies had issued its stock to effect the combination. If another combining company has outstanding debt or equity securities other than voting common stock that are not considered residual equity interests, the issuing company would meet the requirements for using the pooling of interests method if those other securities are handled in any of the following ways. The issuing company may:

1. Assume outstanding debt securities or allow debt securities or equity securities other than common stock to remain outstanding,

2. Exchange substantially identical securities or voting common stock for outstanding debt and equity securities other than common stock of the other combining company, or

3. Retire the outstanding debt or securities other than common stock by paying cash if the securities are callable or redeemable.

An issuing company may not give consideration other than voting common stock in exchange for outstanding debt or equity securities other than common stock if they were issued in exchange for voting common stock during the two-year period prior to the date of initiation. Any issuing company may issue voting common stock in exchange for the net assets of another combining company. Some assets may be retained by another combining company to settle liabilities if any assets remaining after settlement are to be conveyed to the issuing company. In a *stock-for-assets* pooling of interests, if another combining company has equity securities other than common stock outstanding, the issuing company may issue only voting common stock or voting common stock and other equity securities in the same proportions as the outstanding equity securities of the other combining company. If intercorporate investments exist in a stock-for-assets pooling of interests, special computations are necessary in the 90% test.

To illustrate, assume that Company A issues 40,000 shares of voting common stock in exchange for the net assets of Company B, of which 6,000 shares apply to interests of preferred stockholders of Company B. Company B has 100,000 shares of voting common stock outstanding. Intercorporate investments are: (a) Company A holds 3,000 shares of Company B voting common stock, and (b) Company B holds 1,800 shares of Company A voting common stock. The computations in Exhibit 5.2 indicate that the 90% test is met.

EXHIBIT 5.2. Illustration of 90% Test for a *Stock-for-Assets* Exchange With Intercorporate Investments

Company A voting common shares issued for net assets of Company B	40,000
Add, voting common shares of Company A held by Company B	1,800
Total Company A voting common shares issued in exchange for net assets of Company B	41,800
Less, Company A voting common shares issued applicable to preferred stock interests in Company B	(6,000)
	35,800
Adjustments for intercorporate investments:	
Company A voting common shares held by Company B	(1,800)
Company B voting common shares held by Company A (restated as equivalent shares of Company A based on the ratio of Company A shares issued for common stock interests of Company B to total outstanding voting common shares of Company B)	(644)
Adjusted Company A voting common shares exchanged for 90% test	33,356
Company A voting common shares exchanged for voting Common stock interests in Company B	35,800
Percentage for 90% test	93%

EITF Issue No. 87-27, *Poolings of Companies That Do Not Have a Controlling Class of Common Stock*, addressed conditions for pooling of interests accounting if the existence of one or more classes of voting preferred stock that are not substantively equivalent to common stock results in no controlling class of common stock. If the company with this situation is not the issuing company, pooling of interests accounting may be used only if the issuing company exchanges common stock for substantially all of the voting common and voting preferred stock of the other combining company. If the issuing company has no controlling class of common stock because of outstanding voting preferred stock, pooling of interests accounting may be used only if the issuing company exchanges common stock for a sufficient portion of the voting preferred stock to result in a controlling class of common stock prior to or at consummation.

Resale restrictions or requirements that shareholders sell some or all of their shares precludes pooling of interests accounting, unless they are due to government regulation. Pooling of interests accounting is precluded if an issuing company receives a right of first refusal to reacquire shares, as indicated in the response to Question No. 4 in FASB Technical Bulletin No. 85-5, *Issues Relating to Accounting for Business Combinations.*

EITF Issue No. 86-10, *Pooling With 10 Percent Cash Payout Determined by Lottery*, addressed accounting for a creative way of structuring business combinations to try to meet the pooling of interests conditions. An issuing company would offer to exchange 90% common stock and cash up to 10% for fractional shares and to dissenters wishing to receive cash. If the requests for cash exceed 10%, then a lottery would be held to determine which dissenters would receive cash up to the 10% limit. The EITF consensus on this issue was that pooling of interests accounting was not precluded. However, pooling of interests accounting should not be used if an issuing company offers to exchange cash, stock, or debt in a combination without a 90% requirement and the result was that the shareholders of the other combining company selected stock to the extent that the 90% test was met. An issuing company's *offer* must comply with the pooling conditions.

Warrants may not be exchanged for cash. They may be exercised and the shares issued exchanged for common stock in a business combination, exchanged directly for stock based on the exchange ratio and the difference between the warrant exercise price and the market value of the stock to be received, or exchanged for similar warrants of the issuing company.

(c) No Changes in Common Equity Interest (Opinion 16, paragraph 47c)

Condition
None of the combining companies changes the equity interest of the voting common stock in contemplation of effecting the combination either within two years before the plan of combination is initiated or between the dates the combination is initiated and consummated; changes in contemplation of effecting the combination may include distributions to stockholders and additional issuances, exchanges, and retirements of securities.

Dividends and other distributions to stockholders in the normal course of business, such as recurring dividend payments, do not result in changes in equity interests that preclude use of the pooling of interests method. A disqualifying change in equity interests will occur if there is a substantial change in terms of outstanding stock options or similar arrangements. Issuance of stock pursuant to a stock option or similar arrangement within two years of consummation is considered a change in equity interest, unless it can be supported that they were for a business purpose other than anticipation of the business combination.

(d) Limitations on Reacquisitions of Stock (Opinion 16, paragraph 47d)

Condition
Each of the combining companies reacquires shares of voting common stock only for purposes other than business combinations, and no company reacquires more than a normal number of shares between the dates the plan of combination is initiated and consummated.

Customary and systematic acquisitions of treasury stock such as those to obtain shares for issuance pursuant to stock option plans do not cause failure to meet this condition for pooling. Acquisitions of an issuing company's stock by other combining companies after initiation of a plan are reacquisitions of stock are added to intercorporate investments at the date of initiation in the 90% test. This condition prevents use of the pooling of interests method if there have been significant reacquisitions of stock of the combining companies, because the previously existing stockholder groups would not have pooled their interests. Instead, a substantial portion of the business combination has been completed by the purchase of stock for cash.

For public companies, shares of treasury stock reacquired within two years prior to the date of initiation, except those reacquired for customary reissuance under stock option and similar plans, are *tainted* for purposes of the business combination pooling of interest conditions. Tainted treasury stock is added to intercorporate investments in the 90% test. Therefore, the 90% test will not be failed if 10% or less of the shares exchanged are tainted shares if no other reductions to shares exchanged are required, such as for intercorporate investments.

A combining company's treasury stock will not be tainted if acquired with *reasonable expectation of issuance* for a specific business purpose such as: (a) an acquisition to be accounted for by the purchase method, (b) issuance of contingently issuable shares in a previous business combination, or (c) other business reasons unrelated to the business combination expected to be accounted for as a pooling of interests. The requirement of reasonable expectation of issuance for the purpose intended also applies to treasury stock not considered tainted because it was acquired in a systematic pattern for issuance upon exercise of stock options, warrants, and the like. In Accounting Series Release (ASR) No. 146, the SEC established that the market price of stock must generally be at least 75% of the exercise price of the options, warrants, or other arrangement for which the treasury stock is being acquired to avoid being considered tainted shares.

After consummation of a business combination, restrictions on reacquisition of treasury stock decline. The SEC staff would not object to pooling of interests accounting as a result of reacquisition of 20% of the shares issued in a business combination within 30 days of consummation, 80% of the shares within 90 days, and there seems to be no limits on reacquisition after 120 days.

(e) Same Ratio of Ownership Interest (Opinion 16, paragraph 47e)

Condition
The ratio of the interest of an individual stockholder to those of other common stockholders in a combining company remains the same as a result of the exchange of stock to effect the combination.

This condition requires that in the combined entity, each stockholder retains the same ownership percentage in proportion to the ownership percentages of other stockholders in the separate company before the combination. The same form of consideration must be given in exchange for the stock of all significant shareholders.

Voting common stock may be given to holders of debt or equity securities other than common stock in reasonable proportion to their previous holdings.

(f) Voting Rights (Opinion 16, paragraph 47f)

Condition
The voting rights to which the common stock ownership interests in the resulting combined corporations are entitled are exercisable by the stockholders; the stockholders are neither deprived of nor restricted in exercising those rights for a period.

This condition requires that there be no restrictions of voting rights, stockholder discretion about the holding or disposal of the stock, or rights regarding the receipt of dividends. The stockholders of the previously separate companies must share pro rata in the rights, risks, and rewards of the combined entity.

The issuance of unrestricted common stock in exchange for restricted stock of the other combining company does not prevent use of the pooling of interests method. Also, any restrictions imposed by legal requirements, such as the inability to sell stock because of delays caused by SEC matters, does not prevent use of the pooling of interests method.

(g) Complete Resolution (Opinion 16, paragraph 47g)

Condition
The combination is resolved at the date the plan is consummated and no provisions of the plan relating to the issue of securities or other consideration are pending.

Consideration may not be contingent on future events, such as if the number of shares issued is subject to adjustment depending on future earnings or stock prices. However, an arrangement may be made for a adjustment of the number of shares issued dependent on resolution of specific unresolved contingencies at the consummation date, such as litigation, possible additional tax liabilities from Internal Revenue Service examinations, or failure to meet general management or balance sheet warranties with respect to one of the combined companies. Contingently issuable stock in a business combination is sometimes placed in escrow, pending resolution of the related matters.

The SEC requires that for business combinations accounted for by the pooling of interests method involving public companies, contingencies from general management warranties cannot extend past the issuance of the first audited statements of the combined entity or one year after consummation, whichever comes first. The SEC has also indicated that possible future adjustments for more than 10% of the shares issued in a business combination make it questionable whether there are sufficient risk-sharing characteristics to justify use of the pooling of interests method.

The SEC's view on the acceptable longevity of general management warranties appears to establish separate standards on pooling of interest conditions for public and private companies. For private companies, general management and balance sheet warranties could remain until resolved as long as they are not related to future events.

Employment contracts may be entered into with former officer-stock-holders of a combining company without cash consideration being deemed to have been paid in the business combination if the related compensation is reasonable in relation to the services provided.

5.4 ABSENCE OF PLANNED TRANSACTIONS

(a) No Reacquisitions of Stock Issued in Combination (Opinion 16, paragraph 48a)

Condition
The combined corporation does not agree directly or indirectly to retire or reacquire all or part of the common stock issued to effect the combination.

An agreement to reacquire shares issued in a business combination for cash, referred to as a *bailout*, results in a cash transaction that must be accounted for by the purchase accounting method. An immediate sale of shares received in a pooling to a party other than the combined companies based on the unrestricted right of shareholders to sell their shares does not disqualify the pooling. There must, however, be no prior arrangements that require the sale of shares to parties of the transaction or to third parties.

In ASRs No. 130 and 135, the SEC restricted the disposal of shares issued in a pooling to require continuity of ownership for at least some period after a pooling. Generally stated, these restrictions provide that any affiliate (as defined in Regulation S-X) receiving shares of common stock in a pooling may not dispose of any of the shares from (a) 30 days prior to consummation to (b) the date of publication of the first combined sales and net income of the combined company covering a period of at least 30 days after the business combination. SEC Staff Accounting Bulletin (SAB)

No. 65 clarified that these restrictions apply to affiliates of issuing and combining companies. SAB No. 76 established that sales by an affiliate will not violate the rules if they do not exceed 10% of the affiliate's holdings prior to the combination and all affiliates of a combining company do not sell more than the equivalent of 1% of that company's outstanding shares prior to the combination. Although this requirement does not apply to poolings of private companies, a problem could exist with SEC acceptance of pooling of interests accounting in a filing for a later public offering if the SEC requirements described above were not followed.

These SEC rulings are not intended to prevent the above-mentioned rights of common stockholders other than affiliates of a pooling company from selling shares to third parties immediately after a pooling.

(b) No Financial Arrangements (Opinion 16, paragraph 48b)

Condition
The combined corporation does not enter into other financial arrangements for the former stockholders of a combining company, such as a guaranty of loans secured by stock issued in the combination, which in effect negates the exchange of equity securities.

This condition provides that the combined corporation may not use its financial strength to effectively *bailout* the stockholders of a combining company. Bailout arrangements could include consulting or employment contracts or special stock option arrangements that effectively provide additional consideration to some of the shareholders of a combining company.

(c) No Plans to Dispose of Significant Assets (Opinion 16, paragraph 48c)

Condition
The combined corporation does not intend or plan to dispose of a significant part of the assets of the combining companies within two years after the combination other than disposals in the ordinary course of business of the formerly separate companies and to eliminate duplicate facilities or excess capacity.

This condition precludes pooling of interests accounting if there are significant disposals of assets of the combining companies because that would result in a significant change in the stockholders' interests. It prevents carrying out a pooling of interests and then recognizing gains from the sale at fair value of components of the combined companies that were carried forward at a lower book value.

In practice, the guidelines of 10% of assets, sales, or profits of FASB Statement No. 14, *Financial Reporting for Segments of a Business Enterprise*, have been used in determining whether a significant disposal of assets has occurred.

The SEC staff has indicated that significant disposals of assets prior to consummation in contemplation of a business combination would also preclude use of the pooling of interests method. Disposals between six months and two years prior to consummation will not be considered in contemplation of the business combination if so confirmed to the SEC in a letter. A registrant must provide evidence that any disposals between three and six months prior to consummation were not in contemplation of a business combination to overcome a presumption that they were. Disposals within three months of consummation are always considered in contemplation of a business combination.

A spin-off of part of a combined company after a business combination may not preclude pooling of interests accounting if the spin-off was not contemplated at the date the combination is consummated, but a spin-off of a significant part of one of the combining companies prior to consummation would preclude pooling. Without evidence to the contrary, a spin-off initiated nine months to a year following a pooling should not call into question the use of pooling of interests accounting.

Disposals as a result of an order of a governmental or judicial authority or to avoid the issuance of such an order are not disposals for purposes of determining if there has been a significant disposal of assets.

5.5 ACCOUNTING BY THE POOLING OF INTERESTS METHOD

(a) General Principles of the Pooling of Interests Method

At the date of the consummation of a business combination accounted for as a pooling of interests, the assets and liabilities of the combined companies are carried forward into the financial statements of the new combined company at their historical book values. Accounting methods of the combined companies may be changed to enable consistent practices throughout the new combined company if the changes are appropriate. Any changes should be accounted for by restatement of prior periods.

The historical balances of stockholders' equity accounts, including retained earnings, are carried forward and combined. Reclassification may be necessary to conform previous capital structures to the capital structure of the new combined company. Reclassification is necessary if, after the business combination, the par or stated value of the outstanding stock of the issuing company exceeds the related amounts of the combining companies prior to the combination. If so, an appropriate amount should be reclassified from additional paid-in capital to the capital stock account. If paid-in capital is eliminated, an additional reclassification should be made from retained earnings.

Exhibit 5.3 illustrates reclassification of stockholders' equity accounts after a pooling of interests.

EXHIBIT 5.3. Reclassification of Stockholders' Equity Accounts After a Pooling of Interests

The capital structures of Company A and Company B are shown below. Company A acquires all the outstanding common stock of Company B in a pooling of interests in exchange for 20,000 shares of newly issued shares of Company A common stock, increasing Company A's outstanding common stock from 50,000 shares to 70,000 shares. The following table demonstrates the adjustments made to equity accounts as a result of the pooling of interests.

	Before Combination		After Combination	
	Company A	Company B	Reclassification	Combined
Common stock:				
50,000 shares, $10 par	$ 500,000			
100,000 shares, $1 par		$100,000		
	500,000	100,000	$ 100,000	$ 700,000
Additional paid-in capital	1,000,000	400,000	(100,000)	1,300,000
Retained earnings	1,000,000	300,000		1,300,000
	$2,500,000	$800,000		$3,300,000

If the components of stockholders' equity of a combining company are adjusted to eliminate a deficit before or as part of the combination, the components of stockholders' equity before the adjustment should be used in accounting for the pooling.

(b) Treasury Stock and Intercorporate Investments

If treasury stock is issued to effect a pooling, the stock should be accounted for as if the stock was retired and then new shares issued.

If an issuing company holds stock of another combining company, that stock will be exchanged for stock of the issuing company in the pooling, resulting in the elimination of the issuer's investment in the other company. After the pooling, the issuer will hold its own shares in place of the previous investment in the other company. That aspect of the combination should be accounted for as a retirement of stock.

Stock of an issuing company held by another combining company is viewed as reacquired by the issuing company in the combination and becomes treasury stock held by the new combined entity.

(c) Costs of a Pooling

(i) FINANCIAL STATEMENTS OF A COMBINED ENTITY

Costs of a business combination accounted for as a pooling of interests should be charged to expense in the income statement of the new combined entity in the period of consummation. Costs of a pooling may include registration fees, costs of providing information to stockholders, professional fees, and costs of combining operations.

(ii) COSTS INCURRED BY COMBINING COMPANIES PRIOR TO COMPLETION OF A POOLING

Costs of a pooling incurred by the separate companies prior to the combination may be deferred until the combination is consummated, after which they would be charged to expense in the income statement of the new combined entity. Deferral by the separate companies is based on the possibility that the acquisition may be accounted for as a purchase, in which case the costs would be included in the acquisition cost. Alternatively the separate companies may charge these costs to expense as incurred.

If at the end of a reporting period, if costs of a possible pooling have been deferred and it is unlikely that the pooling will be completed, the deferred costs should be charged to expense in the income statement of the separate company for that period.

(iii) COSTS OF A POOLING PAID BY STOCKHOLDERS

If costs of a pooling are paid by stockholders, a capital contribution should be recorded by the combining company and the costs should be accounted for as described in Sections 5.5(c)(i) and (ii). For poolings involving public companies, the SEC staff requires that all costs paid by stockholders be accounted for that way, even if the costs are not legal liabilities of the combining companies.

(d) Foreign Currency Translation in a Pooling

Foreign operations in a pooling are accounted for as if the companies had always been combined. The historical values of assets, liabilities, revenues, expenses, gains, and losses are translated from the functional currency of the foreign operation into the functional currency of the acquirer for all periods presented, including current and restated prior period financial statements, in accordance with FASB Statement No. 52, *Foreign Currency Translation.*

(e) Lock-Up Arrangements

In lock-up arrangement, a potential acquirer is given an option to acquire a potential acquiree or a specified portion of an acquiree and provides that the potential acquirer will be compensated if another party acquires the potential acquiree or the specified portion of it. Lock-up arrangements are entered into to protect a potential acquirer by discouraging other parties from acquiring the potential acquiree or the specified portion of it.

The pooling of interests method can be used to account for a subsequent merger between parties to a lock-up arrangement if: (a) no consideration is paid for the arrangement, and (b) the rights of the potential acquirer under the arrangement are not exercised.

If a lock-up arrangement is established after initiation of a business combination that involves only an exchange of voting common stock for voting common stock, there is no violation of the conditions for pooling.

An arrangement may provide for placing a potential acquirer's cash and the potential acquiree's stock in escrow upon exercise of a lock-up option. If prior to release from escrow, there is a merger between the parties and the arrangement provides that the escrow transaction is voided, then the pooling of interests method may be used for the merger if all pooling conditions are met.

(f) Standstill Agreements

(i) STANDSTILL AGREEMENT NOT IN CONTEMPLATION OF A BUSINESS COMBINATION

A standstill agreement provides that a shareholder will not acquire additional shares in a company for a specified period of time. The consensus on EITF Issue No. 87-15, *Effect of a Standstill Agreement on Pooling of Interests Accounting*, provides that pooling of interests accounting is not precluded as a result of a standstill agreement with a less than majority owner of either an issuing or combining company if the agreement is not in contemplation of a specific business combination.

(ii) STANDSTILL AGREEMENT IN CONTEMPLATION OF A BUSINESS COMBINATION

The consensus on EITF Issue No. 87-15 provides that if a standstill agreement is entered into in contemplation of a specific business combination with a shareholder that will own more than 10% of the combined entity, pooling of interests accounting is precluded. If the aggregate interest of a party entering into the standstill agreement and dissenters to the transaction exceeds 10%, then pooling of interests accounting is also precluded.

(g) Taxable Poolings

An acquisition accounted for as a pooling of interests may not be tax-free for tax purposes, resulting in a step-up of the tax basis of assets. These circumstances can arise from the sale of stock by shareholders after a pooling, which can result in the transaction meeting the conditions for pooling of interests accounting, but not qualifying for tax-free treatment.

Any tax benefits recognized at the consummation date are adjustments of paid-in capital. Any subsequent tax benefits that result from the increased tax basis are recognized as reductions of the provision for income taxes.

5.6 FINANCIAL REPORTING OF A POOLING OF INTERESTS

(a) Financial Statement Presentation

For financial statement purposes, a new combined entity is established on the date of consummation of a pooling of interests. The combined financial position and results of operations of the previously separate companies are reported as if the pooled companies had always been combined. Financial statements for prior periods are restated, including those for the fiscal year of consummation.

If the combined companies previously had different year-ends, it is acceptable to consolidate prior financial statements using different year-ends as long as the difference is not more than 93 days.

(b) Intercompany Transactions

In restating prior period financial statements for a pooling, it is not necessary to eliminate intercompany transactions related to long-term assets and long-term liabilities. Any intercompany transactions that are not eliminated should be discussed in notes to the financial statements, including their effects on earnings per share.

(c) Required Disclosures for a Pooling of Interests

Notes to the financial statements for the year in which a pooling has been consummated should indicate that a pooling has taken place. The basis of combined presentation and restatement of financial statements of prior periods should be discussed either in notes to the financial statements or by appropriate captions in the statements. Exhibit 5.4 lists the disclosure requirements for a pooling, which are set forth in Opinion 16, paragraph 64.

The information listed in Exhibit 5.4 should be included, on a pro forma basis, in information that is provided to stockholders regarding a proposed business combination that is expected to be accounted for as a pooling of interests.

Exhibit 5.5 illustrates notes to financial statements that comply with the disclosure requirements for a pooling of interests.

(d) Reporting In-Progress Poolings

Special reporting issues apply if (a) a pooling is consummated after the end of a financial reporting period but before issuance of the financial statements, or (b) a pooling has been initiated but not consummated as of the date of the financial statements and the company is reasonably assured that the combination will meet the conditions of a pooling.

Because a pooling is recognized in the financial statements as of the date of consummation, if a pooling is consummated after the end of the fiscal period but before issuance of a combining company's financial statements,

EXHIBIT 5.4. Disclosure Requirements for a Pooling of Interests

A. Name and brief description of the companies combined, except a corporation whose name is carried forward to the combining corporation.
B. Method of accounting for the combination—that is, by the pooling of interests method.
C. Description and number of shares of stock issued in the business combination.
D. Details of the results of operations of the previously separate companies for the period before the combination is consummated that are included in the current combined net income. The details should include revenue, extraordinary items, net income, other changes in stockholders' equity, and amounts of and manner of accounting for intercompany transactions.
E. Descriptions of the nature of adjustments of net assets of the combining companies to adopt the same accounting practices and the effects of the changes on net income reported previously by the separate companies and now presented in comparative financial statements.
F. Details of an increase or decrease in retained earnings from changing the fiscal year of a combining company. The details should at least include revenue, expenses, extraordinary items, net income, and other changes in stockholders' equity for the period excluded from the reported results of operations.
G. Reconciliations of amounts of revenue and earning previously reported by the corporation that issues the stock to effect the combination with the combined amounts currently presented in financial statements and summaries. A new corporation formed to effect a combination may, instead, disclose the earnings of the separate companies which comprise combined earnings for prior periods.

those financial statements are not restated to give effect to the business combination. The restatement is not made until financial statements covering the period of consummation are issued. The separate financial statements of the combining company for the fiscal period preceding the consummation should include supplemental disclosures of the details of the combination and the effects on financial position and results of operations,

EXHIBIT 5.5. Illustration of Financial Statement Notes for a Pooling of Interests

---

Note 2—Business Combination

On August 10, 1996, Company A issued 625,000 shares of its common stock in exchange for substantially all the common stock of Company B. The business combination was accounted for as a pooling of interests and the consolidated financial statements for all periods presented have been restated to include the accounts of Company B. Sales and net income of Company B were $17,850,000 and $1,670,000, respectively, in 1995 and were $14,800,000 and $2,830,000, respectively, in 1996 from the beginning of the year to the date of the combination.

Prior to the business combination, Company B reported on the basis of a fiscal year ending on June 30. The restated consolidated financial statement of income for 1995 includes the results of Company A for the twelve months ended December 31, 1995 combined with the results of Company B for the 12 months ended June 30, 1996. The consolidated statement of income for 1996 includes the results of both companies for the 12 months ended December 31, 1996. Retained earnings have been adjusted for the net income of Company B for the six months ended June 30, 1996 of $1,650,000, which has been duplicated in the restated consolidated statement of income. See Note 8 for the effects of the business combination on stockholders' equity.

Note 8—Changes in Stockholders' Equity

Following are the changes in stockholders' equity for the years ended December 31, 1995 and 1996.

	Common Stock	Additional Paid-in Capital	Retained Earnings	Total
Balance, January 1, 1995, as previously reported	$2,200,000	$15,400,000	$28,700,000	$46,300,000
Adjustment from pooling of interests (see Note 2)	625,000	1,500,000	8,600,000	10,725,000
Balance, January 1, 1995, as restated	2,825,000	16,900,000	37,300,000	57,025,000
Net income for the year			7,200,000	7,200,000
Balance, December 31, 1995	2,825,000	16,900,000	44,500,000	64,225,000
Net income for the year			9,100,000	9,100,000
Adjustment to conform pooled company's fiscal year (see Note 2)			(1,650,000)	(1,650,000)
Balance, December 31, 1996	$2,825,000	$16,900,000	$51,950,000	$71,675,000

---

either in the financial statements or notes. These should include the effects on revenue, net income, earnings per share, and also the effects of anticipated retroactive changes in accounting methods to conform with those to be used by the combined company.

For in-progress poolings in 1933 Act SEC registration statements, in addition to the historical financial statements included in the annual report to stockholders, supplemental pro forma statements giving retroactive effect to the pooling are required, which must be covered by an audit opinion. Generally, only the historical financial statements, including the disclosures about the pooling described above are required for the annual report to stockholders, although in some cases pro forma financial statements should also be filed. Form 10-K filings require the same information as the annual report to stockholders, except that if a registration statement was previously filed with the SEC that contained pro forma combined financial statements, reference should be made in the Form 10-K to those financial statements. The foregoing generally describes the SEC reporting requirements for these in progress poolings situations. Specific requirements for a particular SEC registration statement and other particular circumstances (such as whether the auditor's report is dated before or after the consummation date, which can affect the financial statement requirements) should be carefully reviewed to determine if pro forma combined financial statements or only note disclosures are required.

If at the end of a fiscal period, a business combination that has been initiated but not consummated, intercorporate investments acquired for cash or other consideration are stated at cost in the balance sheet of the separate company. Stock acquired in exchange for stock of the issuing company is recorded at the proportionate share of the underlying net assets of the investee at the date acquired. Until the pooling is consummated and the pooling method determined to be appropriate, the investor company should recognize its share of net income or loss of the investee company using the principles of the equity method. Disclosure should be made of the effects of restatement of results of operations for all periods presented that will be made if the combination is later consummated and meets the conditions requiring use of the pooling of interests method.

Reporting for a pooling simplifies significantly after financial statements for the period of consummation have been issued—only combined statements for the current period and restated combined statements for prior periods are issued. This applies to both annual and quarterly financial statements.

An illustration of note disclosure of consummation of a pooling consummated after the end of a fiscal period and prior to issuance of the financial statements is provided in Exhibit 5.6.

EXHIBIT 5.6. Note Disclosure of a Pooling Consummated After the Balance Sheet Date and Prior to the Issuance of Financial Statements

Note 10. Subsequent Event—Business Combination

In January 1997, Company A exchanged 1,400,000 shares of its common stock for all the outstanding common stock of Company B. The transaction will be accounted for as a pooling of interests and in the first quarter of 1997, all prior periods will be restated to give retroactive effect to the combination. Certain changes are expected to be made to conform to the accounting practices of the companies. The effects of the changes are not expected to be significant. The following pro forma information indicates the effects of the combination on the financial position and results of operations of Company A and Company B.

Financial Position at December 31, 1996:

	Company A	Company B	Combined
Working capital	$17,300,000	$ 7,200,000	$24,500,000
Property, plant and equipment, net	39,700,000	16,500,000	56,200,000
Long-term debt	24,800,000	3,000,000	27,800,000
Stockholders' equity	33,500,000	17,300,000	50,800,000

Results of Operations:

	Year Ended December 31,	
	1996	1995
Net sales:		
Company A	$178,000,000	$167,000,000
Company B	64,000,000	51,000,000
Combined	$242,000,000	$218,000,000
Net income:		
Company A	$ 18,625,000	$ 17,600,000
Company B	2,900,000	2,600,000
Combined	$ 21,525,000	$ 20,200,000
Net income per share:		
Company A	$ 6.21	$ 5.87
Company B (based on Company A shares issued in business combination)	2.07	1.86
Combined	$ 8.28	$ 7.73

CHAPTER SIX

Purchase Accounting

6.1 GENERAL PRINCIPLES OF PURCHASE ACCOUNTING

The purchase method must be used to account for any business combination that does not meet *all* the conditions that require use of the pooling of interests method. The purchase method is also used to account for the purchase of some or all of the stock of a minority interest and also to account for acquisitions of stock accounted for by the equity method. The principles of the purchase method are similar to the general principles of accounting for acquisitions of assets and issuances of stock.

A general overview of the purchase method follows:

(a) The total cost of the acquisition is determined.

(b) The cost is allocated to identifiable assets acquired and liabilities assumed, including deferred taxes, in accordance with their respective fair values.

(c) If total acquisition cost exceeds the fair value of net identifiable assets, the excess is allocated to goodwill; any excess of total fair value of net identifiable assets over total cost is first applied as a pro rata reduction of long-term assets.

(d) Goodwill is amortized over a period not exceeding 40 years.

(e) Prior periods are not restated; however, certain supplemental disclosures may be required.

Determining the cost of an acquisition and allocating the purchase price to assets acquired and liabilities assumed requires application of specialized acquisition accounting concepts and procedures, which are discussed throughout this chapter.

6.2 DETERMINING THE COST OF AN ACQUISITION

(a) General

The general approach to determining the cost of a purchase acquisition follows the following the general principles for accounting for acquisitions of assets.

(1) An asset acquired in exchange for cash or other assets is recorded at cost, that is, at the amount of cash disbursed or the fair value of other assets distributed.

(2) An asset acquired by incurring liabilities is recorded at cost, that is, at the present value of the amounts to be paid.

(3) An asset acquired by issuing shares of stock of the acquiring corporation is recorded at the fair value of the asset, that is, shares of stock issued are recorded at the fair value of the consideration received for stock.

(b) Stock Issued in Payment of Purchase Price

Many acquisitions are paid for by exchanging cash or incurring liabilities for the net assets or stock of another company. Alternatively, equity securities of an acquiring company are often issued in exchange for the assets or stock of an acquired company. The fair value of net assets acquired in exchange for stock that has determinable value is usually measured by the value of the stock at the date of acquisition. However, market prices for a reasonable period of time before and after the date an acquisition is agreed to and announced should be considered in establishing the value to be assigned to the securities to avoid volatility of stock prices unduly affecting accounting for the acquisition. If restricted securities are issued, an appraisal of value by qualified professionals, such as investment bankers, may be necessary to establish value.

If fair the value of stock is not readily determinable, other indicators of value should be used, such as an estimate of the value of the assets received, including an estimate of goodwill.

(c) Direct Costs of Acquisitions Other than Purchase Price

Acquisition cost includes all direct costs related to an acquisition, such as finders' and directly related professional fees (for example, legal, accounting, and appraisal fees) and incremental costs that were directly caused by and related to the acquisition. The fixed costs of an internal acquisitions department or officers and employees who work on acquisitions should not be included in acquisition cost, because they are not incremental.

(d) Premium or Discount

Purchase accounting requires recognition of the time value of money in computing total acquisition cost, as well as in determining the fair market values of assets acquired and liabilities assumed. Premium or discount on a debt security issued or assumed should be imputed to adjust the liability to present value based on current market interest or yield rates if stated interest or yield rates vary significantly from current market rates. Assigning fair value to individual assets and liabilities (generally receivables or payables) may require discounting to present value or assigning a premium allocation. After an acquisition, interest expense or income should be recorded by amortization of the premium or discount using the interest method.

(e) Assets Exchanged

Assets given to a seller as consideration should be included in total acquisition cost at fair value. Any deferred taxes related to assets given up should be removed from the balance sheet and accounted for as a reduction of total acquisition cost.

(f) Contingent Consideration

Consideration that is contingent on future earnings of an acquiree should be added to acquisition cost when amounts are determinable beyond a reasonable doubt. Acquisition cost should be increased, with the additional cost should be allocated to net assets acquired in accordance with the purchase method. This often results in an adjustment to long-term assets or goodwill. The additional cost should be depreciated or amortized prospectively over the remaining useful lives of the assets to which the additional cost was assigned. If stock has been given in consideration for an acquisition with a contingency requiring the issuance of additional shares or payments of cash dependent on future security prices, issuance of additional shares does not result in an adjustment of acquisition cost. The recorded amount of shares previously issued is reduced by an amount equal to the fair value of the additional consideration (cash, stock, or other) paid upon resolution of the contingency.

Interest and dividends paid to an escrow agent on contingently issuable debt or equity securities should not be accounted for as interest or dividends. Upon resolution of the contingency, if payment of the escrowed funds by the agent to the seller is required, the amounts should be recorded as additional acquisition cost if the contingency was based on earnings. If the contingency was based on security prices, the accounting is the same as for contingently issuable securities—the value of securities previously issued is reduced and there is no change to total acquisition cost.

(g) Preacquisition Contingencies

The effect of the assumption of a contingency, whether or not there was an identifiable adjustment to the purchase price, should result in an allocation to a liability assumed. Certain resolutions of contingencies after the acquisition can result in adjustments to acquisition costs. See § 6.4(c).

6.3 RECORDING ASSETS ACQUIRED AND LIABILITIES ASSUMED

(a) General

In purchase accounting, total acquisition cost is allocated to assets acquired and liabilities assumed on the basis of their respective fair values. If total acquisition cost exceeds the fair values of identifiable net assets, the excess is allocated to goodwill. If the fair values of identifiable net assets and liabilities exceeds acquisition cost, referred to as *negative goodwill*, the deficiency is applied as a pro rata reduction of the assigned costs of long-term assets, except for long-term investments in marketable securities. If the deficiency results in the elimination of long-term assets, any remaining negative goodwill is recorded as a deferred credit and amortized over a period not to exceed 40 years. FASB Statement No. 109, *Accounting for Income Taxes*, issued in 1992, provides requirements and procedures for establishing deferred taxes as part of an allocation of total acquisition cost in both goodwill and negative goodwill situations.

In a less than 100% of an acquisition, adjustments to carrying value of identifiable net assets are made only for the proportionate share acquired. The portion of the acquired company attributable to the remaining minority interest continues to be accounted for on a historical basis.

(b) Appraisals

Independent appraisals are often the primary way of determining estimated fair values to be used in assigning costs, especially for significant acquisitions. In the absence of evidence of better estimates, the appraised values are often used as the fair values.

In some formal appraisals, an amount may be assigned to goodwill. Goodwill can be attributed to many attributes of a going concern, including the existence of a customer base or market share, an assembled and trained work force, high barriers to entry of competition, or other intangibles of value. The appraiser may estimate the fair value of appraised goodwill based on guidelines, including percentages of goodwill to total acquisition cost evidenced in recent comparable acquisitions.

If the total of the appraised values of identifiable assets varies significantly from total acquisition cost, there should be an identifiable reason. For example, the acquisition cost of an highly profitable business may include a higher than normal amount of goodwill. Conversely, the acquisition cost of an operation that has been experiencing losses or that a seller must for some reason sell under distress conditions may be less than the fair values of the individual assets, resulting in negative goodwill.

In some cases the appraised values of individual assets must be adjusted to reflect additional information that is more indicative of fair value, such as a subsequent sale of one or more of the acquired assets at an amount differing from the appraised value.

The author was a consultant to an acquirer in a particularly fascinating situation in which an acquirer had arranged a bulk sale of inventory of an acquiree for $2,000,000 to obtain a portion of the funds used to pay for an acquisition. The inventory had a cost to the acquiree of $2,800,000, which would have been adjusted in the purchase accounting allocation to $3,200,000 to add a manufacturing profit in accordance with the procedures described in § 6.4(a)(i). Two opposing views were expressed about how this situation should be accounted for:

(1) The cost assigned to the inventory should be $2,000,000 because the most compelling evidence of value is the price received in the sale concurrent with the acquisition. The result would be no gain or loss in the postacquisition income statement.

(2) The cost assigned to the inventory should be $3,200,000 in accordance with normal purchase accounting allocation procedures, resulting in a pretax loss of $1,200,000 in the postacquisition income statement.

After extensive debate, the author and the acquirer were unable to resolve this issue with the acquirer's auditing firm, some of whose partners were adamant that the proper accounting was the second approach, in which case the acquirer would have to report a $2,000,000 loss in the postacquisition income statement. The author prepared a description of the transaction and arguments in support of the acquirer's view that the first approach was correct. The issue was presented as a technical inquiry to the FASB staff. After some discussion, the FASB staff supported the first approach, saying that the proper application of Opinion 16 is to view a price obtained in a sale of an asset after an acquisition and in this case concurrent with the acquisition as the compelling amount to be used in allocating acquisition cost.

(c) Opinion 16 Guidelines for Allocating Acquisition Cost to Individual Assets and Liabilities

(i) GENERAL

The guidelines of paragraph 87 of Opinion 16 for allocating acquisition cost to assets acquired and liabilities assumed are provided below, along with comments about implementing the guidelines in practice.

(ii) MARKETABLE SECURITIES

Marketable securities should be recorded at current net realizable values.

(iii) RECEIVABLES

Receivables should be recorded at present values of amounts to be received determined at appropriate current interest rates, less allowances for uncollectibility and collection costs, if necessary.

In practice, acquired trade accounts receivable expected to be collected within normal collection cycles for a particular industry are not discounted to present value. However, if a receivable is expected to remain outstanding for a length of time that results in a significant discount factor, the discount should be reflected in the acquisition accounting. Notes receivable with interest rates that vary significantly from current market rates for similar notes should be adjusted for imputed discount or premium.

Adjustment for discount or premium results in an increase or decrease to interest income from the date of acquisition to date of collection to value the receivable equal to present value of the amount to be collected on the basis of market interest rates the date of acquisition.

(iv) INVENTORIES

Finished goods and merchandise should be recorded at estimated selling prices less the sum of: (a) costs of disposal; and (b) a reasonable profit allowance for the selling effort of the acquiring corporation. Work in progress should be recorded at estimated selling prices of finished goods less the sum of: (a) costs to complete; (b) costs of disposal; and (c) a reasonable profit allowance for the completing and selling effort of the acquiring corporation based on profit for similar finished goods. Raw materials should be recorded at current replacement costs.

Special aspects of purchase accounting for inventories are discussed in § 6.4(a).

(v) PLANT AND EQUIPMENT

Plant and equipment to be used should be recorded at current replacement costs for similar capacity, unless the expected future use of the asset indicates a lower value to the acquirer. Plant and equipment to be sold or held for later sale should be recorded at current net realizable value. Plant and equipment to be used temporarily should be recorded at current net realizable value, recognizing future depreciation for the expected period of use.

If the total fair value of identifiable net assets exceeds the total acquisition cost, the difference is applied as a proportionate reduction of the values assigned to long-term assets, including fixed assets. None of the excess is allocated to long-term marketable securities or to other long-term assets that have effective cash equivalency with easy conversion. This allocation interacts with computing deferred taxes related to long-term assets as described in § 6.5(b)(iii) and illustrated in Exhibit 6.5.

(vi) INTANGIBLE ASSETS

Intangible assets that can be identified and named, including contracts, patents, franchises, customer and supplier lists, and favorable leases, should be recorded at appraised values.

Identifiable intangible assets should be valued before amounts are allocated to goodwill. In addition to those mentioned above, identifiable intangible assets include customer lists, technology rights, patents and trademarks, computer programs, and software.

If a purchase agreement includes a covenant that a seller will not compete with an acquirer for a specified period of time, a portion of the purchase price should be assigned to the covenant as an identifiable intangible that is amortized over the period of the covenant.

FASB Interpretation No. 4, *Applicability of FASB Statement No. 2 to Business Combinations Accounted for by the Purchase Method*, requires allocation of part of acquisition cost to assets resulting from research and development activities including:

(a) Assets acquired in the combination that result from research and development activities of the acquired enterprise (such as patents, blueprints, formulas, and designs for new products).

(b) Assets acquired to be used in research and development activities of the combined enterprise (such as materials, supplies, equipment, and specific research projects in process).

If a substantial portion of acquisition cost is allocable to research and development projects in progress, such amount should be charged to research and development expense in the income statement of the acquirer for the period in which the acquisition occurs.

(vii) OTHER ASSETS

Other assets, including land, natural resources, and nonmarketable securities, should be recorded at appraised values.

(viii) ACCOUNTS AND NOTES PAYABLE

Accounts and notes payable, long-term debt, and other claims payable should be recorded at present values of amounts to be paid determined at appropriate current interest rates. The possible need to impute premium or discount to adjust stated interest rates to current market rates should be considered.

Considerations for accounts and notes payable are similar to those discussed in § 6.3(c)(iii) for receivables. Adjustment for premium or discount, if necessary, would be recognized as adjustments of postacquisition interest expense.

(ix) ACCRUED LIABILITIES

Liabilities and accruals, such as accruals for pension cost, warranties, vacation pay, and deferred compensation should be recorded at present values of amounts to be paid determined at appropriate current interest rates.

Pension Costs. Purchase agreements sometimes obligate that an acquirer to provide retirement benefits for employees of an acquired company. Pension plans and related fund assets may be transferred intact to provide continuation of the existing plan or the employees may be included in a pension plan maintained by the acquirer. A purchase agreement may require adjustments to the purchase price for future benefits to be provided for preacquisition service. A seller may be required to make a payment to an acquirer or to a pension fund of an amount equal to any excess of vested benefits over pension fund assets as of the acquisition date. The acquirer should include a liability in the acquired balance sheet for the present value of the excess of vested benefits over pension fund assets, to the extent the seller does not eliminate such an excess.

Vacation Pay and Compensated Absences. Purchase agreements sometimes provide for a reduction of the purchase price for earned compensated absences, such as vested vacation pay to be paid after the acquisition date. FASB Statement No. 43, *Accounting for Compensated Absences*, provides accounting standards for accounting for compensated absences. Vacation pay and other compensated absences must be recorded as balance sheet liabilities if employees have earned vested right to such payments. Any earned compensated absences should be included as liabilities in the balance sheet at the acquisition date.

(x) OTHER LIABILITIES

Other liabilities and commitments, including unfavorable leases, contracts, and plant closing expense incident to the acquisition should be recorded at present values of amounts to be paid determined at appropriate current interest rates.

6.4 PURCHASE ACCOUNTING IN SPECIAL AREAS

(a) Inventories

(i) ALLOCATION OF ACQUISITION COST INCLUDING SELLER'S PROFIT

The guidelines for recording acquired inventories are similar to the guidelines for other assets in that they are intended to result in assigning the amount an acquirer theoretically would have had to pay to acquire the assets individually in their current state. For inventory, the amount paid would be expected to include compensating a manufacturer for the profit earned for manufacturing work performed on work-in-process and finished goods inventories. Therefore, cost allocable to inventories is often higher than the acquiree's book value because of equivalent or higher replacement costs for raw materials combined with the addition of a profit factor attributable to manufacturing work performed by the seller.

Allocating cost to inventory, as discussed above, often results in a lower reported gross profit percentage in the income statement of an acquirer for the period following the acquisition because inventories sold in that period bear a higher-than-normal cost. The lower profit reflects that the earning process performed by an acquirer with respect to acquired finished goods and work-in-process does not include a profit factor for the manufacturing effort of the acquiree prior to the acquisition. This effect is illustrated in Exhibit 6.1.

(ii) INVENTORY PURCHASED IN SEPARATE CONTRACT

The author has seen a few acquisitions that were structured so that inventory was acquired in a specific contract separate from the purchase agreement and for a separate and distinct payment for an amount equal to the book value of the inventories in the financial statements of the seller, or some

EXHIBIT 6.1 Illustration of Reduced Gross Profit Percentage in Period Following an Acquisition

An acquired manufacturing company normally sells at a 40% markup, 15% of which is considered to relate to manufacturing and 25% to selling activities. The estimated sales amount to be realized from the sale of inventory is $2,000,000, 75% of which related to finished goods and 25% to work-in-process. The cost to complete the work-in-process is estimated at $50,000 and the work-in-process is 50% completed with respect to manufacturing operations. Costs of disposal are immaterial and are ignored. The table below indicates the manufacturing and selling profits that would normally be reported.

	Finished Goods	Work-in-Process
Cost (when completed)	$1,071,429	$357,143
Profit factors:		
Manufacturing (15%)	160,713	53,571
Selling (25%)	267,858	89,286
Selling price	$1,500,000	$500,000

Following is a computation of the amounts to be assigned to the acquired inventories using the purchase method:

Finished goods:	
Estimated selling price	$1,500,000
Less, normal selling profit	(267,858)
Amount to be allocated	$1,232,142
Work-in-process:	
Estimated selling price	$ 500,000
Less, normal selling profit	(89,286)
Less, manufacturing profit on 50% of work-in-process	(26,786)
Cost to complete	(50,000)
Amount to be allocated	$ 333,928

EXHIBIT 6.1 (*Continued*)

The following computes the amounts that would be reported in the income statement of the acquirer in the period after the acquisition for the sale of the acquired inventory:

	Total	Finished Goods	Work-in-Process
Sales	$2,000,000	$1,500,000	$500,000
Cost of sales:			
Allocated amounts	1,566,070	1,232,142	333,928
Completion costs	50,000		50,000
	1,616,070	1,232,142	383,928
Gross profit	$ 383,930	$ 267,858	$116,072
Gross profit percentage	19.2%		

The gross profit of 19.2% in the period following the acquisition is unusually low for this business. The following table computes the normal income statement effect of the sale of this inventory if a purchase price allocation had not been made:

Sales	$2,000,000
Cost of sales	
($2,000,000/1.40)	1,428,571
Gross profit	$ 571,429
Gross profit percentage	28.6%

other negotiated amount that was less than the amount that would be allocated based on the procedures described in § 6.4(a)(i). The result was that the one-time lower gross profit percentage described in § 6.4(a)(i) did not occur. The specific circumstances of any such transactions must be evaluated to determine if it is appropriate to account for the inventory acquisition separately from the acquisition of the other assets. In some cases, separate accounting may be appropriate. However, if an acquisition has been broken into pieces only to avoid a higher allocation of purchase price to inventory, the author believes that the separate transactions should be *collapsed* into one, with an allocation of total acquisition cost to all the assets, including inventory, as required by Opinion 16, despite the specific price documented for inventory in a separate contract.

(iii) LAST-IN FIRST-OUT (LIFO) INVENTORY

A business combination may: (a) be accounted for by the purchase method but be tax-free or (b) be accounted for by the pooling of interests method but be taxable. In these situations, differences in the value assigned for accounting and tax purposes to LIFO inventories can result.

In a purchase method acquisition, an acquirer is required to revalue the inventories to fair value at acquisition date and the entire inventory is treated as a single LIFO layer acquired in the year of acquisition. If the transaction has been a tax-free exchange, the previous LIFO inventory layers and values may be carried forward for tax purposes. This would ordinarily cause the book LIFO inventory balance to be higher than the tax LIFO inventory. If a taxable transaction is accounted for as a pooling of interests, the reverse would ordinarily occur—the tax LIFO inventory amount would be higher than the book LIFO inventory amount.

The resulting differences between book and tax LIFO values and layers are carried forward from the date of acquisition. If inventory levels increase thereafter, book and tax cost of sales will generally be the same because the costs of current year purchases or production will be the basis for cost of sales for both tax and accounting purposes.

Different values allocated to fixed assets for tax and accounting purposes can cause significant differences in depreciation charges allocated to production costs. These different depreciation amounts will cause different accounting and tax cost of sales and incremental LIFO inventory layer in periods after the acquisition. These differences, however, may exist where FIFO inventories, as well as LIFO inventories, are present.

(b) Leases

(i) Unfavorable Leases

Consistent with the principle that liabilities assumed should be recorded at fair value, if a lease assumed in a purchase bears a rental rate higher or lower than the current market rate for a similar lease, an intangible asset has been acquired or an intangible liability has been assumed. Accordingly, the difference between rentals required by the assumed lease and current market rental rates, discounted to present value, should be included as an asset acquired or liability assumed in the acquired balance sheet. These are referred to as *unfavorable lease obligations*. Exhibit 6.2 illustrates computations related to an unfavorable lease assumed in an acquisition.

As a result of the computations in Exhibit 6.2, the aquirer would record a liability at the acquisition date of $92,135, equal to the present value of the unfavorable portion lease commitment. As each payment of $12,500 is

EXHIBIT 6.2 Computation of an Unfavorable Lease Obligation

An acquirer assumes a lease on a 10,000 square foot factory building with an annual rental rate of $15 per square foot. Due to a decline in real estate values, similar properties can be rented at an average of $10 per square foot. The remaining term of the lease is two years and rents are payable at the beginning of each month. A discount rate of 8% is appropriate.

Month	Rent Payment	Market Value Rent	Unfavorable Lease Obligation		
			Total	Interest	Principal
1	$12,500	$8,333	$4,167	$ 614	$ 3,553
2	$12,500	$8,333	4,167	591	3,576
3	$12,500	$8,333	4,167	567	3,600
4	$12,500	$8,333	4,167	543	3,624
5	$12,500	$8,333	4,167	519	3,648
6	$12,500	$8,333	4,167	494	3,673
7	$12,500	$8,333	4,167	470	3,697
8	$12,500	$8,333	4,167	445	3,722
9	$12,500	$8,333	4,167	420	3,747
10	$12,500	$8,333	4,167	395	3,772
11	$12,500	$8,333	4,167	370	3,797
12	$12,500	$8,333	4,167	345	3,822
13	$12,500	$8,333	4,167	319	3,848
14	$12,500	$8,333	4,167	294	3,873
15	$12,500	$8,333	4,167	268	3,899
16	$12,500	$8,333	4,167	242	3,925
17	$12,500	$8,333	4,167	216	3,951
18	$12,500	$8,333	4,167	189	3,978
19	$12,500	$8,333	4,167	163	4,004
20	$12,500	$8,333	4,167	136	4,031
21	$12,500	$8,333	4,167	109	4,058
22	$12,500	$8,333	4,167	82	4,085
23	$12,500	$8,333	4,167	55	4,112
24	$12,500	$8,333	4,167	28	4,139
			$100,008	$7,874	$92,134

made, rent expense would be charged for $8,333, interest expense would be charged for the corresponding amount in the *interest* column, and the unfavorable lease liability would be charged by the corresponding amount in the *principal* column.

If an acquirer is required to assume a lease for an asset or facility that is of no use, the present value of the entire lease may be established as a liability assumed. If only part of a leased facility or asset is of use to an acquirer, an unfavorable lease obligation should be established for the present value of the portion of future rent obligations attributable to the part of the facility or asset that is of no use.

(ii) FAVORABLE LEASES

If future rent on an assumed lease is below the market rate, the acquirer should record an asset, sometimes referred to as a *favorable lease*, equal to the present value of the difference between the required rental rate and the market rate at the date of acquisition. That amount should be amortized to rent expense ratably over the remaining term of the lease. As in the case of an unfavorable lease, this allocation is made to result in accounting for the lease on equal footing with leases in the current market.

(iii) LEASE CLASSIFICATION

A lease assumed in an acquisition that was classified as an operating lease by the seller in accordance with FASB Statement No. 13, *Accounting for Leases*, should be accounted for as an operating lease by an acquirer if no changes are made to the terms of the lease. If the lease is modified, the amended lease is considered to be a new lease and should be accounted for based on the criteria of Statement 13. A reclassification of a lease does not eliminate the requirement to establish an asset or liability for an unfavorable or favorable lease commitment.

(iv) ASSUMPTION OF A LEVERAGED LEASE AS LESSOR

A leveraged lease involves financing provided by a long-term creditor that is nonrecourse to the general credit of the lessor. The creditor may have recourse only to the leased property and rentals on it. These transactions provide the lessor with *significant leverage*.

If an acquirer assumes a leveraged lease, the lease retains its classification. The acquirer should assign a net amount to the investment in the leveraged lease based on remaining cash flows adjusted for estimated future tax effects. The net investment should be divided into the following components: (a) net rentals receivable, (b) estimated residual value, and (c) unearned income, including discount to adjust the other components to present value. Thereafter, leveraged lease accounting, as described in Statement 13, should be used. This accounting is discussed and illustrated in FASB Interpretation No. 21, *Accounting for Leases in a Business Combination.*

(c) Preacquisition Contingencies

Accounting principles for preacquisition contingencies are provided in FASB Statement No. 38, *Accounting for Preacquisition Contingencies of Purchased Enterprises.* A preacquisition contingency is:

> ". . . (a) contingency of an enterprise that is acquired in a business combination accounted for by the purchase method and that is in existence before the consummation of the combination. A preacquisition contingency can be a contingent asset, a contingent liability, or a contingent impairment of an asset. . ." [FASB Statement No. 38, paragraph 4]

An assumed preacquisition contingency should be established as a liability in an amount equal to fair value. Fair value can be determined by the cost of resolution of a contingency during the *allocation* period or, if applicable, the amount that the parties agreed to in negotiation as an adjustment of the purchase price as a result of the existence of the contingency.

The allocation period for finalizing the amount to assign to a preacquisition contingency extends from the date of acquisition to when an acquirer is no longer waiting for information that it has arranged to obtain and that is known to be available or obtainable. The allocation period should usually not exceed one year from the date of the acquisition. Until the allocation period ends, the purchase price allocation should be adjusted for the effects of additional information about contingencies. After the allocation period, any changes in the estimated fair values of contingencies should be included in determining net income for the period in which the change is determined.

If the fair value of a contingency cannot be determined during the allocation period, the contingency should be assigned an amount determined in accordance with the following criteria:

(1) Information available prior to the end of the *allocation period* indicates that it is probable that an asset existed, a liability had been incurred, or an asset had been impaired at the consummation of the business combination. It is implicit in this condition that it must be probable that one or more future events will occur confirming the existence of the asset, liability, or impairment.

(2) The amount of the asset or liability can be reasonably estimated. [FASB Statement No. 38, paragraph 5]

If this approach of paragraph 5 of Statement 38 is used in valuing the contingency, the determination should be made in accordance with FASB Statement No. 5, *Accounting for Contingencies* and the related FASB Interpretation No. 14, *Reasonable Estimation of the Amount of a Loss.*

(d) Foreign Currency Translation

In a purchase method acquisition of a foreign operation, assets acquired and liabilities assumed are adjusted to fair values in foreign currency at the date of acquisition and translated at the foreign currency exchange rate on the date of acquisition. Any difference between the total cost of the acquisition in dollars and the translated net assets is accounted for as goodwill or negative goodwill. Future balance sheets are translated by converting the fair values at acquisition date into dollars using the exchange rate at the balance sheet date. Any differences caused by changes in exchange rates after the acquisition are accounted for in accordance with FASB Statement No. 52, *Foreign Currency Translation.*

(e) Minority Interests

If a minority interest exists after an acquisition, the adjustments of assets acquired and liabilities assumed to fair value under the purchase method are made only to the extent of an acquirer's proportionate share of the acquired company. The assets and liabilities prior to the acquisition and related future accounting effects remain on an historical basis to the extent of the percentage of minority interest remaining outstanding.

Exhibit 6.3 illustrates the computation of acquisition adjustments if a minority interest remains outstanding. The illustration does not take into account complexities that might exist as a result of deferred taxes, in order to focus more directly on the procedure of making purchase accounting adjustments only for the acquirer's interest.

If an acquirer purchases additional interests in an acquiree some or all of a minority interest after initial application of the purchase accounting

EXHIBIT 6.3   Purchase Accounting With a Minority Interest

Company A purchases 75% of the stock of Company B for $7,500,000 cash. The historical carrying value of Company B's assets and liabilities are indicated below. Following is Company A's accounting for the acquisition in its consolidated financial statements.

	Historical Company B Amounts	Fair Market Value	Excess Fair Market Value	Consolidation Entries	Amounts Included in Financial Statements
Current assets	$ 3,000,000	$ 3,500,000	$ 500,000	$ 375,000 (a)	$ 3,375,000
Fixed assets	7,000,000	9,000,000	2,000,000	1,500,000 (a)	8,500,000
Goodwill				1,500,000 (b)	1,500,000
	$10,000,000	$12,500,000	$2,500,000	$3,375,000	$13,375,000
Current liabilities	$ 2,000,000	$ 2,000,000	$	$	$ 2,000,000
Long-term debt	2,500,000	2,500,000			2,500,000
Stockholders' equity	5,500,000	8,000,000	2,500,000	2,000,000 (c)	7,500,000
Minority interest				1,375,000 (d)	1,375,000
	$10,000,000	$12,500,000	$2,500,000	$3,375,000	$13,375,000

Notes to Consolidated Entries:

(a) Excess fair market value allocations:

	Excess Fair Market Value	Acquirer's Percentage Interest	Acquirer's Share of Excess
Current assets	$ 500,000	75%	$ 375,000
Fixed assets	2,000,000	75%	1,500,000

(b) Computation of goodwill:

Purchase price		$7,500,000
Fair value of net assets	8,000,000	
Percentage interest acquired	× 75%	6,000,000
Goodwill		$1,500,000

(c) Computation of adjustment to equity:

Company A investment in Company B	$7,500,000
Company B historical equity amount	5,500,000
	$2,000,000

(d) Minority interest:

Company B historical equity	$5,500,000
Minority interest percentage	× 25%
	$1,375,000

method, sometimes referred to as an *incremental* acquisition, a separate determination of fair values of identifiable assets and liabilities is made at the time of each separate purchase. Those fair values are used in assigning the cost of the partial interest acquired in each purchase, including separate goodwill calculations for each incremental purchase.

6.5 INCOME TAX ACCOUNTING

(a) General

Accounting for the effects of income taxes in purchase method acquisitions is covered by FASB Statement No. 109, *Accounting for Income Taxes*, which was issued in 1992. Prior to the issuance in 1987 of FASB Statement No. 96, *Accounting for Income Taxes*, accounting for income taxes in purchase acquisitions had been covered by Opinion 16. Statement 96 significantly changed the approach of Opinion 16 and Statement 109 essentially continues the new methods established in Statement 96.

(b) Deferred Taxes

(i) GENERAL

Statement 109 requires that deferred taxes be established in a purchase method allocation for tax effects of temporary differences between amounts to be used for financial reporting of assets and liabilities and their tax bases. That approach is quite different from previous accounting under Opinion 16, which required that tax effects of differences between book and tax bases be recognized as an adjustment of the fair market value of applicable individual assets and liabilities.

Statement 109 provides that deferred taxes are not established for book-tax differences for goodwill to the extent that goodwill is not deductible for tax purposes. Deferred taxes are also not established for negative goodwill that is recorded as a deferred credit to the extent it is not amortizable for tax purposes. Deferred taxes are also not established for leveraged leases acquired in a purchase acquisition.

Statement 109 also indicates that deferred taxes should not be discounted to present value from the date the tax effect is expected to be realized.

Under Opinion 16, discounting of the tax effect was appropriate in determining the adjustment to be made to the fair market value of the applicable asset or liability.

(ii) DEFERRED TAXES IN GOODWILL SITUATIONS

If acquisition cost exceeds the fair value of net identifiable assets, Statement 109 requires use of the *gross* method of purchase price allocation. Under the gross method, purchase price is allocated as follows:

(a) Determine the fair market values of identifiable assets and liabilities.

(b) Identify temporary differences related to identifiable assets and liabilities.

(c) Determine and recognize deferred tax assets and liabilities for deductible and taxable temporary differences.

(d) Determine and recognize deferred tax assets for net operating loss and tax credit carryforwards.

(e) Determine and recognize a valuation allowance to reduce the value of deferred tax assets using the *more likely than not* criteria of Statement 109.

(f) Recognize goodwill for the difference between the total purchase price and the sum of net fair values of identifiable assets and liabilities and the deferred taxes that have been determined, net of valuation allowance.

Computation of deferred taxes in a goodwill situation is illustrated as part of Exhibit 6.5.

(iii) DEFERRED TAXES IN NEGATIVE GOODWILL SITUATIONS

Statement 109 requires that deferred taxes be established for temporary differences related to the allocation to long-term assets of an excess of fair values of net identifiable assets over total acquisition cost, commonly referred to as *negative goodwill*. To compute the amounts to be assigned to the long-term assets and the deferred taxes, it is necessary to use a simultaneous equation. The simultaneous equation on page 201 will apply to most acquisitions, although it may need modification if an acquiree has operations in more than one tax jurisdiction or if the acquirer's and acquiree's temporary differences, net operating loss carryforwards, tax credit carryforwards, and valuation allowances interact so as to require modification to the simultaneous equation approach.

$$\text{Net temporary difference} \times \frac{\text{Tax rate}}{(1 - \text{tax rate})} = \begin{array}{l} \text{Adjustment to} \\ \text{deferred tax assets} \\ \text{and liabilities and} \\ \text{noncurrent assets} \end{array}$$

If tax benefits are recognized as a result of interaction of the tax positions of an acquirer and an acquiree, goodwill is reduced in the allocation of acquisition cost. If goodwill is reduced to zero, then other long-term assets are reduced as described in Section 6.5(b)(ii).

(c) Postacquisition Recognition of Net Operating Loss and Tax Credit Carryforwards

Some or all of the tax benefits of an acquiree's net operating loss or tax credit carryforwards may be recognized as a result of an acquisition if the *more likely than not* criterion is met at the acquisition date. If so, the result is a reduction of goodwill in the allocation of acquisition cost. If not, subsequent recognition of the tax benefits of an acquiree's net operating loss or tax credit carryforwards should be accounted for as follows:

(a) Goodwill from the acquisition is reduced.

(b) If goodwill is completely eliminated, then other noncurrent intangible assets are reduced until fully eliminated.

(c) Any further tax benefits are recorded as a reduction of the provision for income taxes.

If tax benefits of an acquired company have been recognized at the acquisition date and it is later determined that a valuation allowance is needed for the applicable items, the establishment of the valuation allowance is recorded as an increase in the provision for income taxes. Retroactive increases to goodwill are not permitted.

If an acquired net operating loss or tax credit carryforward is utilized in a future period but is offset by a new temporary difference *and* the tax benefit of the new temporary difference is in turn recognized in a future period, the benefit is viewed as attributable to the acquired net operating loss or tax credit carryforward. Goodwill is reduced, even though there was an intervening temporary difference that delayed the ultimate tax effect of the net operating loss or tax credit carryforward.

Applicable tax law should be followed in determining the order in which net operating loss and tax credit carryforwards are utilized. This has accounting significance because postacquisition realization of an acquirer's net operating loss or tax credit carryforwards are recorded as a reduction of the provision for income taxes. Realization of those of an acquiree are recorded as reductions of goodwill. If applicable tax laws do not provide the order of utilization, then the utilization should be prorated based on the proportion of the acquirer's and acquiree's respective shares of the carryforwards utilized.

If a tax benefit from excess of tax basis of an acquired asset over the amount assigned to the asset (excess tax basis) in a purchase method allocation is not recognized in the acquisition accounting at acquisition date, subsequent recognition of that tax benefit is accounted for the same as a postacquisition recognition of an acquiree's net operating loss or tax credit carryforward, as described above.

(d) Goodwill

In taxable acquisitions, sometimes an allocation to goodwill for accounting purposes relates partly to amounts allocated to another asset that for tax purposes are deductible through amortization or otherwise. In that situation, the other asset is viewed as having excess tax basis, resulting in a temporary difference. The tax benefit of the tax deduction attributable to that other asset is accounted for as purchased excess tax basis at either the acquisition date or after the acquisition date.

Temporary differences are not recognizable for goodwill for which deductions may not be taken for tax purposes. Likewise, temporary differences are not recognized for negative goodwill.

For taxing jurisdictions in which goodwill is deductible for taxes, book and tax goodwill is divided into two categories: (1) the lesser of book or tax deductible goodwill and, (2) the remainder of any book or tax goodwill. For category (1) goodwill, any basis difference (e.g., from different amortization amounts or write-downs) that arises in postacquisition periods is accounted for as a temporary difference.

For category (2), if tax deductible goodwill exceeds book goodwill, there will be no category (2) book goodwill and category (2) tax goodwill will be equal to the excess of tax deductible goodwill over book goodwill. If book goodwill exceeds tax deductible goodwill, there will be no category (2) tax goodwill and category (2) book goodwill will be equal to the excess of book goodwill over tax deductible goodwill. Deferred taxes are not recognized for category (2) goodwill. If category (2) goodwill consists of tax deductible goodwill, when the benefits are realized, they are first recognized as a reduction of book goodwill, then as a reduction of other acquired noncurrent intangible assets, and lastly as a reduction of the provision for income taxes.

The Omnibus Budget Reconciliation Act of 1993 changed previous tax rules that did not allow deductions for goodwill. Now, goodwill may be amortized over 15 years for tax purposes. How to account for the new aspect of tax deductible goodwill from business combinations is described in EITF Issue No. 93-12, *Recognition and Measurement of the Tax Benefit of Excess Tax-Deductible Goodwill Resulting from a Retroactive Change in Tax Law*. Also of interest on this subject is that one of the reasons indicated for not establishing deferred taxes related to goodwill in an acquisition was that goodwill, by its nature, was not tax deductible. Even though goodwill can be deductible under the new law, deferred taxes should not be established and goodwill increased as an ultimate balancing amount if goodwill will not be deductible because the inside tax basis of an acquired corporation is not changed in the acquisition.

(e) Aggressive Tax Positions

Deferred taxes established at the date of an acquisition should be determined using management's estimate of tax positions that will be ultimately accepted by tax authorities, notwithstanding the fact that more aggressive positions may be reported on tax returns. The same approach should be used in determining deferred taxes in postacquisition periods. Changes to management's estimate or final resolution by closing of tax years should be accounted for by first adjusting goodwill, then by adjusting other acquired noncurrent intangible assets, and finally by adjusting the provision for income taxes.

(f) Miscellaneous

(i) IDENTIFIABLE INTANGIBLES

Deferred taxes are established for all identifiable intangible assets, both at the acquisition date and for postacquisition temporary differences.

(ii) LIFO INVENTORIES

A difference between the book and tax basis of LIFO inventories is a temporary difference and should be included in the computation of deferred taxes at the acquisition date.

(iii) TAX RATES

Under Statement 109, enacted tax rates should be used in computing deferred taxes at the acquisition date even if rate changes are anticipated. Postacquisition rate changes would result in changes to the deferred tax balances, which would be reported as an adjustment of the provision for income taxes.

(g) Effects of Consolidated Tax Implications

If an acquired company will be included in the acquirer's consolidated tax return, deferred taxes attributable to the acquisition are determined based on the consolidated tax position after the acquisition using the *more likely than not* criterion. The interaction of an acquirer's and acquiree's temporary differences, net operating loss carryforwards, and tax credit carryforwards can result in the elimination of a valuation allowance for deferred tax assets that would have been required without the acquisition. Filing a consolidated return may qualify as a *tax strategy* that enables the realization of tax benefits.

In determining whether the *more likely than not* criterion is met, consideration should be given to the rules related to separate return limitation year

(SRLY) restrictions, limitations on built-in gains, and limitations on usage of net operating loss and tax credit carryforwards.

6.6   RECORD KEEPING FOR PURCHASE ACCOUNTING ACQUISITIONS

If the stock of a company has been purchased, two approaches for the record keeping aspects of the revaluations required by purchase accounting are:

(a) The accounting records of the acquired company are left the same as prior to the acquisition and the revaluations and related effects on future income and expenses are recorded as consolidation adjustments.

(b) The revaluations are recorded directly in the accounts of the acquired company to establish a new basis of accounting.

The term *push-down accounting* refers to preparing separate postacquisition financial statements of the acquired entity that include the purchase accounting adjustments arising from the acquisition. The first approach can be used if separate financial statements of the acquired company are prepared using historical amounts. However, the books of an acquirer can be kept on an historical basis and financial statements of the acquiree can be prepared using *push-down accounting* by adjusting the acquiree's historical general ledger balances for purchase accounting adjustments on a worksheet basis and then using the adjusted amounts in preparing the financial statements. The second approach takes the effects of *push-down accounting* and records them in the books of the acquired company and may be sensible to use only if historical financial statements of the acquired company are not needed.

Also, in deciding whether to push the purchase accounting adjustments into an acquiree's primary books, an acquirer should consider whether historical amounts will be needed for preparation of tax returns. If the acquisition has not resulted in change to the *inside basis* of the acquired company for tax purposes or if there is a continuing minority interest, the author recommends using historical balances in the books and worksheet adjustments in preparing separate financial statements of the acquired company if *push-down accounting* financial statements are to be prepared.

6.7 FINANCIAL REPORTING OF A PURCHASE ACQUISITION

An acquirer includes the assets, liabilities, and results of operations of an acquired company in its financial statements, from the date of acquisition. Notes to the acquirer's financial statements should include the following disclosures, required by Opinion 16, paragraph 95, for the period in which an acquisition accounted for by the purchase method is completed:

(a) Name and a brief description of the acquired company.

(b) Method of accounting for the combination—that is, by the purchase method.

(c) Period for which results of operations of the acquired company are included in the income statement of the acquiring corporation.

(d) Cost of the acquired company and, if applicable, the number of shares of stock issued or issuable and the amount assigned to the issued and issuable shares.

(e) Description of the plan for amortization of acquired goodwill, the amortization method, and period.

(f) Contingent payments, options, or commit
ments specified in the acquisition agreement and their proposed accounting treatment.

Opinion 16, paragraph 96, as amended by FASB Statement No. 79, *Elimination of Certain Disclosures for Business Combinations Accounted for by the Purchase Method*, requires that if an acquirer is a publicly held company, notes to the financial statements for the period in which a purchase method acquisition occurs must also include the following, as supplemental pro forma information:

(a) Results of operations for the current period as though the companies had combined at the beginning of the period, unless the acquisition was at or near the beginning of the period.

(b) Results of operations for the immediately preceding period as though the companies had combined at the beginning of that period if comparable financial statements are presented.

The pro forma information must be presented for the period of combination and the immediately preceding period. Information required includes revenues, income before extraordinary items, net income, and earnings per share. In computing the pro forma results, purchase accounting adjustments should be assumed to have taken place at the beginning of the period prior to the acquisition. The pro forma amounts should include any required changes to interest, income taxes, preferred stock dividends, depreciation, and amortization.

Exhibit 6.4 illustrates disclosure of a purchase method acquisition in notes to a publicly held acquirer's financial statements.

EXHIBIT 6.4   Illustration of Footnote for a Purchase Method Acquisition

NOTE 5. Acquisition of Company B

On June 1, 19X7, the Company acquired all the stock of Company B, a manufacturer of automotive accessories, for $12,000,000 in cash. The acquisition has been accounted for as a purchase and the net assets and results of operations of Company B have been included in the consolidated financial statements since the acquisition date. The excess of cost over net assets acquired amounted to $670,000 and is being amortized over 40 years. Following is unaudited pro forma consolidated results of operations assuming the acquisition had occurred on January 1, 19X6, including the effects of all significant adjustments related to the acquisition. Interest expense has been assumed from January 1, 19X6 on $5,000,000 of 12% subordinated debentures issued by Company A on May 1, 19X7, to obtain funds for the acquisition.

	19X7	19X6
Net sales	$84,500,000	$77,600,000
Net income	6,750,000	6,200,000
Net income per common share	1.93	1.77

6.8 ILLUSTRATIONS OF PURCHASE ACCOUNTING

(a) Positive Goodwill Situation

Exhibit 6.5 illustrates purchase accounting in a positive goodwill situation.

(b) Negative Goodwill Situation

Exhibit 6.6 illustrates the computation of deferred taxes and amounts to assign to long-term assets in a negative goodwill situation.

EXHIBIT 6.5 Illustration of Purchase Accounting in a Positive Goodwill Situation

Company A acquired all the stock of Company B for $12,300,000 cash. Company A also incurred costs of the acquisition of $200,000, resulting in total acquisition cost of $12,500,000. For tax purposes, the basis of assets and liabilities of Company B are carried over, but for accounting purposes the assets must be revalued using the purchase accounting method. The balance sheets of Company B for book and tax purposes at the date of acquisition are shown below. Independent appraisals indicated fair values of identifiable assets as follows: fixed assets, $10 million; other assets (including trademarks and patents), $1 million. Inventories are valued at $3 million in accordance with purchase accounting. Assume a combined U.S. federal and state tax rate of 37%. A discount rate of 8% is considered appropriate for present value computations.

	Historical Company B Book Value	Tax Basis
Cash and receivables	$1,000,000	$1,000,000
Inventory	2,500,000	2,500,000
Fixed assets	5,000,000	2,500,000
Other assets	600,000	6,300,000
	$9,100,000	$6,300,000
Current liabilities	$1,200,000	$1,200,000
Deferred taxes	1,000,000	
Long-term debt	2,000,000	2,000,000
Stockholders' equity	4,900,000	3,100,000
	$9,100,000	$6,300,000

	Historical Company B Book Value	Fair Market Value of Identifiables	Purchase Accounting Adjustment	Acquisition Cost
Cash and receivables	$1,000,000	$ 1,000,000		$ 1,000,000
Inventory	2,500,000	3,000,000	$ 500,000 (a)	3,000,000
Fixed assets	5,000,000	10,000,000	5,000,000 (b)	10,000,000
Other assets	600,000	1,000,000	400,000 (c)	1,000,000
Goodwill			3,120,000 (g)	3,120,000
	$9,100,000	$15,000,000	$9,020,000	$18,120,000
Current liabilities	$1,200,000	$ 1,200,000		$ 1,200,000
Unfavorable lease		200,000	$ 200,000 (d)	200,000
Deferred taxes	1,000,000		1,220,000 (e)	2,220,000
Long-term debt	2,000,000	2,000,000		2,000,000
Stockholders' equity	4,900,000	11,600,000	7,600,000 (f)	12,500,000
	$9,100,000	$15,000,000	$9,020,000	$18,120,000

EXHIBIT 6.5 *(Continued)*

Purchase Accounting Adjustments:

(a) Inventory:

Fair market value including seller's profit	$ 3,000,000
Historical book value	2,500,000
Purchase accounting adjustment	$ 500,000

(b) Fixed assets:

Appraised value of fixed assets	$10,000,000
Historical book value	5,000,000
Purchase accounting adjustment	$ 5,000,000

(c) Other assets:

	Trademarks	Miscellaneous	Total
Appraised value	$400,000	$ 600,000	$1,000,000
Historical book value	—	600,000	600,000
Purchase accounting adjustment	$400,000	$ —	$ 400,000

(d) Unfavorable lease:

Present value (8% discount) of excess of future lease obligations over market value	$ 200,000

(e) Deferred taxes:

	Purchase Price Acquisition Cost Allocation	Tax Basis	Temporary Difference	Deferred Tax (37%)
Inventory	$ 3,000,000	$2,500,000	$ (500,000)	$ (185,000)
Fixed assets	10,000,000	5,000,000	(5,000,000)	(1,850,000)
Other assets	1,000,000	300,000	(700,000)	(259,000)
Unfavorable lease	(200,000)		200,000	74,000
			$(6,000,000)	(2,220,000)
Historical deferred tax balance				(1,000,000)
Purchase accounting adjustment				$(1,220,000)

(f) Equity:

Acquisition cost	$12,500,000
Historical equity of Company B	4,900,000
	$ 7,600,000

(g) Goodwill:

Goodwill is the amount needed to balance the purchase accounting adjustments.

EXHIBIT 6.6 Illustration of Purchase Accounting in a Negative Goodwill Situation

Company A acquired all the stock of Company B for $7,300,000 cash. Company A also incurred costs of the acquisition of $200,000, resulting in total acquisition cost of $7,500,000. For tax purposes, the basis of assets and liabilities of Company B are carried over, but for accounting purposes the assets must be revalued using the purchase accounting method. The balance sheets of Company B for book and tax purposes at the date of acquisition are shown below. Independent appraisals indicated fair values of identifiable assets as follows: fixed assets, $10 million; other assets (including trademarks and patents), $1 million. Inventories are valued at $3 million in accordance with purchase accounting. Assume a combined U.S. federal and state tax rate of 37%. A discount rate of 8% is considered appropriate for present value computations.

	Historical Company B Book Value	Tax Basis
Cash and receivables	$1,000,000	$1,000,000
Inventory	2,500,000	2,500,000
Fixed assets	5,000,000	2,500,000
Other assets	600,000	300,000
	$9,100,000	$6,300,000
Current liabilities	$1,200,000	$1,200,000
Deferred taxes	1,000,000	
Long-term debt	2,000,000	2,000,000
Stockholders' equity	4,900,000	3,100,000
	$9,100,000	$6,300,000

	Historical Company B Book Value	Fair Market Value of Identifiables	Purchase Accounting Adjustment	Purchase Price Allocation
Cash and receivables	$1,000,000	$ 1,000,000		$ 1,000,000
Inventory	2,500,000	3,000,000	$ 500,000 (a)	3,000,000
Fixed assets	5,000,000	10,000,000	3,622,000 (d)	8,622,000
Other assets	600,000	1,000,000	262,000 (d)	862,000
	$9,100,000	$15,000,000	$4,384,000	$13,484,000
Current liabilities	$1,200,000	$ 1,200,000		$ 1,200,000
Unfavorable lease		200,000	$ 200,000 (b)	200,000
Deferred taxes:				
Current			111,000 (c)	111,000
Long-term	1,000,000		1,473,000 (d)	2,473,000
Long-term debt	2,000,000	2,000,000		2,000,000
Stockholders' equity	4,900,000	11,600,000	2,600,000 (e)	7,500,000
	$9,100,000	$15,000,000	$4,384,000	$13,484,000

EXHIBIT 6.6 (Continued)

Purchase Accounting Adjustments:

(a) Inventory:

Fair market value including seller's profit	$3,000,000
Historical book value	2,500,000
Purchase accounting adjustment	$ 500,000

(b) Unfavorable lease:

Present value (8% discount) of payments over market	$ 200,000

(c) Deferred taxes related to current assets and all liabilities:

	Cost Allocation	Tax Basis	Temporary Difference	Deferred Tax (37%)
Inventory	$3,000,000	$2,500,000	$(500,000)	$185,000
Unfavorable lease	(200,000)		200,000	(74,000)
				$111,000

(d) Purchase accounting adjustments for long-term assets and related deferred taxes:

	Total	Fixed Assets	Other Assets
Acquisition cost	$ 7,500,000		
Tax basis	3,100,000		
Temporary differences before adjustment	4,400,000		
Factor (see calculation below)	.5873		
Total adjustment	$ 2,584,000		
Fair value of identifiable net assets (not intended to foot across)	$11,600,000	$10,000,000	$1,000,000
Total acquisition cost	7,500,000		
Unadjusted negative goodwill	$ 4,100,000	(3,727,000)	(373,000)
Unadjusted acquisition cost allocation (to fixed assets and other assets only)	$ 6,900,000	6,273,000	627,000
Adjustment	2,584,000	2,349,000	235,000
Adjusted acquisition cost allocation	9,484,000	8,622,000	862,000
Historical book value	5,600,000	(5,000,000)	(600,000)
Purchase accounting adjustment	$ 3,884,000	$ 3,622,000	262,000
Adjusted acquisition cost allocation	$ 9,484,000	$ 8,622,000	$ 862,000
Tax basis	2,800,000	2,500,000	300,000
Temporary difference	$ 6,684,000	$ 6,122,000	$ 562,000
Deferred taxes at 37%	$ 2,473,000	$ 2,265,000	$ 208,000
Less, historical deferred taxes	(1,000,000)		
Purchase accounting adjustment	$ 1,473,000		

EXHIBIT 6.6 *(Continued)*

Calculation of adjustment factor:

$$\frac{.37}{(1 - .37)} = .5873$$

Cross check by application of complete simultaneous equation:

Net temporary difference	$\times$	$\dfrac{\text{Tax rate}}{(1 - \text{tax rate})}$	$=$	Adjustment to deferred tax assets and liabilities and noncurrent assets
$4,400,000	$\times$	$\dfrac{.37}{(1 - .37)}$	$=$	$2,584,000

(e) Equity:

Acquisition cost	$7,500,000
Historical equity of Company B	4,900,000
	$2,600,000

APPENDIX 6-A

Checklist of Disclosure Requirements— Purchase Method Acquisitions

(Information relating to several relatively minor acquisitions may be combined.)

1. Name and brief description of purchase method acquisitions during the latest period; cost and, if applicable, the number of shares issued or issuable, and amount assigned thereto; and the period for which results of operations are included in the income statement.
2. Contingent payments, options, or commitments and their proposed accounting treatment.
3. Plan for amortization (including method and period) of any acquired goodwill or any excess of acquired net assets over cost (negative goodwill).
4. For publicly held companies, supplemental pro forma information on results of operations for the:
   a. Current period as though the companies had combined at the beginning of the period, unless the acquisition took place at or near that date.
   b. Immediately preceding period as though the companies had combined at the beginning of that period if comparative financial statements are presented.

CHAPTER SEVEN

Accounting for Leveraged Acquisitions

James N. Brendel
Hein + Associates LLP

7.1   INTRODUCTION

This chapter addresses special accounting issues applicable to *leveraged acquisitions*, often referred to as LBOs.

Accounting for leveraged acquisitions was somewhat inconsistent during the early and mid 1980s. The FASB's Emerging Issues Task Force (EITF) first considered the topic in 1986 and reached a consensus that was published in EITF Issue No. 86-16, *Carryover of Predecessor Basis in Leveraged Buyout Transactions*. That consensus primarily addressed leveraged acquisitions in which existing shareholders increased their ownership interest by using borrowed funds.

In 1988 the EITF undertook a broader consideration of leveraged acquisition accounting issues to resolve inconsistency in practice in accounting for both increases and decreases in owners' interests. Consensus was reached in May 1989, when the EITF published a consensus on EITF Issue No. 88-16, *Basis in Leveraged Buyout Transactions*, which superseded the consensus on Issue No. 86-16 and established rules considered adequate to result in consistent accounting for all leveraged acquisitions.

On a conceptual basis, the consensus on Issue 88-16 has received some criticism. It was reached in 1989, when the FASB was working on its major project to study when a company should be included in consolidated financial statements and how to account in the consolidated statements for a subsidiary's assets, liabilities, revenues, expenses, gains, and losses. That study included exhaustive consideration of alternative approaches to acquisition accounting. The FASB did not favor setting arbitrary thresholds for such things as extent of ownership interest in determining whether an acquisition had occurred. The consensus on Issue 88-16 sets arbitrary thresholds that the EITF believed would be sufficient for standardizing, in a reasonable way, practice in accounting for leveraged acquisitions.

Some challenge the conceptual soundness of rules that provide that a transaction in which a shareholder has a 5% interest should be accounted for quite differently than if that shareholder has a 4% interest. Also, the same economic results as those of a leveraged acquisition can be achieved in a transaction in which a new company is not created, but quite different accounting will result. Transactions have and will be structured to meet or not meet the requirements of the consensus, leading to a desired accounting result that may not be representative in comparison to other substantively similar transactions.

Critics say that the consensus on Issue 88-16 results in acquisition accounting on a part-purchase, part-pooling basis, which is not permitted by APB Opinion No. 16, *Business Combinations*. That is because the consensus provides for bringing forward part of the financial statements of an acquired company on an historical basis and adjusting the other part to fair values based on the purchase price. Some of these critics also object to complex determinations and calculations required by the consensus. Some believe that it would be both conceptually sound and more practical to have rules that provide that either an acquisition has occurred or not and that the new company should be recorded either entirely at fair value or entirely at predecessor cost. Others believe that the hybrid accounting is more characteristic of accounting for a step acquisition, and is appropriate for these transactions.

Notwithstanding these criticisms, the EITF achieved its goal of setting a somewhat workable, although complex, set of rules for standardizing the accounting for the preponderance of transactions meeting the criteria for a leveraged acquisition.

7.2 APPLICATION OF EITF ISSUE NO. 88-16

(a) Identifying a Leveraged Acquisition

Issue No. 88-16 distinguishes the leveraged acquisition from other business acquisitions by the following characteristics:

(1) It is effected in a single highly leveraged transaction or a series of related highly leveraged transactions.

(2) The acquirer is a holding company with no substantive operations.

(3) The acquirer obtains all previously outstanding common stock of an operating company and there can be no remaining minority interest.

Although the EITF did not specify the amount of debt utilization that is required to constitute a *highly leveraged transaction*, informal discussion between the author and SEC staff members indicates that the SEC staff will consider an acquisition that is financed 60% or more with debt to be highly leveraged. The SEC staff would presume an acquisition financed with 50% to 60% debt to be highly leveraged and substantial evidence to the contrary would be necessary to overcome that presumption. If an acquisition is financed with less than 50% debt, the facts and circumstances must be carefully analyzed to determine whether the transaction is highly leveraged. However, with less than 50% debt, an acquisition would usually not be considered highly leveraged.

Issues have also risen concerning what is meant by a *holding company with no substantive operations*. The SEC staff has informally indicated that they consider this term to apply to a company that has had no major capital raising activities or has spent insignificant funds on the development of a business, with the exception of companies formed to acquire a business. They have indicated that leveraged acquisition status would also apply to a company that has ceased operations and as a result is a shell company. Leveraged acquisition status would not be applied to companies that had performed significant fund raising activities and had spent significant funds developing their business, even if the business had no revenue generating activities, as long as the development of the business was ongoing.

(b) General Accounting Conclusions

EITF Issue No. 88-16 provides the following conclusions:

(1) A partial or complete change in accounting basis is appropriate only when there has been a change in control of voting interest; that is, a new controlling shareholder or group of shareholders must be established.

(2) The form of transaction by which the investor obtains its interest in NEWCO does not change the accounting to be applied. In general, if an investor in NEWCO owned a residual interest in OLDCO, then the lesser of that investor's residual interest in OLDCO or NEWCO is carried over at the investor's predecessor basis.

(3) The fair value of any securities issued by NEWCO to OLDCO should be objectively determinable. Fair value should not be used, whether or not the NEWCO securities are publicly traded, unless at least 80% of the fair value of consideration paid to acquire OLDCO equity interests comprises monetary consideration.

Leveraged acquisitions do not meet the conditions for pooling of interests accounting since they utilize debt to finance the purchase of the operating company's stock. Therefore, leveraged acquisitions are always accounted for by the purchase method, with allocation of the purchase price to assets acquired and liabilities assumed.

(c) Change in Control

The consensus defines *unilateral control* as:

> "Ownership of more than 50% of the voting interests of a business enterprise, unless the voting rights are legally or externally restricted in such a way that the ability to exercise the normal rights and privileges associated with voting control is absent."

For leveraged acquisition accounting to apply, resulting in changes to the carrying values of an acquired company's assets and liabilities, there must be a change in control that is substantive, genuine, and not temporary. This requirement is not unique to leveraged acquisition accounting—it applies to purchase accounting in general. Without a change in control, any difference between purchase price and historical cost of net assets is accounted for as an adjustment of stockholders' equity, similar to an investment by or distribution to owners.

For a change in control to occur, the consensus of Issue 88-16 requires that one of the following must occur:

(1) A single shareholder, who did not have control must gain control. The single shareholder may be a member of management. This condition may also apply to management as a group; or

(2) A group of new shareholders that meets the definition for inclusion in the new control group, obtains control. This group may include management. For purposes of this condition, management is viewed as a single shareholder; or

(3) The new control group may have no subset that already had unilateral control at the time of the transaction.

(d) Identifying the New Control Group

The new company's shareholders are divided into three groups for purposes of determining inclusion or exclusion from the new control group:

(1) Management,

(2) Shareholders with a greater percentage interest in the new company than they had in the old company, and

(3) Shareholders with the same or a lower percentage interest in the new company than they had in the old company.

Management consists of employees of the old company or persons holding management positions and an interest in the new company. Additional guidance in identifying management is included in Item 401 of SEC Regulation S-K. Management is presumed to be part of the new control group. This presumption can be overcome if management does not participate in promoting the leveraged acquisition. In this event, management is considered to be one shareholder subject to the other tests applicable to shareholders.

A shareholder with a greater percentage interest in the new company than in the old company is included in the new control group if that shareholder holds a 5% or greater interest in the new company. This test is designed to prevent public shareholders from being considered part of the new control group.

A shareholder with the same or a lower percentage interest in the new company than in the old company is subject to two tests: (a) the *voting-interest test*; and (b) the *capital-at-risk test*. Under the voting interest test, any shareholder with a voting interest of 20% or more on a fully diluted basis is considered part of the new control group. Under the capital at risk test, any shareholder with 20% or more of the fair value of cumulative capital at risk in the new company is included in the new control group. Capital at risk includes all debt and equity securities.

See Exhibit 7.1 for an illustration of a voting-interest test.

Exhibit 7.2 is an illustration of the capital-at-risk test.

(e) Determining the Percentages of a Leveraged Acquisition to Record at Fair Value and Predecessor Basis

If a transaction has resulted in a change in control, the holding company's investment in the old company is determined as follows:

EXHIBIT 7.1 Illustration of Voting-Interest Test

Investor A, the 100% owner of a company, sells his stock to a new company for: (a) cash; (b) 1,500 shares of the new company's stock; and (c) options to purchase an additional 500 shares. Including the aforementioned shares and options, the new company has a total of 10,000 shares outstanding and has issued options to purchase an additional 2,000 shares. Investor A has the following voting interest on a fully diluted basis, assuming all options are exercised.

	Investor A	Total	Percentage
Common stock	1,500	10,000	
Options	500	2,000	
Total	2,000	12,000	16.7%

Because Investor A's voting interest of 16.7% is less than 20%, Investor A is not part of the new control group.

(1) For interests held by the new control group, predecessor basis is used to the extent of the lesser of interests held in the new company or the old company.

(2) For interests held by 5% or greater shareholders who are not in the new control group and whose percentage interests decreased, predecessor basis is used if the percentage interests of such shareholders is at least 20% in the aggregate.

(3) Fair value is used for all other interests, subject to the *monetary test*.

The monetary test provides that if less than 80% of the fair value of consideration paid to acquire the old company's equity interests consists of monetary consideration, the percentage of the new company that can be recorded at fair value is limited to the percentage of monetary consideration. If at least 80% of the fair value of the consideration is monetary all of the new company can be recorded at fair value except for the interests of the new control group and certain 5% shareholders, as described above.

Monetary consideration includes debt and similar obligations, and cash. However, proceeds of a loan by the old company to controlling shareholders

EXHIBIT 7.2   Illustration of Capital-at-Risk Test

XYZ Company, which has completed an acquisition of the stock of another company, has the following capital structure:

	Shares	Fair Value
Voting common stock	200,000	$ 2,000,000
Preferred stock	100,000	500,000
Long-term debt (collateralized)		10,000,000
		$12,500,000

Investor B, who owned 15% of the old company's common stock, owns 20,000 shares of XYZ Company's common stock, 1,000 shares of the preferred stock, and $2,000,000 of the collateralized long-term debt. The capital-at-risk test is computed as follows:

	Fair Value		Cumulative Capital-at-Risk
	Investor B	Total	
Voting common stock	$ 200,000	$ 2,000,000	10%
Preferred stock	50,000	500,000	10%
Long-term debt (collateralized)	2,000,000	10,000,000	18%
	$2,250,000	$12,500,000	

Since Investor B has less than 20% of the total fair value of new capitalization at each cumulative risk level, starting with the lowest priority in liquidation, Investor B is not part of the new control group.

of the new company to use in obtaining their controlling interest in the new company are not included in monetary consideration.

7.3   SEC ACCOUNTING GUIDANCE

The SEC staff has also provided guidance on the following issues that either directly or indirectly can affect accounting for leveraged acquisitions:

(a) SEC Staff Accounting Bulletin (SAB) No. 48 requires that assets acquired by a newly established holding company from a promoter or shareholder in exchange for stock should be recorded at predecessor cost.

(b) Takeover costs should generally not be classified as extraordinary items.

(c) If an underwriter requires promoters or shareholders to place stock in escrow as a condition of a public offering and the stock is to be released if the company meets specified performance criteria, release of the stock results in compensation expense equal to the fair value of the stock at the time of release.

7.4 ILLUSTRATION OF ACCOUNTING FOR A LEVERAGED ACQUISITION

Exhibit 7.3 provides an illustration of accounting for a leveraged acquisition following the guidance of the consensus on EITF Issue No. 88-16.

EXHIBIT 7.3 Illustration of Accounting for a Leveraged Acquisition

Company A is a public company with established operations. Its stock trades at $20 per share, and there are 30,000 shares outstanding. Management owns 3,000 shares, or 10%. Net book value is $250,000. The fair market value of Company A's fixed assets exceeds book value by $200,000, and the fair market value of all other assets approximates book value.

An unrelated investor acquires an interest in Company A as follows. Company B is formed and capitalized with $480,000 of bank debt and $60,000 contributed by the individual for 1,000 shares of Company B stock. Management of Company A exchanges its 3,000 shares of Company A (worth $60,000) for 1,000 shares of Company B. The $540,000 cash of Company B is used to acquire the 27,000 shares of Company A owned by the public. Company A and Company B then merge. Management now has a 50% interest in the resulting entity.

Management and the investor will act together in controlling the new entity, constituting a new control group. The leveraged acquisition would be accounted for as follows:

| | | | Eliminations | | |
	Company A	Company B	Entry (1)	Entry (2)	Consolidated
Cash	$ 200,000				$ 200,000
Receivables	250,000				250,000
Inventory	600,000				600,000
Fixed assets	50,000		$ 200,000	$(20,000)	230,000
Investment in					
Company A		$600,000	(600,000)		
Goodwill			230,000	(23,000)	207,000
	$1,100,000	$600,000	$(170,000)	$(43,000)	$1,487,000
Payables	$ 850,000				$ 850,000
Bank debt		$480,000			480,000
Deferred taxes			80,000	(8,000)	72,000
Equity	250,000	120,000	(250,000)	(35,000)	85,000
	$1,100,000	$600,000	$(170,000)	$(43,000)	$1,487,000

Explanation of Entries:

(1) To eliminate Company B's investment in Company A, step up the value of Company A's fixed assets to fair market value of $250,000, record related deferred taxes, and to record goodwill.

(2) Since management is a member of the new control group, predecessor basis for its 10% interest (the lesser of its interest in Company A or Company B) must be included in determining Consolidated Company B's equity. This entry records the disregarded portion of the step-up in basis as a reduction of equity.

EITF ISSUE NO. 88-16, BASIS IN LEVERAGED BUYOUT TRANSACTIONS

EITF Abstracts

Issue No. 88-16

Title: Basis in Leveraged Buyout Transactions

Dates Discussed: June 2, 1988; July 14, 1988; August 25–26, 1988; October 6, 1988; January 12–13, 1989; February 23, 1989; May 18, 1989; June 29, 1989

References: FASB Statement No. 57, *Related Party Disclosures*
FASB Technical Bulletin No. 85-5, *Issues Relating to Accounting for Business Combinations*
AICPA Accounting Research Bulletin No. 51, *Consolidated Financial Statements*
APB Opinion No. 16, *Business Combinations*
AICPA Accounting Interpretation 26, *Acquisition of Minority Interest*, of APB Opinion No. 16
AICPA Accounting Interpretation 39, *Transfers and Exchanges between Companies under Common Control*, of APB Opinion No. 16
AICPA Issues Paper, *"Push Down" Accounting*, dated October 30, 1979
SEC Staff Accounting Bulletin No. 30, *Accounting for Divestiture of a Subsidiary or Other Business Operation*
SEC Staff Accounting Bulletin No. 48, *Transfers of Assets by Promoters and Shareholders*
SEC Staff Accounting Bulletin No. 54, *Application of "Push Down" Basis of Accounting in Financial Statements of Subsidiaries Acquired by Purchase*

ISSUE

A holding company (NEWCO) with no substantive operations acquires an operating company (OLDCO) in a leveraged buyout (LBO) transaction.

The issue is what basis should be used by NEWCO to value its interest in OLDCO; that is, whether the acquisition of shares of OLDCO establishes a new basis of accounting or whether predecessor basis, OLDCO book value, or some combination should be used.[1]

The underlying substance of the transaction must be evaluated to determine whether it constitutes:

1. A financial restructuring-recapitalization for which no change in accounting basis would be appropriate
2. A step acquisition for which a partial change in accounting basis would be appropriate
3. A purchase by new controlling investors for which a partial or complete change in basis based on the fair value of the transaction would be appropriate.

Scope

To distinguish an LBO transaction within the scope of this Issue from other business combinations, the LBO should be effected in a single highly leveraged transaction or a series of related and anticipated highly leveraged transactions that result in the acquisition by NEWCO of all previously outstanding common stock of OLDCO; that is, there can be no remaining minority interest.[2] This Issue excludes LBO transactions in which existing majority stockholders utilize a holding company to acquire all of the shares of OLDCO not previously owned. Step acquisition accounting continues to be appropriate in such transactions.

Definitions

For purposes of this Issue, certain terms are defined as follows:

Continuing shareholder
A NEWCO shareholder that owned a residual interest in OLDCO.

---

[1] Issues concerning recognizing a new basis in the financial statements of OLDCO or recording an owner's basis in the financial statements of OLDCO are outside the scope of this Issue.
[2] The concepts of Opinion 16 and consolidation require that 100 percent of the outstanding common stock of a target entity be acquired to potentially justify a 100 percent change in accounting basis.

Dilutive securities

Options, warrants, convertible securities, or any other financial instrument through which a person or entity may increase its voting or residual interest.

Management

Management comprises OLDCO employees or management that hold management positions and a residual interest in NEWCO. Regulation S-K, Item 401 should be considered when determining which individuals are included in management.

Monetary consideration

Cash, debt, and debt-type instruments such as mandatorily redeemable preferred stock.

Predecessor basis

A shareholder's basis in an interest in a business enterprise, that is, original cost of the investment in the business enterprise plus that shareholder's proportionate share of earnings or losses less dividends and any other distributions received by that shareholder from the business enterprise since the date of acquisition. A difference between a shareholder's cost of an investment and the amount of underlying equity in net assets of the business enterprise should be accounted for as if the business enterprise were a consolidated subsidiary for purposes of determining predecessor basis. The shareholder's proportionate equity in the book value of the business enterprise may be an acceptable substitute measure of predecessor basis, but only in circumstances for which it is impracticable to recompute predecessor basis. Predecessor basis in a stock option is the amount of cash or other tangible assets paid by the holder to obtain the option.

Residual interest

An investor's proportionate share (expressed as a percentage and after conversion or exercise of dilutive securities) of the net assets of a business enterprise after satisfaction of equity securities with redemption or liquidation features (see Exhibit 88-16A).

Shareholder

A residual interest holder.

Unilateral control

Ownership of more than 50 percent of the voting interest of a business enterprise unless the voting rights are legally or externally restricted in such a way that the ability to exercise the normal rights and privileges associated with voting control is absent.

EITF DISCUSSION

The Task Force reached the following consensus, which supersedes the consensus reached on Issue No. 86-16, "Carryover of Predecessor Cost in Leveraged Buyout Transactions." See the SEC Observer's comments on page 441.

Section 1. A partial or complete change in accounting basis is appropriate only when there has been a change in control of voting interest; that is, a new controlling shareholder or group of shareholders must be established.[3]

Consensus Guidance. For purposes of this consensus, the following guidance should be followed in evaluating whether a new controlling shareholder or control group has been established (related parties as defined in Statement 57 are considered a single individual shareholder unless the parties are related only by ownership of OLDCO):

a. A change in control has occurred if *any* one of the following conditions is met (see Exhibit 88-16B):

    i. A single shareholder, that may be an individual member of management, obtains unilateral control of NEWCO, and that shareholder did not have unilateral control of OLDCO. This condition is met when either an individual member of management or management as a group obtains unilateral control of NEWCO and did not have unilateral control of OLDCO.

    ii. A group of *new* shareholders (shareholders with no residual interest in OLDCO), that may include management, that meets the definition for inclusion in the NEWCO control group (see Section 1(c) below for criteria for inclusion in the control group) obtains unilateral control of NEWCO. For purposes of this test, there is a rebuttable presumption that management as a group is considered a single shareholder.

---

[3]*Underlying Authoritative Support.* In form, LBO transactions within the scope of this Issue are analogous to purchase business combinations. Certain purchase business combinations are, essentially, recapitalization-restructuring transactions or simply a change in the legal form or ownership structure. Interpretation 39 of Opinion 16 specifies that a change in basis is not appropriate if the transfer of net assets or exchange of shares is between entities under common control.

To justify using a new basis of accounting to record the acquisition of the target in an LBO transaction (a transaction that can be analogized to the purchase of a subsidiary), the transaction must result in a change of control; that is, an investor or group of investors that previously did not have unilateral control over the target entity must now have such control. The rationale for using a new basis of accounting to record the acquisition of the target in an LBO transaction is supported by the view that the target entity becomes a subsidiary of NEWCO, which is controlled by the new controlling shareholder or control group.

The establishment of a new controlling shareholder or control group results in a transaction similar to a purchase business combination as opposed to a recapitalization-restructuring transaction for which a change in basis is not appropriate.

iii. The NEWCO control group (see Section 1(c)) obtains unilateral control of NEWCO, and no subset of the NEWCO control group had unilateral control of OLDCO.

b. The change in controlling voting interest must be substantive, genuine, and not temporary. The new controlling shareholder or shareholder group must have the ability to implement major operating and financial policies such as refinancing debt and selling or acquiring assets. At the date of the transaction, it must be probable that the controlling voting interest will not revert to the OLDCO share-holders. In addition, there should be no plans or intentions within a short period of time after consummation of the transaction (for example, one year) for either (i) a controlling shareholder or shareholder group to sell all or a portion of its interest such that the conditions for control would no longer be met or (ii) NEWCO to issue additional voting securities such that the conditions for control would no longer be met. The requirement specified in the preceding sentence would not be considered for purposes of determining change in control if the shareholder is committed to transferring its investment only to another member of the controlling shareholder group or if the voting rights of the securities held by the controlling shareholders enable the other members of the controlling shareholder group to retain control even if the voting interest is sold (see Ex-hibits 88-16E and 88-16F, Example 6).

i. NEWCO dilutive securities other than options or warrants that are substan-tially equivalent to voting interests of NEWCO that are issued to or held by investors that are not members of the controlling shareholder group (as de-termined in Section 1(a)) should be considered when evaluating whether control has changed. Factors to consider in determining substantial equiva-lency to voting interests include, but are not limited to, voting rights, time until exercise or conversion, probability of events triggering exercise or con-version, and the relationship between exercise or conversion price and fair value of NEWCO voting interests.

ii. NEWCO warrants and options to acquire voting interests that are issued to or held by investors that are not members of the controlling shareholder group (as determined in Section 1(a)) are presumed to be equivalent to vot-ing interests. Factors to consider in overcoming that presumption include whether such securities can be exercised only after an extended period of time, only after future service is provided over a period of years, or whether such securities can be exercised solely for the purpose of selling the voting securities obtained through exercise (for example, in a public offering). An-other factor to consider is the relationship between the exercise price of the NEWCO warrants or options and the fair value of the NEWCO voting in-terest; however, because of the volatility of new highly leveraged securities, this factor by itself may not be persuasive.

c. For purposes of determining inclusion in or exclusion from the NEWCO control group, NEWCO shareholders, including continuing shareholders, are divided into three groups—management, shareholders with a greater percentage of residual interest in NEWCO than they held in OLDCO, and shareholders with the same or lower percentage of residual interest in NEWCO than they held in OLDCO—and are treated as follows:

    i. There is a rebuttable presumption that the management group is part of the NEWCO control group. That presumption may be overcome if management did not participate in promoting the LBO transaction. In that unusual circumstance, the entire management group is considered an individual shareholder and is subject to the additional tests in items (ii) or (iii) below.

    ii. Individual shareholders (related parties as previously defined are a single individual shareholder) with a greater percentage of residual interest in NEWCO than they held in OLDCO and (a) that hold a 5 percent or greater residual interest in NEWCO are automatically included in the NEWCO control group or (b) that hold less than a 5 percent residual interest in NEWCO are automatically excluded from the NEWCO control group.

    iii. The following voting-interest test and capital-at-risk test[4] are to be applied to individual shareholders with the same or lower percentage of residual interest in NEWCO than they held in OLDCO to determine their inclusion in or exclusion from the NEWCO control group. If the shareholder's interest meets or exceeds the stated percentage in *either* the voting-interest test or the capital-at-risk test, the shareholder is automatically included in the NEWCO control group and, conversely, if the shareholder does not meet or exceed the stated percentage in both of those tests, the shareholder is automatically excluded from the NEWCO control group.

        a. Shareholders with a voting interest, assuming exercise or conversion of all dilutive securities held by that shareholder, of 20 percent or more of the total voting interests of NEWCO are automatically included in the NEWCO control group. Dilutive securities held by other than the individual continuing shareholder should be assumed to be exercised or converted to the extent that the terms of those dilutive securities are no less favorable than the terms of the dilutive securities held by the continuing shareholder. However, the effect of including the dilutive securities held by other than the continuing shareholder may not reduce the continuing shareholder's percentage of voting interest below its percentage of outstanding voting interest. Rights held by a shareholder to purchase additional NEWCO common stock at fair value as determined at the time of

---

[4]Capital at risk includes all debt and equity securities of consolidated NEWCO, including short-term debt, long-term debt, notes payable, and capital lease obligations.

exercise should be ignored if the right is not exercisable until NEWCO has had an extended period of substantive operations (see Exhibit 88-16C).

b. Shareholders with 20 percent or more of the fair value of cumulative capital at risk in NEWCO at any risk level (starting with the security with the lowest priority in liquidation and continuing to the security with the highest priority in liquidation owned by the shareholder), based on ownership of NEWCO equity and debt securities as well as on the maximum amount of any direct or indirect guarantees (such as commitments to infuse cash under certain conditions) made by the shareholder on behalf of NEWCO or its shareholders, are automatically included in the NEWCO control group. The maximum amount of any guarantees should be included in the capital-at-risk test at the risk level of the security guaranteed (see Exhibit 88-16D).

d. If a change in control is deemed not to have occurred as a result of applying the above guidance, the transaction should be considered a recapitalization-restructuring for which a change in accounting basis is not appropriate.

Section 2. The form of a transaction by which the investor obtains its interest in NEWCO does not change the accounting to be applied. In general, if an investor in NEWCO owned a residual interest in OLDCO, then the lesser of that investor's residual interest in OLDCO or NEWCO is carried over at the investor's predecessor basis.[5]

Consensus Guidance. For purposes of this consensus, the following guidance should be followed:

a. Whether OLDCO shares or other OLDCO interests that convert to residual interests are contributed to NEWCO or purchased outright by NEWCO is irrelevant. The governing factor is whether residual interests are held both before and after the transaction.

b. If a change in control has occurred, the carrying amount of NEWCO's investment in OLDCO should be determined as follows:

---

[5]*Underlying Authoritative Support.* To the extent that a shareholder owns the same level of residual interest before and after the LBO transaction, no event has occurred with respect to that retained residual interest. That general notion is consistent with ARB 51, paragraph 10, which establishes accounting principles applicable to a step acquisition. NEWCO's basis in OLDCO in LBO transactions in which one or more of the continuing shareholders has a greater percentage residual interest in NEWCO than they held in OLDCO is generally determined in a manner that is similar to a step acquisition.

i. The lesser of the continuing shareholder's residual interest[6] (members of management are considered individual shareholders and related parties as previously defined are a single shareholder) in OLDCO or NEWCO is carried over at the continuing shareholder's predecessor basis, except as explained below for shareholders that are *not* a part of the NEWCO control group.

    a. The residual interests of individual continuing shareholders that have less than a 5 percent residual interest in NEWCO should (subject to the monetary test that is discussed in Section 3) be valued at fair value.

    b. The residual interests of all individual continuing shareholders with the same or lower percentage of residual interest in NEWCO than they held in OLDCO that individually have a 5 percent or more residual interest in NEWCO and that *in the aggregate* have less than a 20 percent residual interest in NEWCO should (subject to the monetary test) be valued at fair value.

ii. The remainder of NEWCO's investment in OLDCO, subject to the monetary test, is based upon fair value; that is, the amount that was or would have been paid in monetary consideration.

Section 3. The fair value of any securities issued by NEWCO to acquire OLDCO should be objectively determinable. Fair value should not be used, whether or not the NEWCO securities are publicly traded, unless at least 80 percent of the fair value of consideration paid to acquire OLDCO equity interests comprises monetary consideration (the monetary test).[7]

Consensus Guideline. The following guidance should be followed for purposes of applying the monetary test:

a. To reflect at fair value the total consideration paid to OLDCO shareholders, monetary consideration, net of any monetary consideration used to acquire equity securities of NEWCO, should constitute 80 percent or more of the total consideration paid to OLDCO shareholders. Any equity securities of NEWCO

---

[6]The computation of the continuing shareholder's residual interest in OLDCO and NEWCO should include the effect of dilutive securities in the same manner as prescribed in Section 1(c)(iii)(a) for voting interests.

[7]*Underlying Authoritative Support.* Opinion 16, paragraphs 72–76, establishes that the fair value of cash, debt, and equity securities issued to purchase a target company (plus costs) should measure the cost of the acquisition. However, the Task Force believes the fair value of equity securities issued by a highly leveraged company may not be objectively determinable.

received at the formation of NEWCO by NEWCO shareholders in exchange for OLDCO securities should be included in the denominator at fair value (that is, the amount that would have been paid in monetary consideration) when applying the 80 percent test.

b. If controlling shareholders of NEWCO obtain their equity interest in NEWCO using proceeds of a loan from OLDCO, the proceeds of that loan should not be considered as monetary consideration. In addition, those proceeds should be classified in the financial statements as a reduction of NEWCO equity (similar to a stock subscription receivable) until paid. Similarly, if a shareholder's investment in NEWCO is obtained from proceeds of an unusual bonus or other unusual payment from OLDCO, those proceeds should not be considered monetary consideration and the charge (net of tax, if appropriate) should be shown as a reduction of NEWCO equity. Such transactions cannot result in new equity because they are not obtained independently of OLDCO.

c. If the criteria of Sections 1 and 2 are met but the 80 percent monetary test is not met, any NEWCO equity securities issued to shareholders to acquire OLDCO interest should be valued at predecessor basis. That is, the portion of NEWCO's investment in OLDCO that can be valued at fair value cannot exceed the percentage of the total consideration that is monetary.

The examples in Exhibits 88-16A through 88-16I are presented to illustrate the application of the consensus.

Comments by the SEC Observer

Subsequent to the May 18, 1989 Task Force meeting, the SEC Observer indicated that the SEC staff will expect registrants to comply with the consensus for all tranactions included in financial statements filed with the SEC after May 18, 1989, unless the transaction was complete or substantially complete as of that date. In those circumstances, if financial statements including the transaction have not been previously filed with the SEC, the SEC staff encourages application of the consensus but will accept accounting in accordance with the guidance provided by the SEC Observer at previous Task Force meetings in which this Issue was discussed (beginning with the June 2, 1988 meeting). See Exhibit 86-16B of Issue 86-16 for that guidance.

The SEC staff will expect registrants to disclose in the notes to the financial statements the accounting policy followed in determining the basis used by NEWCO to value its interest in OLDCO and the rationale therefor.

STATUS

No further EITF discussion is planned. A related issue was discussed in Issue No. 90-12, "Allocating Basis to Individual Assets and Liabilities for Transactions within the Scope of Issue No. 88-16."

CHAPTER EIGHT

Federal Income Taxation of Acquisitions

Mark A. Blackton
Thermo Companies
E. Christopher Lang
Hughes Clikeman and Associates

8.1 GENERAL

(a) Overview

This chapter will discuss U.S. federal income tax considerations related to corporate acquisitions, based on the Internal Revenue Code (IRC) of 1986, including the Omnibus Budget Reconciliation Act of 1993 and subsequent changes through 1994.

Tax considerations often influence the structure of acquisitions, but they are secondary in importance to overriding business, legal, and economic considerations. However, even if compelling business, legal or economic considerations are present, it is important to quantify the tax cost or tax savings of possible alternate structures. Major questions about the tax aspects of an acquisition include:

(1) Is the transaction taxable or nontaxable?

(2) In transactions that are taxable, how much of any realized gain or loss will be ordinary and how much will be capital gain or loss?

(3) To what extent will tax attributes, such as net operating loss and tax credit carryforwards, be usable against future taxable income?

The Code defines gross income as ". . . all income from whatever source derived . . ." The Internal Revenue Service (IRS) and the tax courts generally start with this definition in considering the taxability of all transactions, including acquisitions. Acquisitions are either taxable, nontaxable, or partially taxable. The taxability of a transaction is dependent on whether the transaction, or part of the transaction, meets the conditions of one or more of the specific tax-free exceptions permitted by the Code. Failing to qualify for an exemption results in the transaction being taxable.

(b) Ordinary Versus Capital Gain or Loss

Generally, the sale of stock creates capital gain or loss. The exception to this is *small business stock*, which may generate ordinary losses under a specific set of rules. The gain or loss resulting from the disposition of all business and non business assets is generally capital in nature. There are exemptions for ordinary income assets such as inventory, certain works created though personal effort, accounts receivable, and recapture assets, such as depreciable personal and real property.

(c) Nontaxable Transactions

In a tax-free transaction involving corporations, the seller (the acquired corporation, or if relevant, its shareholders) generally recognizes no gain or loss. The buyer (the acquiring corporation) carries over the seller's tax basis, holding period, and other tax attributes subject to certain limitations. The tax deferral achieved in a tax-free acquisition can result in significant cash savings for the seller. Additionally, retained and usable tax attributes, such as net operating loss and tax credit carryforwards, may benefit the buyer in the future.

(d) IRS Powers

The structure of a merger or acquisition will determine the tax ramifications for both parties to the transaction. However, the IRS and the courts have the capability of denying taxpayers anticipated tax benefits, even in carefully structured transactions. The IRS has broad powers to reallocate income, deductions, and credits among the parties. Judicial concepts such as *no business purpose, sham transaction*, and *substance versus form* are powerful weapons used by the IRS and the Courts in unexpectedly reshaping a transaction for tax purposes, much to the disappointment and financial loss of the taxpayers. The IRC has integrated these concepts to apply to acquisitions, as well as all other transactions. These judicial and statutory danger zones warrant careful consideration during analysis of potential transaction structures. *Substance versus form* is particularly difficult in the area of corporate acquisitions. In that area there are often choices of form that have similar, at times identical, economic consequences. Clearly, in these situations the tax planner must exercise additional care in documenting the intended form.

(e) Buyer-Seller Conflict

Generally, the buyer and seller will be in conflict over tax considerations. This conflict stems from the general concept that what is advantageous for one is usually not so for the other. However, there are times when the tax goals of the parties provide the tax planner with an opportunity to obtain tax benefits for both. A transaction structured in a way that enables both parties to derive tax advantages may be subject to close IRS scrutiny. The tax planner must be ready to demonstrate that a transaction's form is consistent with the transactions economic substance.

(f) A Note of Caution

The reader should note that these topics involve complex considerations, many of which are not apparent to other than a highly qualified tax specialist. It is important that a tax specialist be consulted regarding the tax aspects of any merger or acquisition.

8.2 OMNIBUS BUDGET RECONCILIATION ACT OF 1993

(a) General

The most recent tax legislation as of the date of preparing this chapter is the Omnibus Budget Reconciliation Act of 1993 (1993 Act), which became law on August 10, 1993. The 1993 Act contains several provisions that affect acquisitions, although not as significantly as other tax legislation in recent years. The 1993 Act raised tax rates, provided tax incentives in the form of capital gain exclusions for qualified small business, and permitted the amortization of intangible assets such as goodwill.

(b) Tax Rates

The highest corporate tax rate increased to 35%, retroactive to January 1, 1993. The highest personal tax rate increased to 39.6%. The 39.6% rate gives effect to a surcharge on taxable income in excess of $250,000 for joint filers. The capital gain tax rate remained at 28% for individuals.

(c) Small Business Stock

The 1993 Act allows noncorporate taxpayers holding *qualified small business stock* for over five years to exclude 50% of any gain on the sale or exchange of that stock, resulting in an effective tax rate of 14%. The gain exclusion is limited to the greater of:

(1) 10 time the taxpayer's basis in the stock; or

(2) $10 million of the gain from the stock in the corporation, applied on a shareholder-by-shareholder basis.

The benefit applies only to *qualified small business stock*. Qualified small business stock must meet the following requirements:

(1) The stock must be acquired at its original issuance, either directly or through an underwriter, in exchange for money or property other than stock. The stock can also be issued as compensation for services provided to the issuing corporation, except for those provided by the stock underwriter.

(2) The issuing corporation must be a *qualified small business* as of the date of issuance and during substantially all of the period that the taxpayer holds the stock.

A qualified small business is a Subchapter C (regular) corporation other than:

(1) a Domestic International Sales Corporation (DISC) or former DISC;

(2) a corporation or a corporation having a subsidiary with a possessions credit election in effect (IRC Section 936);

(3) a regulated investment company (mutual fund);

(4) a Real Estate Investment Trust (REIT);

(5) a Real Estate Mortgage Investment Conduit (REMIC); or

(6) a cooperative.

The corporation is not allowed to own:

(1) real property with a value amount exceeding 10% of the total value of the corporation's assets; or

(2) stock or securities with a value exceeding 10% of the corporation's total assets over liabilities.

Also, at least 80% of the value of the corporation's gross assets must be used in the active conduct of one or more qualified trades or businesses.

A qualified trade or business is any trade or business which does not involve the performance of serving in the fields of health, law, engineering, architecture, accounting, actuarial science, performing arts, consulting, athletics, financial services, brokerage services or any trade or business in which the principal asset is the reputation or skill force of one or more of its employees. Also excluded from this definition is any banking, insurance, leasing, financing, investing, or similar business, farming business, business involving the production or extraction of products with respect to which percentage depletion is allowable, or any business involving the operation of a hotel, motel, restaurant, or similar business.

(d) Amortization of Goodwill and Other Intangible Assets

One of the most important changes affecting acquisitions is that the 1993 Act allows tax deductions that amortize acquired goodwill and similar intangibles over 15 years. The following intangibles are eligible for this deduction:

(1) goodwill;

(2) going concern value of business;

(3) work force in place;

(4) information bases;

(5) licenses, permits and other rights granted by the government or one of its agencies;

(6) covenants not to compete; and

(7) franchises, trademarks, or trade names.

This change in the law will certainly benefit businesses that have significant goodwill, going concern, and trade name value by making them more appealing to potential buyers and thus, giving them an overall higher value. This increased value arises from the fact that the buyer can now reduce future tax payments by amortizing and deducting previously nondeductible items.

8.3 TAXABLE ACQUISITIONS

(a) General

Taxable acquisitions occur in two forms: (1) a purchase of stock; or (2) a purchase of assets. Considerations in deciding whether to complete an acquisition as a purchase of stock or a purchase of assets will be briefly discussed in this section.

Acquisitions of stock are generally easier to carry out than acquisitions of assets. Asset acquisitions involve such complications as asset title transfers and creditor notifications. The acquisition of assets can also trigger transfer taxes. Further, there are times that only a sale of stock can preserve nonassignable rights such as a licenses, leases, trademarks, or other favorable contractual arrangements.

Consideration of unknown or contingent liabilities also affects the stock versus asset purchase decision. The seller may wish to pass risk of these possible liabilities on to the acquirer through the sale of stock. However, the acquirer may prefer to limit any exposure and be unwilling to accept responsibility for the unknown by purchasing assets. Having the seller indemnify the acquirer of stock for any undisclosed liabilities will sometimes allow a stock sale when other factors also favor a stock sale. Other considerations may also determine the form of the transaction. Minority shareholders and undesirable assets that the buyer does not wish to purchase may require an asset acquisition instead of a stock acquisition.

General tax factors to consider when deciding the form of an acquisition transaction include the following. Generally, only the seller recognizes taxable gain. The sale of stock results in only a single tax, generally at capital gain tax rates. The sale of assets normally results in two taxes. The first tax is at the corporate level upon the sale or distribution of appreciated assets. The second tax is at the shareholder level upon the distribution of the proceeds from sale of the asset or the liquidation of the corporation.

The tax basis of the assets acquired is a primary concern of an acquirer. In a purchase of stock, the historical tax bases of the underlying assets are carried over and are not stepped up to reflect the purchase price of the stock. This situation will not allow the acquirer to benefit from increased depreciation or amortization expenses of *inside basis* commensurate with the purchase price. The acquirer can obtain stepped-up inside basis equal to purchase price only through a liquidation of the corporation or an election made pursuant to IRC § 338. Each of these actions results in additional corporate level tax.

(b) Structures of Taxable Asset Acquisitions

Asset acquisitions can follow two patterns: (1) a selling corporation may sell its assets directly to a purchaser and distribute the proceeds and any unsold assets to its shareholders in complete liquidation; or alternatively (2) a corporation may distribute its assets in complete liquidation to its shareholders after which the shareholders sell the assets. The order of liquidation should be structured dependent on tax and nontax issues. Nontax issues include dealing with minority shareholders and potential title transfer problems.

(c) Corporate Liquidations

The tax treatment of a direct sale of assets or a distribution in complete liquidation has similar effects to a selling or distributing corporation. IRC § 336 provides that a corporation must recognize gain or loss on the distribution of property in complete liquidation. The gain or loss must be computed as if such property were sold at fair market value. A sale of the assets or distribution to shareholders of a business is a sale or distribution of each separate tangible and intangible asset in that business. This is true even though the buyer may view the transaction as the sale of a single going concern. It is necessary to identify the value and tax basis of each asset to compute a selling or distributing corporations' gain or loss and to establish the acquirer's tax basis in the acquired assets.

There is an exception to the general rule that gain is recognized by a corporation and its shareholders upon the complete liquidation of the corporation. IRC § 337 and § 332 provide that a complete liquidation to an 80% corporate shareholder (an 80% distributee) does not result in gain or loss to the corporation or the shareholder. The corporate shareholder receives assets with carryover tax basis. Any *built in* gain or loss attributable to the assets is deferred until the shareholder sells the assets. Therefore, a tax planning opportunity exists for closely held corporations. If a single corporate shareholder has or can acquire the stock necessary to hold 80% of a selling corporation, there is an opportunity to avoid the double taxation caused by corporate liquidation. In such an instance, a corporation could be liquidated tax-free. The 80% distributee could then sell the assets, recognizing tax only at the shareholder level. This rule does not apply to partial liquidations.

(d) Allocation of Purchase Price in Asset Acquisitions

IRC § 1001(b) provides that the ". . . amount received from the sale or other disposition of property shall be the sum of any money received plus the fair market value of the property other than money received . . .". Also included in the amount received by a seller are any liabilities of the seller or liabilities associated with the transferred property that are assumed by the buyer. The amount received (sales or purchase price) is allocated to each asset. An acquirer of assets will usually wish to maximize purchase price to depreciable and amortizable assets so as to maximize future tax deductions. Conversely, a seller of assets will often wish to minimize the allocation to the same assets to reduce the tax effect of recapture items and will therefore prefer to allocate the purchase price to intangible assets such as goodwill. Before the 1993 Act, the allocation of purchase price to intangible items was particularly detrimental to acquirers because amounts allocated to intangible assets, such as goodwill or going concern value, were not amortizable for tax purposes. The 1993 Act has reduced this conflict through its provision allowing acquirers to amortize these intangibles for tax purposes over 15 years. It is important to note that IRC § 1060 requires that purchase price allocation be based on fair market value. However, fair market can be subjective, which leads to negotiation of fair market value amounts.

IRC § 1060 requires that the purchase price of assets be allocated by the acquirer and seller using the *residual* method. The residual method allocates the purchase price first to the tangible and intangible assets, other than goodwill or going-concern value (up to their fair market values), with any premiums being allocated to goodwill or going-concern value. The IRC has devised four classes of assets for allocation purposes. Class I assets are basically cash items, such as cash, demand deposits, and similar accounts in banks or other depository institutions. Class II assets are highly liquid, cash-like assets, such as certificates of deposit, U.S. Government Securities, readily marketable stock or securities and foreign currency. Class III assets are those assets being purchased other than Classes I, II and IV assets. Intangible assets that are goodwill in nature are Class IV assets.

Exhibit 8.1 illustrates the application of the residual method of allocation of purchase price for tax purposes in an acquisition.

EXHIBIT 8.1   Residual Method of Allocation of Purchase Price for Tax Purposes

Assume that Company A acquires the business of Company B in an asset purchase for $10,000,000. The asset classes of the acquired assets consist of:

	Tax Basis	Fair Market Value	Purchase Price Allocation
Cash (Class 1 Asset)	$20,000	$20,000	$20,000
Equipment (Class 3 Asset)	$4,000,000	5,000,000	5,000,000
Goodwill (Class 4 Asset)	None	Not Directly Determinable	4,980,000

(e) Gain or Loss of the Seller in Asset Acquisitions

(i) DETERMINING AMOUNT AND CHARACTER OF GAIN OR LOSS

After allocating the sales price to the individual assets, the seller's gain or loss is determined by subtracting each asset's tax basis from its allocated portion of the purchase price. The tax basis of each asset, under IRC § 1011 and related sections, is the seller's original cost less the seller's allowed or allowable depreciation benefits. The resulting amount is the seller's adjusted tax basis.

A seller's gain or loss will either be ordinary gain or loss or capital gain or loss. Sellers generally prefer to have all income characterized as capital gains (taxed at preferred rates) and losses taxed as ordinary losses, which have higher tax benefits because of the higher tax rates on ordinary income. Determining the character of a gain or loss involves many factors. The most important factors are the nature and use of the asset sold. Generally, if the asset sold is a capital asset as defined in IRC § 1221, the seller will receive long-term capital gain tax treatment. Note that assets must be held more than one year and used in the trade or business of the seller to qualify for favorable long-term capital gain tax rates.

(ii) RECAPTURE

Assets subject to an allowance for depreciation or depletion are subject to the recapture provisions under IRC § 1245 and § 1250. These provisions override all other sections, including IRC § 1231 and § 453, resulting in ordinary income to the extent of prior tax depreciation deductions. See Exhibit 8.2 for an illustration.

The gain computed in Exhibit 8.2 would result in federal income tax totaling $20,573, based on ordinary income of $38,780 taxed at 35% and the capital gain of $25,000 taxed at 28%.

EXHIBIT 8.2   Gain on Sale of Equipment

For example, assume that Company A purchased new equipment for $100,000. The equipment has a seven-year MACRS life and is depreciated for tax purposes using the double declining balance method. After two years, Company A has claimed depreciation deductions totaling $38,780. At the beginning of the third year, Company B purchases the equipment from Company A as part of the acquisition of a business. The equipment receives a $125,000 allocation of the purchase price. The following table illustrates the computation of Company A's taxable gain attributable to the sale of the equipment:

Net proceeds received	$125,000
Adjusted basis:	
Cost	100,000
Depreciation allowed	(38,780)
	61,220
Gain	$ 63,780
Character of gain:	
Ordinary income (equal to prior depreciation)	$ 38,780
Capital gain	25,000
	$ 63,780

(iii) EFFECT ON SHAREHOLDERS OF COMPLETE LIQUIDATION AFTER SALE OF ASSETS BY A CORPORATION

After a corporation's assets are acquired by another, the shareholders must decide what to do with the sales proceeds. If the shareholders have common investment goals, they may decide to continue to operate a new venture in the continuing corporation. In that event, the corporation reinvests its sales proceeds and continues to exist as an ongoing entity. Note that some state legal provisions related to the continuity of doing business could apply. There could also be complications in using tax attributes, such as net operating loss and tax credit carryforwards, from the old trade or business against income earned in a new trade or business. These tax attribute issues are discussed later in the chapter.

Sometimes shareholders want the cash that has accumulated in the corporation, in which case the cash is simply distributed to the shareholders in complete liquidation of the corporation. The complete liquidation of a corporation can result in two levels of tax. The sale of assets by the corporation triggers the corporate level tax on gain, which is discussed above. The subsequent distribution of assets by the corporation to its shareholders causes the second level of tax. Generally, the distribution of assets from a corporation to its shareholders constitutes a dividend. The dividends create ordinary income to shareholders to the extent of accumulated corporate earning and profits. However, special rules apply to the process of complete liquidation that permit capital gain treatment of liquidating distributions.

The intent to cease doing business and liquidate all remaining corporate assets causes the corporation to enter the *status of liquidation* as explained by IRC Regulation § 1.332-2(c). The status of liquidation does not require a written plan of liquidation or that a corporation dissolve and end its legal existence. If factors suggest the intention to liquidate, the liquidation provisions apply. Provisions under IRC § 331 allow for complete liquidation to constitute a sale of stock, providing capital gain treatment to the shareholders.

The fair market value of the assets received is the full payment for the surrender of stock. Under IRC § 1001, shareholder gain or loss is equal to the difference between the net fair market value of the property received (fair market value of the assets received less any liabilities assumed by the shareholder) and the shareholder's basis of the stock surrendered. The basis of noncash assets received by a shareholder is equal to the fair market value on the date of distribution, under IRC § 334(a).

If a shareholder has acquired shares at different times and for different amounts, each group of shares will require a separate gain or loss computation. The allocation of the liquidating distribution is based on the number of shares within each group. This individual group treatment can cause situations in which one group has capital gain, while another group may have a capital loss. This is covered in IRC Regulation Section 1.331-1(e) and Revenue Rule 68-348, 68-2 C.B. 141.

A shareholder who receives all liquidating distributions in a single year reports the total gain or loss in the year of receipt. However, it is possible for a liquidation of a corporation to take several years. The recognition of gain or loss in this situation requires the used of the cost recovery method for recognition of gain or loss, as explained by Revenue Rule 68-348, 68-2 C.B. 141. This method allows the first proceeds received to reduce the shareholder's basis of the stock held. After the shareholder's stock basis is zero, all subsequent receipts represent taxable gain. Liquidations that cause a loss to the shareholder require that no loss be recognized until the final distribution.

(f) Taxable Stock Acquisitions

The tax aspects of a stock acquisition are relatively straight forward in comparison to those related to asset acquisitions. If an acquirer purchases stock, the acquirer receives stock with a tax basis equal to the amount paid for the stock. The selling corporate shareholders recognize gain or loss determined by deducting their tax basis in the stock from the amount they receive. The acquired corporation did not participate in the sale transaction and generally will not recognize gain or loss related to the acquisition. The acquired corporation continues to exist and continues to hold assets with their historical tax basis and with tax attributes unchanged. The utility of the tax attributes will likely be limited due to the application of IRC § 382 to be discussed later in the chapter.

After an acquisition, the acquired corporation may be liquidated. The effect of a post-stock acquisition liquidation, barring the exception to 80% corporate shareholders as previously discussed, is that the acquiring shareholders will hold the asset directly with a stepped up basis. Since these shareholders owned the corporation at the time of the liquidation, they bear the burden of the tax triggered upon liquidation. The practical application of this strategy for noncorporate and non-80% corporate shareholders is limited due to the obvious high tax cost.

8.4   IRC SECTION 338

(a) General

Generally, the assets held by a corporation acquired in a stock acquisition retain their historic tax basis. The historical tax basis of the acquired corporation's assets may be stepped up by elective or deemed application of IRC § 338 or an election under IRC § 338(h)(10).

(b) Regular Section 338 Election

IRC § 338 allows a corporation acquiring at least 80% of the stock of another corporation during a 12 month period (a *qualified stock purchase*) to elect to treat the stock acquisition as an asset acquisition. If a corporate acquirer elects under regular IRC § 338, the acquired corporation is deemed to have sold all of its assets, subject to its liabilities, to a newly formed corporation. The acquired corporation is then deemed to have liquidated. The sale and liquidation have taken place after the purchase of the stock. Therefore, from the selling shareholder's perspective, this is a stock sale. The acquirer receives the step up in tax basis in the assets acquired that is generally associated with an asset purchase.

The primary distinction between an asset sale and a deemed asset sale under IRC § 338 is that the selling shareholders do not bear the burden for the tax triggered by the sale of the assets. This is due to the fact that the deemed sale occurs after the selling shareholders have transferred their stock.

If acquired corporation was not a member of a controlled group prior to the acquisition, the deemed sale of the assets takes place in the final return of the acquired corporation. The final return of the acquired corporation will have a tax year that closes on the acquisition date. If the acquired corporation was a member of a controlled group prior to the acquisition, the acquired corporation will need to file two tax returns. The first tax return is for inclusion with the affiliated group, with a tax year ending on the date of acquisition. The other will be a special *one day* tax return, which will include the gain on the sale and no other transactions.

The result of these rules is that the gain on the deemed sale is taxed to the acquired corporation. There is no shelter for this tax other than by tax attributes of the acquired corporation.

The results of a regular IRC § 338 election are generally unwanted. The additional tax to the acquired corporation is generally a high price to pay for a step up in underlying asset tax basis, unless the acquired corporation has adequate tax attributes to shelter the gain.

IRC § 338 provides a special rule that deems a regular § 338 election to have been made. This deemed election could have serious negative tax effects. The regular IRC § 338 election is deemed to have been made if the acquiring corporation acquires any assets of the acquired corporation within the *consistency period*. The *consistency period* starts one year before the first purchase of stock constituting a qualified stock purchase and ending one year after the qualified stock purchase has been accomplished (IRC § 338(h)(4)). Note that there are some exceptions for acquisition of assets in the ordinary course of business and other circumstances.

A *protective carryover basis election* is available under Temporary Regulation 1.338-4t(f)(6). This protective election will avoid a deemed regular § 338 election. This election requires that all assets acquired by the acquirer within the consistency period have a carryover tax basis. The Proposed Regulation would reduce the scope of the consistency rules and eliminate the necessity of making a protective carryover basis election. The filing of a protective election for all qualified stock purchases is recommended until the new rules become effective.

(c) Section 338(h)(10) Election

The election available under IRC § 338(h)(10) is similar to a regular IRC § 338 election. The IRC § 338(h)(10) election provides special benefits for acquisitions of corporations out of affiliated groups. Unlike a regular IRC § 338 election, the deemed sale takes place while the acquired corporation is still a member of the affiliated group, followed by the distribution of the sale proceeds in liquidation of the acquired corporation. These events allow for two advantages over a regular IRC § 338 election.

The first advantage relates to the gain associated with the deemed sale of assets. As this gain is deemed to occur while the acquired corporation is still a member of the affiliated group, this gain is reported on the affiliated groups consolidated tax return. This allows the gain to be sheltered by the combined tax attributes of the affiliated group.

The second advantage relates to the liquidation treatment of the sales proceeds under an IRC § 338(h)(10) election. This liquidating distribution is governed by IRC § 332 and § 337. The parent corporation would qualify as an 80% distributee, as explained above, making the liquidation tax free.

The overall result of an IRC § 338(h)(10) election is that a single level of tax is imposed to the acquired corporation's old consolidated group. This tax may be sheltered by the consolidated tax attributes of the affiliated group. Note that this gain is not generally larger than the gain the consolidated group would have recognized on sale of the acquired corporation's stock. The acquiring corporation receives a corporation holding assets with a tax basis stepped-up to the purchase price of the stock.

8.5 TAX-FREE MERGERS AND ACQUISITIONS

(a) General Concepts and Requirements

IRC § 368(a)(1) defines and describes forms of corporate reorganizations for which U.S. federal taxation does not occur. Each form of corporate reorganization has specific requirements, several of which are common to most forms of tax-free reorganization. Some of the reorganizations have well-known variances such as *forward* and *reverse* triangular mergers under IRC Section 368(a)(2)(D) and (E).

Reorganizations that involve the transfer of assets generally require that *substantially all* of the assets of the seller be transferred to the acquirer. By transferring specified minimum percentages of assets, transactions can fall within defined safe harbors for qualifying as substantially all of the assets. However, the type of assets transferred (e.g., operating assets or investment assets) is also important in determining whether substantially all of the assets of the seller have been transferred to the buyer.

Reorganizations involving exchanges of stock require that the acquirer gains *control* over the seller. Control is generally defined as acquiring 80% or more of the voting and nonvoting stock (IRC § 368(c)(1)).

Another concept that is common to most forms of reorganizations is the doctrine of *continuity of interest.* In order to satisfy the doctrine of continuity of interest, the sellers must maintain specified minimum proprietary interests in the business after the reorganization is completed. Determining whether the continuity of interest requirement is met can be complex. IRC Reg. § 1.368-1(d) provides guidance on the application of this doctrine. In theory, a tax-free reorganization involves only a structural change in a business without changing ownership. The doctrine of continuity of interest is a test for determining whether the transaction is only a structural change, or whether the purported reorganization is in reality a winding up of the business affairs of the entity, which may be treated as a taxable liquidation.

Statutory provisions under IRC § 269 and § 482 also provide broad powers to the IRS to restructure a purported tax-free transaction into a taxable event that conforms to the underlying economic reality of such a transaction. These provisions will be discussed in detail later in this chapter.

In some reorganizations, a buyer and seller are permitted to exchange, in addition to stock, limited amounts of other property to which, although taxable to the extent of such other property, will not cause the transaction to fail as a reorganization. This property, which is partially taxable in an otherwise tax-free exchange, is called *boot.*

The courts and the IRS can utilize a variety of judicial doctrines and statutory provisions that enable them to restructure an attempted tax-free transaction into a taxable event if they believe such is appropriate. For example, *form over substance, sham transaction,* and *no business purpose* are three separate (although related) doctrines that look to the underlying economic reality of a transaction in determining tax consequences. Additionally, under the *step transaction doctrine,* a series of legally separate transactions, completed pursuant to a common plan or goal, can be collapsed into a single transaction and taxed accordingly by the IRS.

These judicial doctrines, statutes, and also technical requirements must be considered by the tax planner in structuring any acquisition to be tax-free.

(b) Types of Tax-Free Reorganizations

(i) TYPE A REORGANIZATION-STATUTORY MERGERS

A *Type A* reorganization is defined as a statutory merger or consolidation meeting the conditions of IRC § 368(a)(1)(A). A statutory merger occurs if an acquired corporation releases all of its assets and liabilities to an acquiring corporation in return for some of the acquiring corporation's stock. After the transaction is completed, only the acquiring corporation survives. A *consolidation* occurs if the two companies release all of their assets to a new corporation in return for stock of the new corporation. Upon completion of this transaction, only the new corporation remains.

Type A reorganizations do not have any statutory limitations on the consideration that an acquiring corporation can issue to the acquired corporation for its assets and liabilities. The acquiring corporation is free to issue any type of common or preferred stock as well as securities. While a *Type A* reorganization is very flexible, it must meet the *continuity of interest* requirement. Thus, the shareholders of the acquired corporation must receive enough stock in the acquiring corporation so that they have a continuing financial interest in the remaining corporation. Furthermore a *Type A* reorganization is subject to all state laws that may have narrower definitions of acceptable consideration to be given up by the acquiring corporation.

Consolidation to a Subsidiary (Drop Down). In cases where it may be disadvantageous for the acquiring corporation to merge with the acquired corporation, the assets of the acquired corporation can be placed into a newly formed subsidiary of the acquiring corporation in a nontaxable IRC § 351 exchange. Normally, the step transaction doctrine would be applicable, combining the two steps, and tax-free *Type A* reorganization treatment would not apply since all the assets are not in one corporation. IRC § 368(a)(2)(C) has allowed this since the 1954 code. This technique is referred to as a *transfer to a* subsidiary, or a *drop down*.

(ii) TYPE B REORGANIZATIONS

A *Type B* reorganization is defined as the acquisition of the stock of one corporation by another. After the transaction, the acquired corporation is a subsidiary of the acquiring corporation. There are two requirements which must be met in order to have a successful *Type B* reorganization

(a) A *stock-for-stock* condition requires that the acquiring corporation must acquire the acquired corporation stock by exchanging only voting stock of the acquiring corporation; and

(b) Immediately following the exchange, the acquiring corporation must be in control of the acquired corporation.

Control is defined under IRC § 368(c) as the acquirer receiving 80% or more of the stock of the acquired corporation (All stock, voting and non-voting). For example, if Company A exchanges 1 share of voting stock for every 10 shares of Company B's voting stock and acquires all of Company B's voting stock, then a successful *Type B* reorganization has occurred. If Company B's shareholders have the *option* of taking $50 in cash or one voting share of Company A's stock, the *Type B* reorganization can not be successful, even if 90 percent of Company B's shareholders accept stock. This is because stock must be exchanged solely for stock, the cash option is fatal to the *Type B* reorganization.

Creeping Control. It is permissible under the regulations to have a *creeping Type B* reorganization. It is so called because the requisite *control* occurs as a result of several transactions. There are several requirements for a successful creeping *Type B* reorganization.

(a) There must be an overall plan to gain control of the acquired corporation and each acquisition transaction must be part of the overall plan; and

(b) This overall plan must only cover a short period of time, generally 12 months or less; and

(c) The acquisition must be made solely for voting stock.

Prior cash purchases are acceptable if they are a separate transaction which is not part of the overall plan.

(iii) TYPE C REORGANIZATIONS

A *Type C* reorganization is defined as a transfer of *substantially all* of the assets of an acquired corporation solely for voting stock of the acquiring corporation. The acquired corporation, generally, must liquidate as part of this type of transaction unless waived by the IRS. There is a similarity between *Type A* and *Type C* reorganizations—*Type C* reorganizations are referred to as *practical Type A reorganizations.* One benefit of a *Type C* reorganization is that the acquiring corporation's shareholders need not approve the acquisition. The acquired corporation's shareholders generally must approve the sale of the assets and the liquidation.

Substantially all of the assets is not defined in the code. Revenue Procedure 77-37, 1977-2 C.B. 568 has set forth governing guidelines that the acquiring corporation must acquire at least 70% of the gross assets and 90% of the net assets of the acquired corporation. Furthermore, it is required that the assets critical to the continuation of the acquired corporation's business must be transferred.

Type C reorganizations have a *solely for voting stock* requirement. Liabilities, in this context, receive special treatment. Assumption of the acquired corporation's liabilities or taking property of the acquired corporation that is subject to a liability is not fatal to a *Type C* reorganization. When voting stock and assumed liabilities are transfered, the assumed liabilities have no effect on the transaction. In transactions which include other forms of *boot*, the assumed liabilites are considered as *boot*.

A minimal amount of boot is acceptable in a *Type C* reorganization. *Boot* is limited to 20% of the total consideration given. Therefore, to have a successful *Type C* reorganization, 80% or more of the fair market value of the assets must be received solely for voting stock. Liabilities assumed are not considered in this equation unless other property (boot) is also given. If the liabilities exceed 20% of the value of the assets, only voting stock can be used since these liabilities are ignored if no other boot is transferred. See Exhibit 8.3 for an illustration.

While it is not possible under a *Type C* reorganization to have a dropping down of the assets to a controlled subsidiary, it is acceptable to have a controlled subsidiary act as the acquiring corporation. If the transaction is structured that way, the acquiring subsidiary may use the voting stock of its parent corporation as considered for the acquisition, instead of its own voting stock. It is not permissible to use both the parent corporation's voting stock and an acquiring subsidiary's voting as consideration in a *Type C* reorganization.

EXHIBIT 8.3   Boot in a Type C Reorganization

> Assume that Company B transfers all of its assets, which have a fair market value of $1,000,000, to Company A in exchange for Company A's voting stock. Company A assumes $350,000 of Company B's liabilities. Even though the liabilities make up 35% of the consideration, the transaction is a valid *Type C* reorganization as long as no other boot is given.

(iv) TYPE D REORGANIZATIONS

There are two kinds of *Type D* reorganizations: (a) acquisitive; and (b) divisive.

Acquisitive Type D Reorganizations. A corporation transfers substantially all of its assets to another corporation in exchange for voting stock of the other corporation. The first corporation must receive enough stock to have control after the exchange. Control in all tax-free reorganizations is set at 80% of the voting stock and 80% of the total number of shares of all other classes of stock. The rest of the first corporation's stock and any other remaining assets are distributed to the other corporation's shareholders. After the transaction, the shareholders of the first corporation become the controlling shareholders of the other. A transaction may meet the requirements for both the *Type C* and a *Type D* reorganization, in which case it is considered *Type D*. See Exhibit 8.4 for illustration.

Divisive Type D Reorganization. In a divisive *Type D* reorganization, before the transaction there is one corporation and after the transaction there are two corporations. One of the most well-known divisive *Type D* reorganizations was the breakup of AT&T. There are various circumstances that lead to divisive *Type D* reorganizations, including federal mandates to avoid monopolies, as seen in the case of AT&T, the need to settle shareholder squabbles, and decisions to separate risky business sectors.

There are two steps to a *Type D* divisive reorganization. The first is to transfer assets of a going concern business to a corporation in exchange for control of that corporation. The second step is the transfer of all the stock and securities of the controlled corporation to the shareholders of the corporation that transferred the assets. How the controlled corporation's stock

EXHIBIT 8.4   Type D Reorganization

For example, assume that Company A wishes to control Company B, with Company B being the survivor. Thus, a *Type D* reorganization is suitable. There are 1,000 shares of Company B voting stock issued and outstanding. Company A transfers all of its assets in exchange for 950 shares of Company B voting stock. Company A then dissolves by issuing Company B stock in exchange for Company A voting stock. Therefore, Company B survives with Company A's stockholders owning the controlling interest of Company B as a result of a *Type D* reorganization.

is divided is key in determining whether the resulting transaction is a spin-off, split-off or a split-up.

Spin-offs. A spin-off is similar to a normal dividend distribution, although a spin-off is taxfree. The controlled corporation's stock is distributed to the controlling corporation's shareholders. The result is that the shareholders own stock in both corporations. A spin-off provides the shareholders with continuing interests in the businesses of both the controlling and controlled corporations through separate stockholdings in each.

Split-offs. A split-off is useful if the shareholders wish to have a continuing interest in only one of the lines of business. In the case of a split-off, only some of the original corporation's shareholders retain the stock in the original corporation. Other shareholders relinquish their stock in the original corporation for stock in the newly formed corporation. The end result is that some shareholders own one corporation while another set of shareholders own the new corporation. This is an effective device if there is animosity present between groups of shareholders.

Split-ups. A split-up is similar to a split-off except that the original corporation liquidates, with two new corporations being formed. The original corporation transfers some of its assets to a new corporation in exchange for all that corporation's stock and the rest of its assets are transfered to another new corporation in exchange for all that other corporation's stock. The original corporation then liquidates, distributing the stock of the two new corporations to its shareholders.

All *Type D* reorganizations are required to meet the additional conditions of IRC § 354, § 355 and § 356. It is in this area of law that the tax planner will have his most difficult task in effecting a successful tax-free *Type D* reorganization. IRC § 354(a)(1) provides that, in general, no gain or loss is recognized if stock or securities in a corporation, a party to a reorganization, are, in pursuance of the plan of reorganization, exchanged solely for stock or securities in such corporation or in another corporation which is a party to the reorganization.

Some exceptions are made regarding securities. These exceptions are intended to protect against a bail out of earnings and profits at the capital gain tax rate. IRC § 354(b) provides that substantially all of the assets of the transferor must be transferred in order to qualify under IRC § 354. Also required is the transfer of all stock, securities, and other property to the transferor's shareholders.

IRC § 355 deals with the distribution of stock and securities. Stock is not required to be exchanged or otherwise redeemed from the shareholders.

This section permits the transfer of less than substantially all of a corporation's assets in an exchange for stock or securities of the transferee. It is not required that distribution of stock be pro rata to all of the shareholders. IRC § 355 includes provisions to protect against the bailout of earnings and profits at the capital gain rate. One of the more common requirements is that the transferor's business must have been engaged in an active trade or business for the previous 5 years.

IRC § 356 provides some flexibility regarding the receipt of boot in a *Type D* reorganization. The general rule is that if *boot* is received, in an exchange that is governed by IRC § 354 or § 355, gain is to be recognized to the extent of the *boot*. *Boot* includes cash and other property. IRC § 356 determines whether the gain is capital or ordinary. In addition it determines whether the exchange has the effect of a dividend.

To summarize, a successful *Type D* reorganization must meet four requirements. The first is that the original corporation must distribute, to its shareholders, stock of a new subsidiary that results in control of that subsidiary. The second is that property distributed by the original corporation must consist solely of stock and securities of the new subsidiary. The third is that, after the distribution has occurred, both companies must be actively engaged in business. The fourth is that the distribution must not be a tax avoidance device used to bailout earnings and profits in either the original corporation or the new subsidiary.

(v) HYBRID REORGANIZATIONS—Triangular Mergers and Reverse Triangular Mergers

General. Triangular merger is a term used to describe a reorganization in which a parent company's subsidiary is acquiring or being acquired by another corporation.

Triangular Merger. There are three requirements of a triangular merger. The first is that the parent corporation must have a controlled subsidiary (80% owned) and must receive substantially all the assets of the acquired corporation in the merger. As discussed previously, substantially means 90% of the fair market value of the net assets and 70% of the fair market value of the gross assets. The second is that the transaction between the subsidiary and the acquired corporation must satisfy all the requirements of a *Type A* reorganization. The third is that no stock of the subsidiary can be used in the transaction. See Exhibit 8.5 for illustration.

EXHIBIT 8.5 Triangular Merger

For example, assume that Company A owns all of the stock of Company B. Company A wishes to acquire Company C. Company C transfers all of its assets to Company B in exchange for 100 shares of Company A stock. Company C's assets have a value of $100,000, all of which have been transferred to Company B. Company C dissolves and transfers its stock in Company A to its shareholders. This transaction qualifies as a valid triangular merger because Company B received more than 90% of the fair market value of the net assets as well as more than 70% of the fair market value of the gross assets of Company C. The second requirement is met because, if Company B had been merged directly into Company A, the merger would have qualified as a *Type A* reorganization. Finally, the only stock transferred to Company C was Company A stock.

Reverse Triangular Merger. This is a variation of the triangular merger. The acquired corporation is the surviving subsidiary instead of the subsidiary of the acquirer. The parent corporation's voting stock is transferred to the acquired corporation in exchange for the acquired corporation's stock, which must retain substantially all of its assets and property. The acquired corporation must acquire substantially all of the assets and property of the acquiring corporations subsidiary and the acquiring corporation must obtain control (80% ownership).

8.6 TAX LOSSES AND TAX CREDIT CARRYOVERS OF ACQUIRED CORPORATIONS

(a) General

At one time, an important motive for many corporate acquisitions or mergers was the availability of tax loss or tax credit carryovers in the acquired corporation that could be used to offset taxable income of the acquiring corporation. *Loss corporations* were often advertised for sale in business magazines and newspapers. The price for a loss corporation often was based on a discounted value of the future tax reductions expected from utilization of the net operating loss or tax credit carryovers. However, a series of tax reforms enacted by Congress, including IRC § 269, § 382, § 383, § 384, and § 482, have greatly restricted the ability to offset an acquirer's taxable income by the tax loss or tax credit carryovers of an acquired corporation.

As a general rule, unused net operating losses may be carried back by the corporation that incurred the losses to each of the three taxable years preceding the taxable year of such loss (IRC § 172(b)(A)). Thereafter, any excess net operating loss may be carried forward to each of the 15 taxable years following the taxable year of such loss (IRC § 172(b)(1)(B)).

IRC § 381, § 382, § 383, and § 384 are the statutory provisions that apply to and govern the carryover and realization of tax benefits related to the carryover of tax losses, as well as tax credits in mergers and acquisitions. Each of these is discussed below.

(b) IRC Section 381

IRC § 381 generally provides that a corporation acquiring the assets of another corporation in a nontaxable reorganization or from the liquidation of a subsidiary shall succeed to and take into account, as of the close of the date of distribution or transfer, that other corporation's net operating loss carryovers, earnings, profits, and capital loss carryovers.

IRC § 381(b) provides three operating rules for the carryover of tax attributes. The first is that in any type of reorganization, except an F reorganization, the taxable year of the transferor ends on the date of the transfer, thus triggering the requirement of filing a tax return for the short taxable year ending on the date of the transfer. The second is that the date of distribution or transfer is the date when the transaction is completed. If the transferor corporation retains some assets, the date of distribution is the date on which substantially all the assets were transferred to the acquiring corporation. The third is that the acquiring corporation may not carryback a net operating loss or a net capital loss from a taxable year ending after the date of transfer to preacquisition years of the transferor corporation. See Exhibit 8.6 for an illustration.

IRC § 381 provides that many tax attributes in a reorganization may be transferred. However, IRC § 269, § 382, § 383, and § 482 set limitations on the benefits available from such tax attributes.

EXHIBIT 8.6 IRC Section 381 Carryback of Net Operating Loss

On December 31, 1994, Company B merges into Company A in a *Type A* nontaxable merger. A loss incurred by Company A in 1995 may not be carried back to offset the income of Company B prior to the merger. The loss may be carried back only to offset taxable income of Company A for years prior to the merger.

(c) IRC Sections 269 and 482

IRC § 269 and § 482 can be best described as *antitax avoidance* provisions. They provide the IRS with substantial power to construe transactions in accordance with their substance rather than form.

IRC § 482 allows the IRS to reallocate (but not disallow) income, deductions, credits, or other allowances between or among related taxpayers. IRC § 269 generally disallows the benefit of any deductions, credit, or other allowance obtained by acquiring property or control of a corporation for the principal purpose of avoiding tax. It should be noted that for IRC § 269, control is defined as ownership of 50% or more. IRC § 269 requires taxpayers to show that the choice of the most favorable tax route was motivated by substantial business reasons in addition to the opportunity to obtain the particular tax benefits inherent in the method selected. Several business purpose criteria are set forth by IRC § 269:

(1) Are the acquiring parties aware of the tax benefits at the time of transfer?

(2) Will the acquired corporation have a continuing business after the acquisition, not just a shell?

(3) Is the acquisition of control or assets necessary or useful to the acquiring corporation's activities?

(4) A comparison of the economic benefit of the acquisition versus the tax benefit of the acquisition.

(5) Could the challenged benefit be used by the taxpayer even if the acquisition did not occur?

(6) Was the type of transaction the most economically feasible way to reach the desired objective?

IRC § 269 may overlap with IRC § 381 and § 383. IRC § 382 and § 383 do not limit the authority present in IRC § 269, but the limitations of IRC § 382 and § 383 can be relevant evidence in determining whether the principal purpose of an acquisition is the evasion or avoidance of income tax (IRC Reg. § 1.269-7).

(d) IRC Section 382

(i) GENERAL

IRC § 382 was established to address perceived abuses from the acquisition of loss corporations. It imposes limitations on the use of net operating loss carryforwards and certain unrealized losses if an *ownership change* has occurred. This requires careful evaluation whenever there have been substantial changes in the stock ownership of a loss corporation.

Under IRC § 382, an ownership change occurs if the percentage of the stock owned by the loss corporation, owned by one or more 5% stockholders, has increased by more than 50% over the lowest percentage of such stock that was owned by those parties at any time during any three-year period. All transactions during the testing period, whether or not related to each other, are considered in determining whether an ownership change has occurred, including increases from multiple acquisitions, even if the percentage ownership between the first and last days of the testing period is the same or has decreased. The attribution rules of IRC § 318 apply to the determination of ownership changes. All ownership changes of less than 5% stockholders are aggregated into a single shareholder unit referred to as the *public*. Any stock sales by the public to a 5% shareholder is included in the measurement of ownership change, whereas sales of stock by the public to other shareholders in the public group are not included in the measurement of ownership change. Public shareholders must be segregated if they receive loss corporation stock as a result of an equity structure shift or nontaxable exchanges of stock for property.

The testing period required by IRC § 382 is a three-year period ending on the day following any ownership change. A loss corporation does not need to include in the measurement of ownership change any transactions that occurred on or before the date of the most recent ownership change in determining if another ownership change has occurred. The testing period does not begin until the corporation becomes a loss corporation—any ownership changes prior to the corporation becoming a loss corporation are not considered. See Exhibit 8.7 for an illustration.

Exhibit 8.7 illustrates a relatively simple IRC § 382 three-year ownership change test. Exhibit 8.8 illustrates how the test is applied to slightly more complicated circumstances.

(ii) THE IRC SECTION 382 LIMITATION

The IRC § 382 limitation is imposed after an ownership change has occurred. The calculation of this limitation is based on two factors: (a) the value of the loss corporation; and (b) the long-term tax exempt rate. The long-term tax exempt rate is the highest of the federal long-term rates determined under IRC § 1274(d), which states:

> "The federal *long-term* rate shall be the rate determined by the Secretary based on the average market yield (during an 1-month period selected by the Secretary and ending in the calendar month in which the determination is made) on outstanding marketable obligations of the United States with remaining periods to maturity of over 9 years."

The maximum annual amount of net operating loss that an acquiring corporation can use to offset taxable income after an ownership change date is an amount equal to the value of the loss corporation immediately before the ownership change multiplied by the long-term tax exempt rate. Exhibit 8.9 illustrates the computation of a Section 382 limitation.

IRC § 382(b)(2) provides that if the amount of net operating loss that may be used in any postownership change year exceeds taxable income for that year, the excess loss permitted by the limitation may be carried forward to the next year and into the future until expiration of the net operating loss carryforward. In Exhibit 8.9, if Company A had only $50,000 of taxable income in 1996, there would be $30,000 ($80,000 less $50,000) of unused IRC § 382 limitation that is carried forward to 1997, making the IRC § 382 limitation for 1997 equal to $110,000, comprised of the $80,000 applicable to 1997 and the $30,000 carried forward from the prior year. If Company A has no taxable income in 1997, the limitation for 1988 would be $190,000 comprised of $80,000 applicable to 1998 and $110,000 carried forward from 1997. The limitation and amounts available for utilization are computed in this cumulative manner until the net operating loss carryfor-

EXHIBIT 8.7   Test for Ownership Change Under Code Section 382

Shareholders A and B each own 40% of the stock of Company Z. The other 20% is owned equally by 100 other shareholders. Company C becomes a loss corporation in 1994. No shares have been traded prior to September 19, 1996. On September 19, 1996, Shareholder C purchases A's stock and on April 16, 1998, purchases B's stock. As of April 16, 1992, there has been an ownership change because C's ownership has changed from zero to 80% during the testing period. The following computes the ownership changes at September 19, 1996 and April 16, 1998:

	Prior to September 19, 1994	September 19, 1996	April 16, 1998
Shareholder A	40%	40%	0%
Shareholder B	40%	0%	0%
Shareholder C	0%	40%	80%
Public (less than 5% shareholders)	20%	20%	20%
Cumulative ownership change	BASE	40%	80%

EXHIBIT 8.8   Test for Ownership Change Under Code Section 382

Company Z is a loss corporation with 200 shares of common stock outstanding. Shareholder A owns 100 shares and Shareholders B and C each own 50 shares. On March 16, 1996, A sells 60 shares of stock to B, which causes B's ownership to increase by 30%, from 25% (50 shares/200 shares) to 55% (110 shares/200 shares). As result of that transaction, A's ownership percentage is reduced to 20% (40 shares/200 shares). On November 10, 1997, A purchases all 50 shares of C's stock, causing A's ownership to increase to 45% (90 shares/200 shares), an increase of 25% in comparison to A's lowest ownership percentage during the testing period, which was 40% after A sold 60 shares to B on March 16, 1996. This increase is a 25% increase in ownership for the three-year ownership change test. Therefore, even though A and B have increased their aggregate ownership percentage by only 25% when compared to the ownership percentages at the beginning of the testing period, an ownership change has occurred because the total of their separate increases from the lowest point of each of their ownership percentages during the testing period totals 55%. The following computes the ownership changes:

	Prior to March 16, 1996	March 16, 1996	Ownership Change	November 10, 1997	Ownership Change
Shareholder A	50%	20%	0%	45%	25%
Shareholder B	25%	55%	30%	55%	30%
Shareholder C	25%	25%	0%	0%	0%
Cumulative ownership change	BASE		30%		55%

EXHIBIT 8.9 IRC Section 382 Limitation

For example, assume that on December 31, 1995, there is an ownership change under IRC Section 382 with respect to Company A, when the long-term tax exempt rate is 8%. The value of Company A's stock is $1,000,000 and Company A has a net operating loss carryforward of $500,000. The IRC Section 382 Limitation is $80,000 ($1,000,000 $\times$ 8%). Accordingly, Company A's net operating loss carryforward may be utilized against future taxable income at a rate of $80,000 per year.

wards expire. Expiration dates continue to be based on the 15-year carryforward period from the dates the losses were incurred. Unless a net operating loss carryforward can be utilized at a rate sufficient to enable its complete utilization within 15 years from the date the losses were incurred by the acquired company, some or all of the net operating loss carryforwards will expire. The proportion of an acquired company's value at date of acquisition to its net operating loss carryforward has become an important ratio that will determine the extent to which net operating losses of an acquired company can be utilized subsequent to the acquisition.

(e) IRC Section 383A

IRC § 383 was implemented to provide limitations on utilization of *preownership change* carryforwards of unused general business credits, unused minimum tax credits, net capital loss carryovers, and unused foreign tax credits. The amount of any credit carryovers that may be used in a postchange year (as defined by IRC § 382) is determined by converting the credits into the tax liability that the credits would offset. This tax liability is then converted to a taxable income amount. This taxable income is then limited to the IRC § 382 limitation for such year.

The ordering provisions of IRC § 383 provides that the IRC § 382 limitation will be used in the following order:

(1) Net capital loss carryovers

(2) NOL carryovers

(3) Foreign tax credits

(4) General Business credits

(5) Minimum tax credits

(f) IRC Section 384A

IRC § 384 was implemented to limit the use of a corporation's losses in situations in which the loss corporation does not undergo an ownership change. This can occur in an IRC § 332 liquidation or a *Type A, Type C,* or *Type D* reorganization. IRC § 384 prohibits the offset of any preacquisition loss against any recognized built in gains in the gain corporation. IRC § 384(b) provides an exception to this general rule. It states

> "Subsection (a) shall not apply to the preacquisition loss of any corporation if such corporation and the gain corporation were members of the same controlled group at all times during the 5-year period ending on the acquisition date."

The definition of a controlled group is set forth in IRC § 1563(a) with the exception that 80% is changed to 50% when dealing with IRC § 384. It is clear that current tax laws significantly limit the availability of tax losses and tax credit carryovers to acquiring corporations. Careful planning and strategy will allow some carryovers to the acquiring corporation.

CHAPTER NINE

The Independent Accountant's Role in Acquisitions

James N. Brendel
Hein + Associates LLP

9.1   INTRODUCTION

This chapter addresses the work in the merger and acquisition environment of independent accountants, referred to in this chapter as *CPAs* or *auditors*. It is intended to provide assistance to CPAs and to be informative to clients and others who interact with CPAs in an acquisition environment. The scope of services rendered by independent CPAs in mergers and acquisitions may range from a minimum effort, such as assisting a client in analyzing available information on an informal basis, to a maximum effort, such as an audit supplemented by a *preacquisition review*.

The preacquisition review procedures of an independent CPA generally include one or more of the following categories:

(a) confirming information about an acquisition candidate,

(b) investigating for and providing relevant information on which the client will rely in making the decision of whether or not to consummate the transaction, and

(c) evaluating the proposed purchase price and terms of the acquisition.

An independent CPA may also act as a consultant and business advisor by assisting in structuring and planning transactions, advising in negotiations, assisting in developing and commencing acquisition programs, searching for acquisition candidates, or referring acquisition candidates to clients.

Careful judgment is required in communications regarding work performed by a CPA related to an acquisition. The form and content of the communication should be determined by the nature and extent of work performed, and in some cases should be expanded due to the sensitivity of merger and acquisition situations and the degree of reliance that may be placed on the report.

Many situations in which a CPA performs less than a full audit, including some preacquisition reviews, can fall under the classification of applying agreed-upon procedures to specified elements, accounts, or items of a financial statement. If the procedures specifically focus on confirming information with respect to expected or actual realizability of specific assets and liabilities for use in finalizing the purchase price, or in verifying representations made by either the purchaser or seller in the agreement, the standards for special reports on applying agreed-upon procedures to specified elements, accounts, or items of a financial statement should be referred to.

If a CPA is asked to give negative assurance on financial statements of an acquisition candidate which have been reviewed, special reporting rules apply.

Another area of concern to CPAs is auditing financial statements of an acquirer after an acquisition has been completed. The last section of this chapter discusses this area.

The references to *AU sections* relate to the *AICPA Professional Standards*, issued by the American Institute of Certified Public Accountants, as of June 30, 1994.

9.2 ACQUISITION AUDITS

(a) Acquisition Audits

An audit of an acquired company's financial statements may be required for various reasons, including purchase price contingencies, the level of comfort desired by buyer, and the amount and quality of financial information about the acquired company that is already available. If the acquirer is an SEC registrant, audited financial statements of the acquired company may be required for inclusion in Form 8-K if the acquisition meets certain materiality thresholds. While an audit may be looked upon as just an additional cost by some acquirers, in many cases acquisition audits have resulted in savings well in excess of the cost from adjustments to the purchase price or the identification of unknown exposure areas, problems, and issues.

Audits of the separate financial statements of companies that may be acquired or have been acquired should in some cases be approached somewhat differently than recurring annual audits. The essential difference is that an audit of the financial statements of an acquisition candidate or recently acquired company may require a relatively low materiality threshold in comparison to materiality considerations in a recurring annual audit of financial statements related to continuing operations and financial position on a going concern basis. A CPA's report on a preacquisition audit can have a bearing on whether or not the acquisition is completed or may have a bearing on the final determination of purchase price. Even a postacquisition audit performed as part of an annual audit of the acquirer may have an effect on the final purchase price if it is subject to adjustments based on the ultimate realizability of assets or liabilities or the resolution of other contingencies.

In view of these factors, a CPA may deem it appropriate or may be requested by the client to perform more extensive audit procedures or establish a lower materiality threshold in planning the scope of audit procedures and evaluating their results. For example, auditing procedures might have additional emphasis on operationally oriented areas.

Extended audit procedures may also be necessary if an audit is the CPA's initial audit of the financial statements of the company or if it is the first audit ever of the company's financial statements, which is often the case in acquisition audits. In such situations, extended procedures will probably be required to establish beginning balances, especially for those accounts having historical accumulations or cutoff implications. Several specific areas where extended procedures may be required are:

(a) Historical costs of fixed assets and accumulated depreciation.

(b) If the income statement is being reported on, beginning balances of inventories, receivables, and payables and investigation for any income or expense items that may have been recognized in prior periods, which should have been recognized in different periods.

(c) Deferred tax balances, giving consideration to the use of proper rates in establishing the deferred tax liability.

Many acquisition agreements require separate audited financial statements of the acquired company for several years after the acquisition to provide information necessary for finalizing the purchase price. A client may also request audits of the acquired company's separate financial statements, especially in cases in which former management of the acquired company has been retained.

(b) Reporting on Audits

If an audit of financial statements has been performed in an acquisition environment, an audit report following the requirements of AU § 508 should be issued. However, an audit performed in an acquisition environment may involve more in-depth procedures and is often expected to provide information of importance to the acquisition transaction, such as final determination of purchase price, and may even be a factor in determining whether the transaction is completed. Therefore, consideration should be given to supplemental communication of the nature and extent of the procedures, the assurances that are being given, and the degree of responsibility the CPA is assuming. The additional communication should be provided to avoid possible misunderstanding about the nature and scope of the audit testing, and the assurances given, even though this information would essentially have been included in the engagement letter.

Communication of a more in-depth description of procedures is discussed in AU § 551.20, which applies to situations in which an auditor is requested by a client to describe the procedures applied to specific items in the financial statements. An auditor would be well-advised to review with the client in advance the proposed contents of an expanded report, whether the report is expanded pursuant to a client request or based on the auditor's suggestion.

Exhibit 9.1 lists possible areas of additional commentary concerning an audit in an acquisition environment.

The communication may be provided in various ways, depending on the importance and extent of the information. For example, communication could be in the form of:

(a) An additional paragraph in the audit report to emphasize a matter, or

(b) A supplemental letter to the client in form similar to a special report on the performance of agreed-upon procedures to specified elements, accounts, or items of a financial statement.

EXHIBIT 9.1 Possible Additional Communications in Conjunction With an Acquisition Audit Report

1. Discussion of significant procedures, audit issues and how they were resolved.
2. Findings of matters that could affect measurement of the purchase price based on terms of the purchase agreement.
3. Discussion of assets and liabilities as to which the ultimate valuation remains uncertain. This may be desirable where the accountant wishes to emphasize that while the financial statements may be fairly stated in all material respects, there are likely to be minor adjustments to assets and liabilities as a result of future experience.
4. Statistical data, explanatory comments, or other informative material, some of which may be of a nonaccounting nature, which the CPA believes is important enough for formal communication.

The reporting guidelines of AU § 551.20 require that additional commentary concerning an audit should not detract from or contradict the description of the scope of audit in the audit report and that they be set forth separately from the information accompanying the basic financial statements.

9.3 PREACQUISITION REVIEWS AND PROCEDURES AND RELATED REPORTING

(a) Preacquisition Reviews and Procedures

Even if a separate audit is not required, a CPA may be engaged to perform procedures to evaluate the ultimate realization of represented values of assets and liabilities, or to evaluate compliance with other covenants or representations in the purchase agreement. These procedures will usually focus on significant or high risk areas such as inventories, accounts receivable, and certain liabilities.

There are no authoritative professional standards that establish guidelines for preacquisition review procedures or specific procedures that should be performed. Preacquisition review procedures must be determined based upon agreement between a CPA and his or her client, with use of sound professional judgment.

Many preacquisition review engagements are in the category of "applying agreed upon procedures to specified elements, accounts or items of a financial statement," as described in AU § 622. In performing that type of service, the CPA applies specified procedures to specified elements, accounts, or items which are not sufficient to enable expressing an opinion on the elements, accounts, or items. AU § 622.02 permits this form of service and reporting provided that:

(1) the parties involved have a clear understanding of the procedures to be performed; and

(2) distribution of the report is to be restricted to named parties involved.

AU § 622.02 provides guidance on how a CPA may ensure that the parties have a clear understanding of the procedures. One of the procedures suggested is the distribution of a draft of the report or a copy of the engagement letter to the parties involved, with a request for their comments prior to issuance of the report. That implies that CPAs have some degree of responsibility to all parties involved and not just to their clients. Careful judgment is required in this area, particularly where full disclosure of the procedures and findings to certain parties (the seller, for example, if the client is the buyer) could be detrimental to the CPA's client.

It should be noted that standards of reporting, including the third standard regarding adequacy of informative disclosure, do not apply to special reports on applying agreed-upon procedures to specified elements, accounts, or items of a financial statement. Even if it did apply, the requirements for adequate disclosure under the third standard of reporting is not intended to require publicizing information that would be detrimental to a CPA's client. If a CPA becomes involved in a difficult reporting situation in which significant issues and questions of disclosure regarding findings related to the carrying out of agreed-upon procedures are involved, the CPA should carefully evaluate his or her actions, giving consideration to all professional standards and ethics, and should consider consulting with his or her own legal counsel.

(b) Reporting on Preacquisition Reviews and Procedures

(i) REPORTING ON AGREED-UPON PROCEDURES

AU § 622.04 specifies the content of a CPA's report on applying agreed-upon procedures to specified elements, accounts, or items of a financial statement, which will be applicable in many cases to special acquisition review procedures. The report should:

- (a) indicate the specified elements, accounts, or items to which the agreed-upon procedures were applied,
- (b) indicate the intended distribution of the report,
- (c) enumerate the procedures performed,
- (d) state the accountant's findings,
- (e) disclaim an opinion with respect to the specified elements, accounts, or items,
- (f) state that the report relates only to the elements, accounts, or items specified, and does not extend to the entity's financial statements taken as a whole.

Exhibit 9.2 is a partial quotation of a report on agreed-upon procedures rendered in connection with a proposed acquisition which is contained in AU § 622.06.

(ii) REPORTING ON OTHER PREACQUISITION REVIEW PROCEDURES

If the scope of a preacquisition review engagement is more general in nature than applying agreed-upon procedures to specified elements, accounts, or items of a financial statement, a form of communication similar to a report on agreed-upon procedures should be provided. Exhibit 9.3 is a suggested list of items to consider in a communication to a client about a preacqui-

EXHIBIT 9.2 Report on Agreed-Upon Procedures in Connection With an Acquisition

---

BOARD OF TRUSTEES
X COMPANY

We have applied certain agreed-upon procedures, as discussed below, to accounting records of Y Company, Inc., as of December 31, 19XX, solely to assist you in connection with the proposed acquisition of Y Company, Inc. It is understood that this report is solely for your information and is not to be referred to or distributed for any purpose to anyone who is not a member of management of X Company, Inc. Our procedures and finding are as follows:

(a) We obtained Y Company's internal financial statements and agreed the amounts therein to supporting general ledger balances.

(b) We reconciled cash on deposit with banks to the balances in the respective general ledger accounts and obtained confirmation of the related balances from the banks. These procedures were performed for the following accounts:

Account	General Ledger Balance
XXXXX	$XXX,XXX

(c) We obtained an aged accounts receivable listing, traced the age and amounts of approximately__% of the accounts to the supporting documents, and agreed the total of the aging to the balance in the related general ledger account. We mailed requests for confirmation of balances to__customers. The differences disclosed in confirmation replies were minor in amount and nature, and we reconciled them to our satisfaction. The results are summarized as follows:

Account	Confirmation Results	
Balance	Requested	Received
Current $XXX,XXX	$XXX,XXX	$XXX,XXX
30 days XXX,XXX	XXX,XXX	XXX,XXX
60 days XXX,XXX	XXX,XXX	XXX,XXX
90+ days XXX,XXX	XXX,XXX	XXX,XXX

EXHIBIT 9.2 *(Continued)*

(d) We obtained the December 31, 19XX physical inventory schedule and traced___items to the Company's count sheets. We agreed the unit cost for an additional___items to supporting documentation and recalculated the extended cost for that inventory item. We also checked the arithmetical accuracy of the total inventory balance per the schedule and agreed the balance to the balance in the related general ledger. These procedures resulted in no exceptions.

Because the above procedures do not constitute an audit made in accordance with generally accepted auditing standards, we do not express an opinion on any of the accounts or items referred to above. In connection with the procedures referred to above, no matters came to our attention that caused us to believe that the specified accounts or items should be adjusted. Had we performed additional procedures or had we made an audit of the financial statements in accordance with generally accepted auditing standards, matters might have come to our attention that would have been reported to you. This report relates only to the accounts and items specified above and does not extend to any financial statements of Y Company, Inc. taken as a whole.

sition review, including general business and investigative matters that do not constitute the performance of agreed-upon procedures.

(c) Comfort Letters

A CPA may issue a comfort letter such as that normally provided to an underwriter with respect to unaudited financial statements, as well as reporting the nature and results of other agreed-upon procedures, in conjunction with an acquisition in which there is an exchange of stock, if requested by an acquirer or seller. A representation letter in the form illustrated in Exhibit 9.4, specified by AU § 634.07, must be obtained from the party requesting the letter.

AU Section 622.04 (footnote 5) permits the inclusion of reports containing results of applying agreed-upon procedures with the entity's financial statements. Appropriate standards, including AU § 504, *Association With*

EXHIBIT 9.3 Suggested List of Items to Include in Communications on Acquisition Related Services

1. Identification of the proposed transaction, and drafts of major agreements reviewed.
2. Description of areas reviewed, nature and extent of procedures performed, and reference to the engagement letter.
3. Officials of the company and acquisition candidate and other specialists (investment bankers, lawyers, etc.) met with and areas discussed, and information provided by each.
4. Disclaimer of opinion and denial of audit responsibility.
5. Key financial data and information, and where it was obtained.
6. An indication of with whom the report has been reviewed and to whom the report may be distributed.
7. Discussion of findings and matters of an accounting, financial, or operational nature that may be of interest to the client, together with any additional information or schedules that are pertinent to the acquisition candidate and might be helpful to the client.

Financial Statements, should be referred to. Also, when negative assurance is given, the standards of Statement of Standards for Accounting and Review Services (SSARS) No. 1 entitled *Compilation and Review of Financial Statements* should be referred to.

(d) Reporting on Financial Statements Prepared in Accordance with Accounting Practice Specified in an Agreement

AU § 9623.17–25 address the CPA's reporting considerations if valuation bases other than generally accepted accounting principles are specified in an agreement for certain assets, such as receivables, inventories, and properties. These situations do not constitute a "comprehensive basis of accounting other than generally accepted accounting principles" in accordance with the provisions of AU § 623.04d.

A CPA is permitted to express an opinion on the fair presentation of such financial statements, provided that the report explains what the presentation is intended to present and states that it is not intended to be a presentation in accordance with generally accepted accounting principles. The basis of presentation should be described in a note to the financial statements.

EXHIBIT 9.4   Representation Letter From a Party Requesting a Comfort Letter in Connection With an Acquisition

(Requesting party), as principal or agent, in the placement of (identify securities) to be issued by Company A, will be reviewing certain information relating to Company A that will be included (incorporated by reference) in the document (if appropriate, the document should be identified), which may be delivered to investors and utilized by them as a basis for their investment decision. This review process, applied to the information relating to the issuer, is (will be) substantially consistent with the due diligence review process that we would perform if this placement of securities were being registered pursuant to the Securities Act of 1933 (the Act). We are knowledgeable with respect to the due diligence review process that would be performed if this placement of securities were being registered pursuant to the Act. We hereby request that you deliver to us a *comfort* letter concerning the financial statements of the issuer and certain statistical and other data included in the offering document. We will contact you to identify the procedures we wish you to follow and the form we wish the comfort letter to take.

Very truly yours,

(Requesting party)

Any significant interpretations of provisions related to the agreement made by the client should be described in a paragraph in the report, or a note to the financial statements which is referred to in the report. The report should also contain a paragraph that restricts its distribution to those involved in the transaction.

(e) Reporting on Special Purpose Financial Presentations

AU § 623.23–25 discuss reporting considerations for special purpose financial presentations not consisting of a complete presentation of financial position or results of operations, such as a schedule of assets to be sold and liabilities to be transferred pursuant to a buy-sell agreement. Such presentations are considered to be financial statements for reporting purposes, and a CPA may express an opinion on the fairness of the presentation of the information in conformity with generally accepted accounting principles, even though certain items required by generally accepted accounting principles are excluded. In expressing the opinion, materiality should be measured based on the presentation taken as a whole. Presentations should differ from complete financial statements only to the extent necessary to meet the special purposes for which they were prepared. The report should state what the presentation is intended to represent, and a suitable title for the presentation should be used. Generally accepted accounting principles, including informative disclosures, should be followed. AU § 623.26 contains the example provided in Exhibit 9.5 of such a special-purpose report:

9.4 CONSULTING AND BUSINESS ADVISORY SERVICES

Additional services performed by CPAs related to mergers and acquisitions include:

1. Assisting clients in developing and commencing acquisition programs.

2. Searching for acquisition candidates or referring companies wishing to be acquired to clients who may be prospective acquirers.

3. Assisting clients in structuring and planning acquisition transactions to meet desired objectives.

4. Providing advice to clients in negotiating the terms of an acquisition.

5. Review of controls and procedures of the acquired company, or providing consulting services connected with integrating the financial and accounting systems of the acquired company with those of the client.

Some public accounting firms maintain separate departments with staffs of specialists in merger and acquisition work who are especially qualified to provide special services in this area. These specialists may also provide services to clients on divestitures.

In rendering special services in mergers and acquisitions, CPAs should be careful to coordinate their services with those of other professionals, such as financial consultants, investment bankers, and lawyers, and to ensure that the client understands the limitations of expertise of the CPA.

Normally, CPAs consider it appropriate to provide advice to clients in setting up acquisition programs, but do not consider it appropriate to be

EXHIBIT 9.5 Report on a Statement of Assets Sold and Liabilities Transferred

We have audited the accompanying statement of net assets sold of ABC Company as of June 8, 19XX. This statement of net assets sold is the responsibility of ABC Company's management. Our responsibility is to express an opinion on the statement of net assets sold based on our audit.

We conducted our audit in accordance with generally accepted auditing standards. Those standards require that we plan and perform the audit to obtain reasonable assurance about whether the statement of net assets sold is free of material misstatements. An audit includes examining, on a test basis, evidence supporting the amounts and disclosures in the statement. An audit also includes assessing the accounting principles used and significant estimates made by management, as well as evaluating the overall presentation of the statement of net assets sold. We believe that our audit provides a reasonable basis for our opinion.

The accompanying statement was prepared to present the net assets of ABC Company sold to XYZ Corporation pursuant to the purchase agreement described in Note X, and is not intended to be a complete presentation of ABC Company's assets and liabilities.

In our opinion, the accompanying statement of net assets sold presents fairly, in all material respects, the net assets of ABC Company, as of June 8, 19XX, sold pursuant to the purchase agreement referred to in Note X, in conformity with generally accepted accounting principles.

This report is intended solely for the information and use of the boards of directors and managements of ABC Company and XYZ Corporation and should not be used for any other purpose.

responsible for carrying out specific programs and actions. For example, an independent CPA would not normally consider it appropriate to negotiate on behalf of the client with the owner of the acquisition candidate, although he or she may provide advice to the client or the client's representatives during the negotiation process.

CPAs generally consider it acceptable to search for acquisition candidates on behalf of clients, or to refer companies seeking to be acquired to prospective acquirers. Some CPAs are reluctant to provide this assistance to companies requesting only this service, who are not already clients. CPAs receiving this type of request should carefully review the circumstances before accepting such an engagement.

9.5 AUDITING POSTACQUISITION FINANCiAL STATEMENTS OF AN ACQUIRER

(a) General

After an acquisition, an auditor will need to evaluate the significance of the acquired company to the consolidated financial statements of the acquirer. Based upon the results of this evaluation, the CPA will decide the nature and extent of audit procedures necessary with respect to the acquired operation in regard to the recurring annual audit of the acquirer's financial statements. Major areas for the CPA to be concerned with are:

(1) The acquirer's accounting for the acquisition, including selection of the applicable accounting method (purchase or pooling), application of the method, and verification of data.

(2) If the purchase method is applicable:
   (a) Results of operations and cash flows of the acquired company after the acquisition date, which are included in the client's reported results.
   (b) Operations of the acquired company prior to the acquisition date needed for combining with results of operations of the acquirer for pro forma disclosure purposes, if the acquirer is a public company.

(3) If the pooling of interests method is applicable, results of operations and changes in financial position of the combined companies after the transaction, and before the transaction, which are reported on a restated basis.

(4) Possible reporting implications regarding the auditor's opinion where other independent auditors have audited prior or current financial statements of the acquired company.

(b) Auditing Independent Appraisals

Because the independent appraisal is a key element in the accounting for an acquisition accounted for under the purchase method, audit procedures in this area should be carefully planned. The provisions of Statement on Auditing Standards No. 73, *Using the Work of a Specialist*, should be followed. Such procedures normally include a review of the appraisers' qualifications, a review of his or her procedures, and test and verification of the data included in the appraisal.

(c) Auditing Operations of an Acquired Company

Several auditing and reporting matters relate to the financial statements of an acquired company in the context of an audit of an acquirer's consolidated financial statements.

If other CPAs have previously audited the financial statements of the acquired company, and continue to do so after the acquisition, the acquirer's CPA must consider the professional standards applicable where part of an audit was made by another independent auditor.

Frequently, if other CPAs have audited the financial statements of the acquired company prior to the acquisition, the CPAs of the acquirer will be engaged to audit the financial statements of the acquired company after the acquisition. In this case, considerations present if part of an audit is performed by other independent auditors will apply to a portion of the prior period restated financial statements for a pooling of interest, and to pro forma data to be disclosed for a purchase acquisition, if the acquirer is a public company.

(d) Audit Reports Following an Acquisition

(i) POOLING OF INTERESTS

A business combination accounted for as a pooling of interests requires that the financial statements of prior periods be restated to reflect the combined entities. The acquisition of an entity is not considered a change in reporting entity for purposes of applying the consistency standard and, therefore, no reference in the auditor's report as to consistency is required.

If a single year report is presented for the year in which a pooling of interests was consummated, footnote disclosures should describe the transaction and set forth the revenues, extraordinary items, and net income of the previously separate companies for the preceding year, on a combined basis. Failure to make these disclosures would require the auditor's report to be qualified for lack of disclosure and may require an explanatory paragraph for lack of consistency. This area is discussed in AU § 420.08–10.

If a pooling of interests has occurred, special reporting considerations are present if some of the financial statements included in the new combined entity for the current and/or prior year were audited by other auditors. The first decision an auditor must make is whether he has audited a sufficient portion of the combined financial statements to serve as principal auditor.

AU § 543.09 contains an example of an appropriate audit report for a situation in which the auditor is satisfied he can properly express an opinion as principal auditor, but has decided to make reference to the audit of the other auditor, which is presented in Exhibit 9.6.

In some situations, after a pooling of interests, an auditor may conclude that he has not audited a sufficient portion of the restated prior year's financial statements to serve as principal auditor, or it may not be possible, or there may be no reason for the auditor to satisfy himself regarding the restated financial statements. AU § 543.16–17 provide for a form of reporting wherein the auditor does not assume responsibility for the work of other auditors, nor for expressing an opinion on the restated financial statements taken as a whole. Instead, the auditor may express an opinion only as to the proper combination of such financial statements. In order to report this way, the auditor must test the clerical accuracy of the restatement and the methods of combination for conformity with generally accepted accounting principles, including intercompany eliminations, combining adjustments and reclassifications, adjustments to make the accounting policies of the entities consistent, and the manner and extent of presentation of required disclosures.

After the satisfactory carrying out of such procedures, AU § 543.16 provides that a paragraph similar to that shown in Exhibit 9.7 may follow the standard audit report for the current year.

EXHIBIT 9.6 Audit Report With Reference to Other Auditors

We have audited the consolidated balance sheet of X Company and subsidiaries as of December 31, 19..., and the related consolidated statements of income and retained earnings and cash flows for the year then ended. These financial statements are the responsibility of the Company's management. Our responsibility is to express an opinion on these financial statements based on our audits. We did not audit the financial statements of B Company, a wholly owned subsidiary, which statements reflect total assets and revenues constituting 20 percent and 22 percent, respectively, of the related consolidated totals. Those statements were audited by other auditors whose report has been furnished to us, and our opinion, insofar as it relates to the amounts include for B Company, is based solely on the report of the other auditors.

We conducted our audit in accordance with generally accepted auditing standards. Those standards require that we plan and perform the audit to obtain reasonable assurance about whether the financial statements are free of material misstatement. An audit includes examining, on a test basis, evidence supporting the amounts and disclosures in the financial statements. An audit also includes assessing the accounting principles used and significant estimates made by management, as well as evaluating the overall financial statement presentation. We believe that our audit and the report of the other auditors provide a reasonable basis for our opinion.

In our opinion, based on our audit and the report of the other auditors, the consolidated financial statements referred to above present fairly, in all material respects, the financial position of X Company as of (at) December 31, 19..., and the results of its operations and its cash flows for the year then ended in conformity with generally accepted accounting principles.

(ii) PURCHASE ACQUISITIONS

Following a purchase acquisition, the standard auditor's report will apply and no reference to consistency is required, since there is no restatement of prior periods. However, consideration should be given to appropriate presentation of the operations of the acquired company prior to the acquisition,

EXHIBIT 9.7 Audit Report Paragraph for Situation in Which Auditor Expresses an Opinion Only as to the Proper Combination of the Restated Financial Statements of the Prior Year

We previously audited and reported on the consolidated statements of income and cash flows of XYZ Company and subsidiaries for the year ended December 31, 19X1, prior to their restatement for the 19X2 pooling of interests. The contribution of XYZ Company and subsidiaries to revenues and net income represented . . . . . percent and . . . . . percent of the respective restated total. Separate financial statements of the other companies included in the 19X1 restated consolidated statements of income and cash flows were audited and reported on separately by other auditors. We also audited the combination of the accompanying consolidated statements of income and cash flows for the year ended December 31, 19X1, after restatement for the 19X2 pooling of interests; in our opinion, such consolidated financial statements have been properly combined on the basis described in Note A of notes to consolidated financial statements.

required in supplemental disclosures where the acquirer is a public company which may have been audited by other accountants, or which may be unaudited.

(iii) AUDIT REPORTS WHERE AN ACQUISITION HAS OCCURRED AFTER THE BALANCE SHEET DATE

AU § 530.04–08 contain guidelines for the auditors in providing reports for situations in which significant subsequent events, such as a business combination, have occurred. In such cases, if a significant business combination has occurred after the completion of fieldwork, but before the issuance of the report, the report should be dual dated, or the procedures for review of subsequent events should be extended to the date of the subsequent event and the report should be dated as of that date.

Unaudited pro forma information may be presented in a footnote if a business combination subsequent to the balance sheet date is significant. The footnote disclosure about the subsequent event should be audited. However, the pro forma information may be unaudited.

In reissuing a previously issued report at a later date, an unaudited note may be presented when a significant business combination occurred between the date of issuance of the original auditor's report and reissuance of the auditor's report.

(iv) UNAUDITED INFORMATION

AU § 508.46 provides that footnotes to financial statements that contain unaudited information, pro forma calculations, or other unaudited information should be identified as unaudited information. If this identification is made, the auditor need not refer to the information in his report.

9.6 PLANNING AND ARRANGEMENTS WITH CLIENTS

In view of the many sensitive considerations the CPA faces when planning an acquisition engagement, it is important that a specific program of procedures be prepared for the engagement. The written program of procedures will present a basis for discussion with the client of the specific scope of the procedures to be performed, and what can be expected from the procedures.

Because of the inherently sensitive nature of work performed by a CPA in a merger or acquisition situation, and the variety of levels of procedures and responsibility that can be present, the CPA should consider issuing an engagement letter in addition to discussing the procedures and role to be assumed. The letter should clearly communicate the scope of the engagement to prevent any subsequent misunderstandings, and, in addition, may describe the form of report that will be furnished. The engagement letter is also a good opportunity to communicate the CPAs understanding of any additional role he or she may take in providing advice to the client in the acquisition negotiations, and the limitations of responsibility with respect to that role.

The reduction in the possibility of a misunderstanding of the CPA's role, which should be achieved by the engagement letter, can reduce the risk of the CPA being subjected to legal liability from an acquisition engagement. In especially difficult or sensitive situations, the CPA should consider reviewing a draft of his or her engagement letter, for work to be performed in connection with a merger or acquisition, with his or her legal counsel.

Illustration of Program for Auditing Purchase Method Accounting

Section One

GENERAL

(a) Review the purchase agreement, contracts assumed or related to the acquisition (leases, employment agreement, etc.) for items of accounting significance. Be alert for any commitments that appear to be at other than current market rates, or do not provide future benefits to the client commensurate with the amounts of commitments.

(b) Identify any contingent consideration and ensure such are properly reflected in the acquisition accounting.

(c) Ascertain whether acquisition adjustments will be recorded in consolidation entries or pushed-down into the accounts of the acquired company, and plan audit procedures accordingly.

(d) Review subsequent results of operations of the acquired company for information having an impact on the acquisition accounting (e.g., disposal of an acquired asset as a loss).

Section Two

INDEPENDENT APPRAISALS

(a) Review the professional qualifications of the appraiser. Not all of the following procedures may be required where the appraiser has strong professional qualifications and is known to use sound procedures.

(b) Ascertain that the basis upon which fair value is being determined is in conformity with the requirements of APB Opinion No. 16.

(c) Review the appraiser's procedures to ensure all acquired assets will be included in the appraisal and that conversions and summarizations will be accurately performed.

(d) Observe the appraiser while in the process of carrying out the appraisal to ensure established procedures are followed.

(e) Verify information and data provided to the appraiser by the client company.

(f) Review the appraisal report and verify for accuracy and theoretical correctness.

Section Three

COMPUTING COST AND ALLOCATION

(a) Review the list of items included in total acquisition cost and ascertain whether such items are properly includable in cost under APB Opinion No. 16.

(b) Examine evidence for significant elements of cost, considering propriety of approach where subjective valuation considerations are present (e.g., stock given in consideration for purchase where a market price for the stock is not readily available).

(c) Compare the book and tax bases of individual assets acquired and liabilities assumed, and ascertain that proper consideration has been given to the tax effects of any differences in basis.

(d) Identify any contingencies and ascertain possible effects on acquisition accounting (e.g., possible need for future restatement for contingency resolution within one year in certain cases, or realization of a net operating loss carryforward).

(e) Ensure imputation of premium or discount has been performed wherever required.

Section Four

TAX MATTERS

(a) Determine if the structure of the transaction is consistent with the tax treatment recognized by the client.

(b) Review propriety of items allocated to cost for tax purposes and consider whether any expenses incurred in connection with the acquisition that the client intends to deduct currently should be capitalized.

(c) Where the acquisition is a taxable transaction, review the allocation of cost to individual assets and liabilities for tax purposes.

Section Five

DISCLOSURES AND AUDIT REPORT

(a) Review and verify data for disclosure of pro forma results prior to acquisition.

(b) Where periods prior to acquisition have been audited by other accountants, or not subjected to complete audits, consider ramification on accountant's report as to whether opinion should make reference to audits by other accountants, whether any should be marked unaudited, or whether any data is so unreliable that no disclosure should be made because such could be misleading.

(c) Review the financial statements to ensure the following required disclosures are made (information related to more than one relatively insignificant acquisition may be aggregated):

   (i)   Name and brief description of acquired company.

   (ii)   Cost, number of shares issued or issuable, and amount assigned to stock.

   (iii)   Period for which results of operations are included in income statement.

   (iv)   Contingent payments, options, or commitments with proposed accounting treatment.

Illustration of Engagement Letter for a Preacquisition Review

Board of Directors
Gentlemen:

This letter confirms our understanding of the terms and objectives of our special engagement to Company A and the nature and limitations of the services we will provide.

The purpose of our special engagement is to assist the Company in performing certain due diligence procedures, as described below, related to the Company's proposed acquisition of Company B.

We will issue a report and provide you with copies of our workpapers. It is understood that such information is solely for your use and is not to be referred to or communicated for any purpose to anyone who is not a member of management or the Board of Directors of Company A.

We will work under the direction of Mr. Smith of Company A. We will perform procedures from the attached outline. This outline was developed by personnel of the Company and us and certain of these procedures may be modified as the project progresses. In addition to these procedures, we will perform certain tax due diligence procedures, which will be under the supervision of Mr. Jones of Company A.

It is understood the procedures to be performed are limited in scope and do not constitute an audit conducted in accordance with generally accepted auditing standards. We make no representation as to the sufficiency of the procedures to be performed for your purposes. In addition, had we been instructed to perform additional procedures or an audit in accordance with generally accepted auditing standards, other matters might come to our attention, which could have relevance on this proposed acquisition.

Illustration of Program for Preacquisition Review by an Independent CPA

Section One

GENERAL INSTRUCTIONS

Use the following program for a guide in areas to be reviewed and general procedures. Specific procedures should be designed based on the circumstances, and expanded procedures carried out as necessary.

Section Two

OVERALL OBJECTIVE

Evaluate most recent balance sheet and income statement for reasonableness, review for contingent liabilities or contingencies and identify trends, if any.

Section Three

PROCEDURES

(a)   Review prior year audit workpapers, make inquiries, and obtain copies of relevant information as necessary.

(b) Obtain most recent internal financial statements and agree to general ledger. Test financial statement accounts as noted below.

(c) Cash

    (i)   Obtain reconciliations, test footing and agree to general ledger.

    (ii)   Agree to bank statements and test significant reconciling items (document scope) including tracing outstanding checks from subsequent bank statements to outstanding check list.

(d) Accounts receivable

    (i)   Obtain aging, test footing and agree to general ledger.

    (ii)   Consider confirmation of customer balances as appropriate.

    (iii)   Agree to subsequent receipts.

    (iv)   Evaluate reasonableness of allowance for doubtful accounts.

(e) Inventory

    (i)   Obtain perpetual inventory listing, test footing and agree to general ledger.

    (ii)   Observe inventory count and document procedures and evaluate their adequacy. Inquire of appropriate personnel regarding their experience with inventory as to any problems, etc. Compare current inventory balance with internal financial statements and obtain explanation for fluctuations.

    (iii)   Document inventory receipt and shipping and accounting for purchases and sales procedures and controls. Perform compliance tests to gain assurance that procedures are functioning as documented.

    (iv)   Perform price testing.

    (v)   Inquire and review for obsolescence and test for lower of cost or market.

(f) Prepaid and other assets—obtain detail listing and inquire as to any material impairment in value.

(g) Property and equipment—obtain detail listing and inquire as to any impairment in value.

(h) Notes payable

    (i)   Obtain agreements and summarize.

    (ii)   Agree balance per general ledger to lender statements.

    (iii)   Review for compliance with covenants.

    (iv)   Test interest expense for reasonableness.

    (v)   Contact loan officer for any indications of problems with account.

(i) Accounts payable
  (i) Obtain listing and reconcile to general ledger.
  (ii) Agree significant items on listing to supporting documentation.
  (iii) Perform search for unrecorded liabilities.
(j) Accrued and other liabilities—obtain listing and test.
(k) Warranty reserve
  (i) Obtain agreements for and understanding of each type of warranty and products and time periods covered.
  (ii) Obtain target company's calculation of reserve and test based on:
      (a) units sold under each type of warranty;
      (b) expected failure rate; and
      (c) average cost of claim. Obtain support for amounts and assumptions used.
(l) Commitments and contingencies
  (i) Review legal invoices for indication of litigation.
  (ii) Obtain inventory purchase agreements and review for potential loss due to over commitment.
  (iii) Obtain major lease agreements and quantify noncancellable obligation.
  (iv) Review agreements with vendors for any commitments.
  (v) Review minutes of board of directors' and shareholders' meetings.
(m) Income taxes—review tax returns and tax issues.
(n) Sales and cost of sales
  (i) Trace a limited number of items through the system.
  (ii) Review subsequent credit memos for possible overstatement of sales.
  (iii) Perform analytic review for indication of trends and compare actual performance to budget.

CHAPTER TEN

Securities and Exchange Commission and Other Regulatory Requirements

Robert J. Puls
Price Waterhouse LLP

10.1 OVERVIEW OF REGULATORY ENVIRONMENT

In the United States, various regulatory bodies have jurisdiction over mergers, acquisitions, and other forms of business combinations, depending on the specifics of the transaction. The determination of what laws and requirements apply is a complex legal matter and must be considered carefully in each and every situation. Some of the more critical requirements follow:

- For public companies, if securities are to be issued or exchanged, registration statements may need to be filed with the Securities and Exchange Commission (SEC). Also, a proxy statement must be prepared if shareholders need to vote on a possible acquisition or merger. Even if no securities are exchanged, a Form 8-K current report may be required to be filed. Further, certain filings are required if a tender offer is made to acquire shares of another company.

- If public shares are issued or issuable in an acquisition or merger, a stock listing application usually would have to be filed with the stock exchange on which the company is listed.

- If certain conditions are met, contemplated mergers and acquisitions must be reported to the Federal Trade Commission and the U.S. Department of Justice prior to consummation. Further, the parties to the transaction must wait at least 30 days after reporting before completing the transaction to allow these organizations to consider the related antitrust implications.

The primary objective of this chapter is to provide the reader with a general awareness of the major regulatory requirements related to mergers or acquisitions. It is not intended to provide a comprehensive treatment, nor a complete presentation of the form or content of the various filings and regulations referred to.

10.2 SECURITIES LAW REQUIREMENTS UPON MERGER OR ACQUISITION

(a) Primary Filing Requirements

Various filings with the SEC can be required if a public company engages in a merger, acquisition, or other form of business combination. The primary filings under both the Securities Act of 1933 (the 1993 Act) and the Securities Exchange Act of 1934 (the 1934 Act) follow:

(1) A 1933 Act registration statement on Form S-1 or Form S-4. Either of these forms may be used to register securities offered in exchange for the securities of a *target* company. Form S-4 may also be used

when a vote is required—by either the security holders of the acquiring company or those of the target company, or both—and a proxy statement is supplied in connection with the solicitation of proxies.

(2) A proxy statement under Regulation 14A of the 1934 Act.

(3) A current report (Form 8-K) under the 1934 Act.

In addition, if a company's securities are listed on a national securities exchange, a stock listing application usually would have to be filed for any securities issued or issuable in the transaction.

(b) Private Sale Exemptions

In some situations, a company may be relieved of the registration requirements of the 1933 Act through Rule 144A if an acquisition does not involve a public offering. The most important factors to assess in determining whether an acquisition involves a public offering are size of the offer (i.e., the number of offerees), the offerees' relationship to the issuer, and whether the offerees will make a secondary distribution of the securities.

(i) SIZE OF OFFER

Although not in itself determinative, the SEC has in many cases agreed that, under ordinary circumstances, an offering to less than 35 persons presumably does not involve a public offering.

(ii) RELATIONSHIP TO ISSUER

The relationship of offerees to an issuer has taken on greater importance since the Supreme Court decided that the basic test of the availability of the private sale exemption was ". . . whether the particular class of persons affected needs the protection of the 1933 Act." In other words, if the offerees of the company to be acquired, because of their relationship as officers, directors, controlling stockholders, or the like, have access to the same type of information that would be available in a 1933 Act registration statement, they need not be regarded as members of the investing public.

(iii) SECONDARY DISTRIBUTION

Equally important is whether an offeree who is to receive the securities will make a secondary distribution of them, thereby falling within the 1933 Act definition of a *statutory underwriter*. If that is the case, the private sale exemption would be unavailable to the issuer. To protect against this, the issuer should obtain from each offeree an *investment letter* in which the offeree represents that he or she is purchasing the securities for investment and not for redistribution. However, although the issuer requests investment letters in a transaction, the courts have made it clear that such letters are of little value to the issuer if they are not adhered to. Some methods that may be used to guard against the possibility of a subsequent sale of the securities nullifying the exemption are:

(a) Require registration of the securities by the issuer if the offeree wants to make a public offering; or

(b) Provide for restrictions on transfer of the securities, such as stamping the face of the securities as unregistered or requiring that the transfer agent not transfer them without instructions from the issuer.

(c) Form S-1 Filings

If Form S-1 is used in an *exchange offer*, potential investors (i.e., offerees) must be provided with sufficient information regarding both companies to enable him or her to arrive at an informed decision.

The most important requirement of Form S-1 is General Instruction III which reads as follows:

> "If any of the securities being registered are to be offered in exchange for securities of any other issuer, the prospectus shall also include the information which would be required by Item 11 if the securities of such other issuer were being registered on this Form. There shall also be included the information concerning such securities of such other issuer which would be called for by Item 9 if such securities were being registered. In connection with this instruction, reference is made to Rule 409."

This means that, in registering securities to be offered in an exchange or other form of acquisition, the financial statement requirements of the company to be acquired are the same as those of the registrant. However, in some circumstances, management of the target may not cooperate in supplying all of the necessary information, such as if management does not approve of the offer. In those situations, an issuer can rely on rule 409 and include in the registration statement only information about the target that is available from public sources, such as annual reports to stockholders and other SEC filings. If a company is to avail itself of this rule, copies of correspondence between the two companies evidencing the request for and the refusal to furnish the necessary financial information must be provided to the SEC.

(d) Form S-4 Filings

Form S-4 was developed to further simplify the 1933 Act registration of securities to be issued in a merger or acquisition. Since, in most situations, a shareholder vote is required for approval of the transaction, Form S-4 is designed to permit use of a proxy statement for the prospectus portion of the registration statement, eliminating the duplication of disclosures otherwise necessary in both a proxy statement and a separate 1933 Act registration statement.

Nonetheless, both a proxy statement and any 1933 Act form that a registrant might be eligible to use in a business combination transaction require a significant level of disclosure for all parties involved in the merger or acquisition.

10.3 SOLICITATION AND PREPARATION OF PROXIES

(a) General

SEC regulations do not require the solicitation of proxies, but do govern procedures for their solicitation through Regulation 14A of the 1934 Act. This Regulation sets forth requirements for form and content of a proxy if it is determined that one is required. A proxy can be required by:

(1) Statutory provisions of the jurisdiction under which a corporation is organized;

(2) Regulations of the stock exchange on which the company's shares are listed;

(3) The company's bylaws; or

(4) Provisions contained in a company's certificate of incorporation or similar controlling instruments.

Both the New York and the American Stock Exchanges require that shareholder approval be obtained through a proxy solicitation if a business is acquired from an *insider*, or if the number of shares to be issued in the acquisition or the market value thereof would exceed 20% of the respective amounts related to presently outstanding shares.

Even though companies may not be required to obtain stockholder approval for a merger or acquisition, they sometimes obtain such approval to avoid potential legal difficulties and criticism in the future.

(b) Information Included in Proxy Statements

As mentioned above, information to be included in a proxy statement relating to acquisitions and mergers is governed by Item 14 of Regulation 14A, which requires the following about the companies involved:

1. A brief description of:
    (a) The plan for merger, consolidation, or acquisition;
    (b) The business—nature of the products or services, methods of production and markets; and
    (c) The plants and other physical properties.

2. A statement as to any:
    (a) Dividend arrearages; or
    (b) Defaults in principal or interest on outstanding securities.

3. A capitalization table for each company and on a pro forma combined basis.

4. Selected financial information for five years for each company and on a pro forma combined basis.

5. A pro forma combined summary of earnings for five years.

6. Financial information relating to the issuer's industry segments.

7. A Management's Discussion and Analysis of Financial Condition and Results of Operations as required by Item 11 of Regulation S-K.

As previously discussed, if an acquiring company cannot obtain all the required information from the target, it may rely on Rule 409 and provide whatever it is able to.

10.4   TENDER OFFERS

(a) General

A tender offer is an active and widespread solicitation of public shareholders for the shares of a company. While there is currently no exact definition of what constitutes a tender offer, the following are often characteristic:

(1) Solicitation made for a substantial percentage of the company's stock;

(2) Offer made at a premium over the prevailing market price;

(3) Terms of offer are firm rather than negotiable;

(4) Offer contingent on receipt of a fixed number of shares and often subject to a maximum;

(5) Offer open for a limited period of time; and

(6) Offeree subjected to pressure to sell his or her stock.

Tender offers fall into two general types: (1) those made by a company to purchase its own securities; and (2) those made by unrelated third parties.

Special disclosure requirements pertain to tender offers to acquire shares of public companies if certain conditions are met. The specific rules regulating tender offers are dependent on the type of offer. The following provides some general guidelines and basic disclosure requirements of certain types.

(b) Purchase of *Own* Securities

Section 13(e) of the 1934 Act contains the rules regulating purchases or tender offers by a company for its own equity securities. These rules also apply when an affiliate makes the purchase or tender. An *affiliate* is a person or entity that, directly or indirectly through one or more intermediaries, controls, is controlled by, or is under common control with such company. The types of transactions covered by Section 13(e) include:

(1) Purchases of securities by a company during a third party tender offer;

(2) *Going private* transactions; and

(3) Other cash tender and exchange offers.

Section 13(e) also specifies disclosures required to be disseminated to security holders for each of the above transactions. Additionally, if the tender offer involves the solicitation of a proxy or distribution of an information statement, the transaction would also be subject to either Regulation 14A or Regulation 14C of the 1934 Act.

(i) PURCHASE DURING A THIRD PARTY TENDER OFFER

If a company has received notice of a third party tender offer filed with the SEC, it can purchase its own securities during the period of the tender only if:

1. A *disclosure document* has been filed with the SEC that contains information regarding the nature of the securities, the purpose of the purchase, the source and amount of funds used or to be used in making the purchase, etc. (no specific form or schedule is required to be filed); and

2. The substance of the information contained in the "disclosure document" has been sent by the company to its equity security holders within the past six months.

(ii) GOING PRIVATE

The effects of *going private* are to cause any class of equity securities of a company:

1. Subject to section 12(g) or section 15(d) of the 1934 Act to be held of record by less than 300 persons; or ·

2. Either listed on a national securities exchange or authorized to be quoted in an interdealer quotation system of a registered national securities association to be neither listed nor authorized to be quoted.

Filing and disclosure requirements for going private are governed by Rule 13e-3. In this regard, Schedule 13E-3 is required to be filed with the SEC containing information regarding the nature of the securities, the terms and purpose of the transaction, the source and amounts of funds or other consideration, etc. In addition to filing with the SEC, Rule 13e-3 generally requires the dissemination of certain disclosures to the record holders of the equity security.

(iii) OTHER SELF TENDERS

A company that makes a tender offer for its own securities for any other purpose is subject to Rule 13e-4. For this catchall, Schedule 13E-4 must be filed with the SEC disclosing information regarding the security, the source and amount of funds or other consideration, the purpose of the tender offer and plans or proposals of the company or affiliate, and other similar information.

In addition, a company making the tender must also disclose: (1) the scheduled termination date of the tender offer and whether it may be extended; (2) withdrawal rights of persons who tender their shares; and (3) if the tender offer is for less than all the securities of a class, the exact dates of the period during which securities will be accepted on a pro rata basis and the manner in which securities will be accepted for payment and in which they may be withdrawn.

(iv) FINANCIAL STATEMENT REQUIREMENTS

Schedules 13E-3 and 4, referred to above, each require the following financial information disclosures concerning the issuing company (any information which has been included in a document previously filed with the SEC may be incorporated by reference):

(1) Audited financial statements for the two fiscal years required to be filed with the company's most recent annual report.

(2) Unaudited balance sheets and comparative year-to-date income statements and statements of cash flows and related earnings per share amounts required to be included in the company's most recent quarterly report.

(3) Ratio of earnings to fixed charges for the two most recent fiscal years and the interim periods provided under 2 above.

(4) Book value per share as of the most recent fiscal year end and as of the date of the latest interim balance sheet provided under 2 above.

(5) If material, pro forma data disclosing the effect of the transaction on:
   (a) The company's balance sheet as of the most recent fiscal year end and the latest interim balance sheet provided under 2 above;
   (b) The company's statement of income, earnings per share amounts, and ratio of earnings to fixed charges for the most recent fiscal year and the latest interim period provided under 2 above; and
   (c) The company's book value per share as of the most recent fiscal year end and as of the lastest interim balance sheet date provided under 2 above.

(c) Third Party Tender Offers

Third party tender offers are one of the most common methods used to acquire control of a target company in a take over attempt. These offers are subject to SEC requirements (Section 14(d) of the 1934 Act) whenever the bidder, upon consummation of the tender offer, would be the beneficial owner of more than 5% of the security of the target.

(i) TENDER OFFER COMMENCEMENT

A tender offer, generally, is deemed to commence when a bidder makes a public announcement through a press release, newspaper advertisement, or public statement or such information is sent or given by the bidder to the security holders of the target company. The information required to be included in the announcement or advertisement is dependent on the type of offer.

If it meets the 5% rule discussed above, the bidder is required to file Schedule 14D-1 with the SEC as soon as practicable after commencement of the offer and is also required to deliver a copy of it to:

(1) The subject company's principal executive office;

(2) Any other bidder which has filed a Schedule 14D-1; and

(3) Each national securities exchange on which the security is registered and to the NASD, if applicable.

Schedule 14D-1 requires disclosure of the security and subject company, source and amount of funds or other consideration, purpose of the tender offer, and plans or proposals of the bidder, etc.

(ii) FINANCIAL STATEMENTS OF CERTAIN BIDDERS

If a bidder is other than a natural person and its financial condition is material to an investment decision, current adequate financial information of the bidder is required.

The financial condition of the bidder is usually considered material if a security holder of the target company receives a security of the bidder as part of the tender offer consideration. If a security of the bidder is part of the consideration, a 1933 Act registration statement must be filed by the bidder. The facts and circumstances concerning a cash only tender offer will determine whether disclosure of financial information of the bidder is necessary.

The financial statements required to be included are determined by the nature of the bidder. Generally, financial statements prepared in compliance with Form 10 are appropriate for a domestic bidder and financial statements prepared in accordance with Item 17 of Form 20-F are appropriate for a foreign bidder. If the bidder is subject to the periodic reporting requirements of the 1934 Act, the financial statements may be incorporated by reference.

10.5   SEC FINANCIAL REPORTING REQUIREMENTS

(a) Historical Financial Statements of Registrants

For filings related to business combinations, Form S-1, Form S-4, and proxy statements must include or incorporate by reference the registrant's financial statements and supplementary financial information required by Regulation S-X. These principally are audited balance sheets as of the end of each of the two most recent fiscal years, and audited statements of income and changes in cash flow for each of the three fiscal years preceding the date of the most recent audited balance sheet.

Depending on the date of the filing, interim financial statements may also be required. These interim statements need not be audited.

(b) Historical Financial Statements of Acquired Entities

Audited financial statements of a business acquired or to be acquired (if probable) are required if either: (1) the combination is accounted for as a purchase (including an investment to be accounted for by the equity method); or (2) the combination is to be accounted for as a pooling. In recognition that acquisitions come in all sizes, Rule 3-05 (see below) utilizes a sliding scale to determine the period(s) for which financial statements are required.

The SEC's requirements for financial statements of businesses acquired or to be acquired are set forth in Rule 3-05 of Regulation S-X. Its requirements for pro forma financial information are included in Article 11 of Regulation S-X. The SEC's interpretive views on such statements are included at FRP § 506.

In the SEC's integrated disclosure system, Form 8-K is intended to provide investors with timely information, including that of businesses acquired. The inability to provide the financial statements or pro forma information within the required time period (generally 15 days, although an automatic 60 day extension to file is provided for) can limit current access to the securities markets.

(c) Probable Acquisitions

SEC guidance in this regard states that "consummation of a transaction is considered to be probable whenever the registrant's financial statements alone would not provide investors with adequate financial information with which to make an investment decision." The SEC has not attempted to provide definitive guidance as to when consummation is deemed probable because of the many variables involved. Each situation must be evaluated based on the specific facts and circumstances.

(d) Periods to Be Presented

Except as discussed below, the sliding scale test determines the number of years audited annual financial statements must be furnished for a business acquired or to be acquired. When audited annual statements are presented, unaudited interim financial statements must also be furnished (Rules 3-01 and 3-02).

If securities are being registered on Forms S-4 or F-4 to be offered to the security holders of the business to be acquired (an exchange offer) or an acquisition/merger proxy statement is being prepared, the sliding scale is not used; rather, 3-year audited financial statements of the acquired business are usually required to be furnished or incorporated by reference, as appropriate. In all other cases, the financial statements to be filed for a significant business acquired or to be acquired should be determined based on the sliding scale test.

The test for significance is based upon a comparison of the most recent annual financial statements of the business acquired or to be acquired, to the registrant's most recent annual consolidated financial statements or in certain instances to the registrant's pro forma financial information. Specific items compared are net book value (after considering the purchase price), total assets, and pretax income. The largest percent relationship derived from these specific comparisons should be compared to Exhibit 10.1, which is a summarization of S-X Rule 3-05(b). This Exhibit indicates the number of years for which audited financial statements of the acquired entity are required.

Any required audited financial statements of the acquired businesses are for its most recent fiscal year(s).

EXHIBIT 10.1   S-X Rule 3-05(b) Summarization

Any comparison criteria:	Number of fiscal years required	
	Balance Sheet	Statements of Income and of Cash Flows
Greater than 10% but less than 20%	1	1
Greater than 20% but less than 40%	2	2
Greater than 40%	2	3

In 1989, the SEC issued Rule 3-06 which codified practice of accepting nine-month statements in satisfaction of one annual period. Pursuant to this Rule, the SEC will accept for the acquired business the filing of audited financial statements covering a period of from nine to twelve months as satisfying a requirement for filing financial statements for a period of one year. However, no period shorter than nine months will be accepted.

(e) Acquisitions of Individually Insignificant Subsidiaries

Rule 3-05 provides that all individually insignificant entities acquired in a fiscal year (i.e., those which do not exceed at least one of the aforementioned tests at the 10% threshold) that have not been included in the audited statement of operations of the registrant for at least nine months, shall be aggregated in the test for significance.

If these aggregated insignificant entities exceed the 20% threshold in the year of acquisition, then financial statements covering at least the *substantial majority* of the businesses acquired shall be furnished. SEC staff believes that a *substantial majority* of the businesses acquired have been furnished when the aggregate of the entities not audited do not exceed any of the tests at the 10% level. Audited financial statements shall be provided for *at least* the most recent annual period and any interim periods required by Rules 3-01 and 3-02.

It is not clear whether a Form 8-K needs to be filed in circumstances where there have been no individually significant acquisitions, but aggregated insignificant acquisitions exceed the 20% threshold. In practice, the aggregate impact of insignificant acquisitions is only considered by most registrants when there is a Securities Act filing which triggers the Rule 3-05 requirements. Notwithstanding, when the aggregate insignificant transactions approach the 20% significance threshold, an 8-K filing should be considered.

The financial statements of insignificant entities may be combined, if appropriate. However, financial statements could not be combined, for example, for entities with different year ends if there were significant intercompany transactions which would not be eliminated because of the timing of such transactions.

(f) What Constitutes a *Business*

Since inception of the Securities Acts, there has been a continuing dialogue within and without the SEC as to the appropriate definition of a *business*. It has not yet been defined, nor is it likely to be in the near future. Registrants often contend that a business has not been acquired and that audited financial statements therefore are not required. In relatively few cases, the staff has agreed. In the overwhelming majority, the SEC considers a business acquisition to have occurred.

The SEC concluded in Financial Reporting Release No. 2 (FRR 2) that it was impracticable to provide a precise definition of *business*. Notwithstanding that position, they provided certain Rule 11-01 guidelines which they deemed relevant to that determination and in 1991, the SEC issued some guidance in Staff Accounting Bulletin No. 89 regarding troubled financial institutions acquired or to be acquired.

Many acquisition-minded companies make audited financial statements a condition of closing. If the buyer is willing to close without audited amounts, a subsequent audit becomes an unavoidable cost of the acquisition. Until the audits are performed, the buyer has the choice of delaying the acquisition or foregoing 1933 Act securities offerings.

(g) Stock Exchange Requirements

If securities are to be issued in connection with an acquisition and listed on the New York or American Stock Exchange, the latest available balance sheet and related statements of income, changes in financial position, and retained earnings (including supplemental interim statements) are required to be audited by independent accountants or certified by the company's principal accounting officer.

(h) Pro Forma Financial Statements

Pro forma financial statements are required in SEC registration statements and proxy statements where business combinations have occurred, are in progress, or are probable. Pro forma financial statements show the results of operations and financial position on an *as if* basis, which assumes the separate entities had always been combined.

In the case of an SEC registration presenting financial statements, including a period for which a purchase method acquisition was made, the pro forma financial statements will present an historical *as if* combining of the previously separate entities prior to the date of the business combination. Where a combination accounted for as a pooling has already occurred, pro forma financial statements are not necessary, because the historical financial statements will have been restated.

(i) ARTICLE 11 PRESENTATION OF PRO FORMA INFORMATION

Rule 11-02 contains instructions for presentation of pro forma information. The rules allow flexibility in order to tailor pro forma information to individual facts and circumstances. The requirements for the pro forma statement of income clearly distinguish between the one-time impact and the ongoing impact of the transaction. Items with a one-time impact should be excluded from the pro forma income statement.

Article 11 requires introductory language, a condensed pro forma balance sheet, condensed income statement, and explanatory notes. The introductory headnote(s) should describe the transaction and the entities involved. The purpose of the pro formas should also be described.

The most recent annual and interim pro forma income statements must be presented. The interim presentation must cover the period from the most recent fiscal year end to the date of the interim balance sheet required. Optionally, a pro forma income statement for the corresponding period in the preceding year may be filed.

Pro forma income information should be presented only through income (loss) from continuing operations. Any amounts relating to discontinued operations, extraordinary items, or the cumulative effect of accounting changes are to be excluded. Material nonrecurring charges or credits which result from the transaction and which will impact the income statement during the next 12 months should not be included in the pro forma income statement. These amounts should be separately discussed in a note or table with a clear indication that they are not reflected in the pro forma income information. For example, if an acquirer decided to shut down an existing plant because it was made redundant by an acquired facility, any resulting charge should only be included in a pro forma footnote disclosure.

Primary and fully diluted earnings per share from continuing operations and the number of shares used in each computation must be shown on the face of the pro forma income statement. In computing the weighted average shares outstanding, effect would be given to shares issued or to be issued as if issuance had taken place at the beginning of the period presented. If any convertible securities are issued as part of the transaction, their dilution must be considered in the primary EPS (if a common stock equivalent) and in the fully diluted EPS calculation.

The pro forma balance sheet should be as of the date of the most recent balance sheet included or incorporated by reference in the registration statement. A pro forma balance sheet is not required if the transaction is reflected in the most recent historical balance sheet filed.

As already noted, only items with an ongoing impact (i.e. those which will continue to affect the income statement 12 months after the transaction) should be income statement adjustments. These typically include items such as goodwill amortization, depreciation charges, estimated changes in interest expense due to debt assumed or retired, and tax provision adjustments due to changes in tax allocation methods. Pro forma adjustments to conform an acquired entity's accounting policies should be made as if the acquisition occurred at the beginning of the year.

(ii) MULTIPLE PRESENTATION FOR SOME TRANSACTIONS

A single pro forma presentation may be inadequate in circumstances where a transaction is subject to several different outcomes with a wide range of possible effects. In this case, several pro formas may be needed to give effect to the range of possible results.

A common example is a tender offer where the seller has options to receive cash or available stock. In this example, the amounts of cash and stock to be ultimately exchanged cannot be accurately determined until consummation of the tender offer. In these situations, two or more pro forma presentations are usually made which represent the outcome considered most probable by management.

10.6 UNIQUE SEC ACCOUNTING REQUIREMENTS

(a) General

With respect to the accounting for mergers and acquisitions, the SEC strictly enforces the provisions of Accounting Principle Board (APB) Opinions No. 16, *Business Combinations*, and 17, *Intangible Assets* and their interpretations, as well as the consensuses of the EITF. In addition, where it believes specific guidance is lacking, the SEC has issued, and will continue to issue, its own interpretations.

(b) Pooling of Interests

(i) GENERAL

Although Opinion 16 is quite complex and contains many detailed rules and conditions, the substance of transactions, and not merely the form, must be considered in determining the appropriate method of accounting for business combinations. In this regard, the SEC has taken a very active role in the refinement of criteria to determine if a business combination should be accounted for as a pooling of interests.

(ii) TREASURY STOCK TRANSACTIONS

Opinion 16 states that all acquisitions of treasury stock during a two-year period prior to the initiation of a business combination (the *restricted period*) would preclude the pooling of interests method from being used, unless the treasury stock acquired is for purposes other than the business combination, including shares for stock option and compensation plans and other recurring distributions. In ASR 146 and 146A, the SEC stated its conclusions regarding the effect of treasury stock transactions on accounting for business combinations as follows:

"The Commission concludes that treasury shares acquired in the restricted period for recurring distributions should be considered "tainted" unless they are acquired in a systematic pattern of reacquisitions established at least two years before the plan of combination is initiated (or coincidentally with the adoption of a new stock option or compensation plan) and there is reasonable expectation that shares will be issued for such purposes.

However, if an equal number of shares are sold prior to the date of consummation, the SEC believes that the treasury shares were not purchased in contemplation of a business combination. Further, acquisition of shares to fulfill contractual obligations or settle outstanding claims does not *taint* shares reacquired.

The AICPA SEC Committee held informal discussions with the SEC staff subsequent to the issuance of ASR 146 and 146A, the results of which were published in the November 1974 Journal of Accountancy. Although not *official*, this article should be consulted if questions arise regarding treasury stock transactions and the related provisions of APB Opinion No. 16.

(iii) RISK SHARING

APB Opinion No. 16 refers to one important element of the spirit of the pooling of interests concept as sharing of risks by the stockholder groups. Risk sharing has also been likened to continuity of ownership and contrasted to *bailout.*

Continuity of ownership by individual shareholders is not a requirement for a pooling of interests under APB 16. Thus, if the conditions of paragraph 48 are met, a pooling will not be precluded simply because shareholders of a combining company sell voting common stock received in a business combination after consummation of the combination.

However, the SEC has imposed a restriction upon the immediate disposition of voting common stock by affiliates of either company in a business combination to be accounted for as a pooling of interests. The restriction stipulated by the SEC requires that no affiliate of either company may reduce its risk relative to its common shareholder position within the period beginning 30 days prior to consummation of the business combination and ending when financial results covering a period of at least 30 days of post-merger operations have been published. A Form 10-Q filing, a post-effective amendment, the issuance of a quarterly earnings report, or the issuance of a press release with sales and earnings information would constitute publication of combined financial results. The financial information should be filed with the SEC on Form 8-K, if not filed otherwise.

The term affiliate is defined in Rule 1-02(b) of Regulation S-X as ". . . a person that directly, or indirectly through one or more intermediaries, controls, or is controlled by, or is under common control with, the person specified." However, for purposes of applying the above restrictions, the SEC has interpreted the term *affiliate* to include officers, directors, and significant shareholders of both of the combining companies.

(c) Pushdown Accounting

(i) NEW BASIS

If an acquired company's operations are maintained in a separate subsidiary after a purchase business combination, the question arises as to whether the new parent's basis resulting from the business combination should be reflected in the financial statements of the subsidiary.

In most circumstances, the SEC believes in the application of *pushdown* accounting for separate financial statements of subsidiaries acquired and recorded by the purchase method. In SAB No. 54, the SEC states that when an entity has become substantially wholly owned, the entire cost of the acquisition should be *pushed down* to the subsidiary's financial statements, thereby creating a new basis of accounting for the purchased assets and liabilities. In situations where outside interests in the form of minority stockholders, or holders of public debt or preferred stock remain, the staff would encourage but generally not insist on the application of *pushdown* accounting.

(ii) PARENT COMPANY DEBT

If a parent company uses borrowed funds to finance the purchase of a subsidiary or to finance a subsidiary's operations, the question arises as to whether the debt should be included in the subsidiary's financial statements. Staff Accounting Bulletin (SAB) Topic 5J expresses the SEC's views that if: (1) the subsidiary is to assume the parent's debt either presently or in a planned transaction in the future; (2) the proceeds of a debt or equity offering of the subsidiary will be used to retire all or a part of the parent's debt; or (3) the subsidiary guarantees or pledges its assets as collateral for the parent's debt, then the parent's debt, related interest expense, and allocable debt issue costs should be included in the subsidiary's financial statements. If the subsidiary has not formally guaranteed the debt and the parent company has no operations to generate cash to pay the debt, the SEC would not insist that the debt be *pushed down*. However, full disclosure of the relationship between the two entities should be made.

10.7 ANTITRUST REGULATIONS

The Hart-Scott-Rodino Antitrust Improvement Act of 1976 requires that certain mergers and acquisitions be reported to the Federal Trade Commission (FTC) and the U.S. Department of Justice prior to consummation. The parties involved must wait at least 30 days before completing the acquisition to allow the governmental agencies time to consider the antitrust implications of the proposed transaction. Premerger notification is made on *Notification and Report Form for Certain Mergers and Acquisitions*, and must be made when:

(a) Either of the acquiring or acquired companies is involved in commerce or in any activity affecting commerce;

(b) The annual net sales or total assets of one company are $10 million or more and of the other company are $100 million or more; and

(c) The acquiring company would gain one of the following:
    (i)   15% or more of the voting securities or assets of the acquired company or more than $15 million worth of both the assets and the voting securities of the acquired company;
    (ii) 15% or more of the issuer's outstanding voting securities which are valued in excess of $15 million;
    (iii) 25% of the issuer's outstanding voting securities; or
    (iv) 50% of the issuer's outstanding voting securites.

Additional notifications must be filed when 15%, 25%, and 50% of the outstanding voting securities of an issuer are about to be acquired. Smaller acquisitions are exempt if the acquiring company will not hold voting securities and assets aggregating more than $15 million.

Information included in the Premerger Notification Form applies only to operations conducted within the United States, including its commonwealths, territories, possessions, and the District of Columbia. Information requested includes a description of the acquisition, assets to be acquired, voting securities to be acquired, and dollar revenues by Standard Industrial Classification (SIC) Code.

If the FTC or Department of Justice believes the merger or acquisition violates antitrust laws, they must file for an injunction requiring the parties to *cease and desist* from consummation of the merger or acquisition. However, these parties do not have the power to stop the merger or acquisition; only a court of law can render a decision on whether or not antitrust laws would be violated.

10.8   OTHER REGULATIONS

(a) Blue Sky Laws

If an acquisition involves the issuance or *sale* of the buyer's securities, the buyer must also comply with blue sky laws in all states where its securities are being offered to selling shareholders.

Sales or exchanges of stock or other securities are regulated by various state and federal laws. Generally, it is illegal to sell or exchange unregistered securities, unless they meet specific exemptions. The burden of proof as to qualifying under the various exemptions lies with the issuer of the security. Exemptions to the federal laws prohibiting transactions in unregistered securities generally apply to limited sales or exchanges of securities by corporations if:

(1) The company is incorporated or doing business in one state and the security is offered or sold only to residents of that state, or

(2) The issue is a private placement. A private placement is where the offer to acquire securities is made to no more than 35 persons. In addition, the purchaser of securities in a private placement must represent that he or she has purchased the securities for investment and not for secondary distribution.

(b) ERISA Filings

ERISA was enacted to protect the interest of participants in employee benefit plans. Filings must be made with the Pension Benefit Guaranty Corp.

(PBGC) and the IRS if pension plans are merged or partially or completely terminated.

(c) IRS Rulings

With a tax-free transaction (see Chapter 8), IRS approval should be sought before a deal is completed. Final approval typically takes several months.

(d) Other Filings

When buying or selling a business in a regulated industry such as banking, public utilities, transportation, or communications, filing and obtaining the necessary approval(s) with applicable regulatory agencies, such as the Federal Reserve Board, Interstate Commerce Commission, Public Utility Commission or Federal Communications Commission, are usually required.

Significant SEC Regulatory and Accounting Pronouncements

THE SECURITIES EXCHANGE ACT OF 1933

Rule 409   Exemption from Requirements for Information Unknown or
            Not Reasonably Available
Rule 145   Mergers and Acquisitions
Rule 3-05 Financial Statements of Businesses Acquired or to be
            Acquired

THE SECURITIES EXCHANGE ACT OF 1934

Regulation 14A   Solicitation of Proxies
Section 13(e)   Purchases or Tender Offers by a Company for its Own
                 Securities
Section 14(d)   Third Party Tender Offers

SEC RELEASES

Accounting Series Releases (ASRs):

ASR 130   Pooling-of-Interests Accounting

ASR 135   Revised Guidelines for the Application of ASR No. 130

ASR 146   Effect of Treasury Stock Transactions on Accounting for Business Combinations

ASR 146-A   Statement of Policy and Interpretations in Regard to ASR No.

Financial Reporting Releases (FRRs):

FRR 2   Guidance as to What Constitutes a "Business"

Staff Accounting Bulletins (SABs):

SAB 54   Pushdown Accounting

SAB 89   Financial Statement Requirements of Certain Troubled Financial Institution Acquisitions

Illustration of Letter of Intent

[Date]

John A. Seller, President
Company B
[Address]

Re: *Purchase of Stock*

Dear Mr. Seller:

This letter sets forth our preliminary understanding with respect to the proposed purchase by Company A of all of the issued and outstanding shares of stock of Company B. For convenience, we will refer to Company B as the "Company," to you individually as the "Seller," and to Company A as the "Buyer."

1. *Purchase and Sale.* Buyer intends to purchase from Seller all of the issued and outstanding stock of the Company and related noncompetition rights for total consideration of $2,000,000. This consideration will be paid by delivery of $1,000,000 in cash at the time of closing and by further delivery of a promissory note in the amount of $1,000,000, bearing interest at 8% per annum, amortized over 10 years, with a five year balloon.

2. *Security for Payment.* The $1,000,000 promissory note will be secured by the following: (i) the unlimited personal liability of Buyer; (ii) a pledge of all the shares of stock of the Company; and (iii) the guarantee of the Company and a security interest in all the furniture, fixtures, and equipment of the Company.

3. *Consulting and Noncompetition.* Seller will enter into a consulting and noncompetition agreement providing for services to be rendered on a part-time basis by the Seller to the Buyer after the date of closing on a mutually

agreed-upon schedule. The Seller will further agree not to compete with the business of the Company for a period of five years and within a radius of 250 miles of the current principal place of business of the Company.

4. *Exchange of Information.* The Buyer will immediately have the right to inspect, through its accountants and other agents, all of the books and records and assets of the Company. The Buyer agrees that all such information is confidential and proprietary to the Seller, and the Buyer will use such information only for the purpose of evaluating its proposed purchase of the Company. The Buyer may disclose such information to its lending bank and its agents, including its accountants and attorneys, but in all other respects, the information shall be held confidential. In the event the purchase does not occur as intended hereunder, all such information shall be returned to the Seller. None of such information shall be used in any manner which is competitive with or adverse to the Company or the Seller.

5. *Final Agreement.* Within 30 days after acceptance of this letter of intent, the Buyer will advise Seller if its inspection of the books and records pursuant to paragraph 4 above has been satisfactory. If so, the Buyer will promptly proceed to have its legal counsel draft a standard Stock Purchase Agreement, including customary representations and warranties on the part of the Seller and the Company for transactions of this type. Such agreement shall be subject in all respects to review and negotiation by the Seller and the Seller's legal counsel.

6. *Confidentiality of Transaction.* The existence of this letter of intent and the intention of the parties to engage in the transactions described herein are confidential and will not be disclosed to any third party except those parties essential to the investigation and negotiation procedures related hereto. In particular, the Buyer will not disclose its intention to purchase the Company to any of the Company's employees, agents, customers or suppliers, except with the prior written consent of the Seller.

7. *Operations Prior to Closing.* Seller will not cause or permit the Company to make any distributions or payments (other than salaries at current levels) to or for the benefit of Seller. Seller shall cause Company to continue to operate its business, consistent with past practice, through the date of closing.

8. *Closing.* The closing for the transactions contemplated by this letter of intent shall occur within 90 days of the date of this letter of intent at a time and place designated by the Buyer.

9. *Exclusive Dealing.* The Seller agrees that, for so long as Buyer is

proceeding in good faith to complete its due diligence and to negotiate in completing an agreement of purchase, the Seller shall not enter into substantive negotiations with any third party for the sale of the Company or any interest therein. The Seller may, however, terminate its obligations hereunder 30 days after acceptance if the Buyer has failed to advise the Seller by that time that it has satisfactorily completed its investigation under paragraph 4, and the Seller may further terminate 60 days hereafter if the parties have not by that date entered into a formal and enforceable Stock Purchase Agreement.

10. *Legal Effect.* This letter agreement represents an expression of intent of the parties only, except that the provisions of paragraph 4 and paragraph 9 shall be enforceable in accordance with their terms. The parties intend to use this letter of intent as a basis for consummating a sale transaction, and both parties agree to use their best efforts to enter into a formal and binding contractual agreement as promptly as possible hereafter.

If you agree with the foregoing, please indicate your concurrence by signing and returning one copy of this letter of intent to the undersigned.

Very truly yours,

Buyer

Agreed to this _____ day of _____, 19_____.

_____
Seller

Illustration of Stock Purchase Agreement Table of Contents

I   PURCHASE AND SALE

II   PURCHASE PRICE AND NONCOMPETITION PAYMENT

III REPRESENTATIONS AND WARRANTIES OF THE SELLER AND THE COMPANY

VII   CONDITIONS TO CLOSING

VIII   CLOSING

IX   TERMINATION

X   MUTUAL INDEMNIFICATION

XI   POST-CLOSING OPERATIONS

XII GENERAL PROVISIONS

Illustration of Stock Purchase Agreement

This Stock Purchase Agreement is made and entered into as of _____ ,199__ , by and among Corporation A, a [Name of State] corporation (hereinafter referred as "Buyer"), John A. Seller (herinafter referred to as the "Seller"), and Corporation B, a [Name of State] corporation (hereinafter called the "Company").

Article I

PURCHASE AND SALE

Subject to the terms and conditions of the Agreement set forth below, Seller agrees to sell, and Buyer agrees to purchase, all of the issued and outstanding shares of stock of the Company.

Article II

PURCHASE PRICE AND NONCOMPETITION PAYMENT

The total consideration for the shares of stock to be purchased and the noncompetition covenant of the Seller hereunder is the sum of $2,000,000, payable as follows:

2.1 *Cash Payment.* At the time of Closing, the Buyer shall pay to the Seller the sum of $750,000 in certified funds, by wire transfer, or in other form satisfactory to the Seller, as a down payment on the stock of the Company.

2.2 *Noncompetition Payment.* At the time of Closing the Buyer shall pay to the Seller the sum of $250,000, in the same manner as the payment made under Section 2.1 above, as consideration for the Seller's noncompetition covenant as provided for in Section 6.2 below.

2.3 *Promissory Note.* The balance of the purchase price of $1,000,000 for the stock will be paid by the Buyer to the Seller by delivery of a promissory note in the form attached hereto as Exhibit A (the "Promissory Note"). The Promissory Note shall provide for the payment of $1,000,000 with interest at the rate of 8% per annum in equal monthly installments, amortizing principal and interest over a term of 10 years, with a balloon payment of all remaining principal and interest due 5 years after Closing.

2.4 *Security.* As security for the payment of the deferred purchase price hereunder, the Buyer shall do the following:

(a) Pledge to the Seller all of the stock purchased hereunder pursuant to the Pledge Agreement in the form attached hereto as Exhibit B (the "Pledge Agreement"); and

(b) Cause the Company to guarantee the payment of the Promissory Note and to grant to the Seller a security interest in the furniture, fixtures, and equipment of the Company, which security interest shall be senior to all other encumbrances and liens on such assets. The security interest in favor of Seller shall be granted pursuant to a Security Agreement in the form attached hereto as Exhibit C (the "Company's Security Agreement").

Article III

REPRESENTATIONS AND WARRANTIES OF THE SELLER AND THE COMPANY

The Seller and the Company jointly and severally represent and warrant to the Buyer as follows:

3.1 *Organization and Good Standing.* The Company is a corporation duly organized, validly existing, and in good standing under the laws of the State of [Name of State]. The Company is not required, by the nature of its assets or business, to qualify as a foreign corporation in any other jurisdiction. The Company has full power to own all of its properties and to carry on its business as it is now being conducted.

3.2 *Corporate Authority.* The Company has the authority, pursuant to its articles of incorporation and bylaws, and pursuant to such additional action as is necessary by its officers, directors, and shareholders, to execute this Agreement and to consummate the transactions provided for herein.

3.3 *Capitalization of the Company.* The Company has only one class of stock authorized by its articles of incorporation. The Seller owns 10,000 shares of the issued and outstanding shares of such stock. Such shares, all of which shall be transferred to the Buyer pursuant to this Agreement, represent all the issued and outstanding shares of stock of the Company. The Company has no stock options, warrants, or other rights to acquire stock outstanding. The shares of the Company's stock to be transferred by the Seller to the Buyer hereunder are free and clear of any liens, security interests, pledges, or other claims or rights on the part of any third party.

3.4 *No Violation of Obligations.* The execution and delivery of this Agreement, and the consummation of the transactions provided for herein, will not violate any agreement or commitment made by the Company, or any requirement binding on the Company, including, without limitation, any lease, contract, loan agreement, promissory note, franchise agreement, court order, judgment, regulatory ruling, or arbitration award.

3.5 *Financial Statements of the Company.* The financial statements of the Company attached hereto as Schedule 3.5 (the "Financial Statements") fairly present the financial position of the Company as of the respective dates thereof and the results of the operations of the Company for the periods indicated. All of the Financial Statements have been prepared in accordance with generally accepted accounting principles applied on a basis consistent with that of preceding years, but those Financial Statements which are internal and unaudited, have been prepared without certain year-end adjustments which are reflected in the audited statements. Neither the audited fiscal year-end Financial Statements nor the interim internal Financial Statements are, to the best knowledge of Seller, misleading in any material respect.

3.6 *Assets.* The Company has good and marketable title to all of the Company's assets reflected on the Financial Statements and to certain other off-book assets (including previously expensed supplies and written off inventory) shown on the attached Schedule 3.6 and collectively referred to as the "Company's Assets." Except as disclosed in the Financial Statements of the Company, the Company's Assets are not subject to any deed of trust, mortgage, security interest, or other liens or claims of any nature whatsoever. All of the Company's Assets are in satisfactory and operational condition, except as otherwise shown on Schedule 3.6. All inventory is shown on the Financial Statements at the lower of current fair market value or cost, and the accounts receivable (net of bad debt reserves) are collectible in full in the ordinary course of the Company's business.

3.7 *Liabilities.* Except as shown on Schedule 3.7, the Company has no liabilities, liquidated, actual, or contingent, except as shown on the Financial Statements and except for liabilities which have arisen in the ordinary course of business from and after the date of the most recent Financial Statement. Any liabilities arising after the date of the Financial Statements have arisen in the ordinary course of business of the Company and are substantially similar as to kind and amount to those shown on the Financial Statements.

3.8 *Operations Since the Financial Statements.* Since the date of the most recent Financial Statement, there has not been and there will not be through the date of Closing:

(a) Any change in the business, results of operations, assets, financial condition, or manner of conducting the business of the Company, which has or may be reasonably expected to have a material adverse effect on such business, results of operations, assets, or financial condition;

(b) Any decrease in the net book value shown on the most recent balance sheet included within the Financial Statements;

(c) Any damage, destruction, or loss (whether or not covered by insurance) which has or may reasonably be expected to have a material adverse effect upon any material asset or the business or operations of the Company;

(d) Any declaration, setting aside, or payment of any dividend or other distribution in respect to the stock of the Company;

(e) Any increase in the compensation payable or to become payable by the Company to any of its officers, directors, employees, or agents;

(f) Any other distribution of any nature whatsoever to or for the benefit of the Seller;

(g) Any issuance of shares of stock of the Company, or any grant of any option to purchase, or other rights to acquire, stock of the Company;

(h) Any employment, bonus, or deferred compensation agreement entered into between the Company and any of its directors, officers, or other employees or consultants;

(i) Any entering into, amendment, or termination by the Company of any material contract, franchise, permit, license, or other agreement;

(j) Any indebtedness incurred by the Company, any commitment to borrow money, or any guarantee by the Company of any third party obligation, or the imposition of any lien on the Company's assets or the grant of any encumbrance by the Company; or

(k) Any amendment of the articles of incorporation or bylaws of the Company.

3.9 *Legal Proceedings.* There are no private or governmental proceedings pending, or to the knowledge of Seller threatened, against the Company, including, without limitation, any investigation, audit, lawsuit, threatened lawsuit, arbitration, or other legal proceedings of any nature whatsoever.

3.10 *Material Agreements.* The Company is not a party to any employment agreement, equipment lease, real property lease, agreement for purchase or sale, franchise agreement, joint venture agreement, or any other contract, agreement, or other obligation, whether or not in writing, except for agreements which individually represent obligations on the part of the Company of less than $5,000 and in the aggregate obligations of not more than $25,000, other than agreements which are terminable at will by the Company and except for those agreements which are listed on Schedule 3.10 attached hereto. Copies of all agreements listed on Schedule 3.10 have been provided to the Buyer. None of such agreements is in default, nor is the Company or the Seller aware of any claim or penalty against the Company which has accrued or which will accrue as a result of the Closing hereunder or for any other reason under any of such agreements.

3.11 *Employees.* Attached hereto as Schedule 3.11 is a list of all the Company's employees and the rate of compensation of each. None of such employees is a party to any employment agreement or other contract with the Company, nor are any of such employees entitled to any fringe benefits or other compensation from the Company except as reflected on Schedule 3.11 or separately reflected in a copy of the Company's employment manual, a current copy of which has been delivered to the Buyer. None of the Company's employees is subject to any collective bargaining agreement or other union agreement, nor is the Company or the Seller aware of any effort to organize any of the work force of the Company. No disputes or claims against the Company exist on behalf of any of its employees, including, but not limited to, claims of employment discrimination, violation of wage and hour laws, or claims relating to past unpaid compensation.

3.12 *Compliance with Law.* The Company is not in violation of any material law, regulation, rule, ordinance, or other governmental requirement relating to its properties or its business. Neither the Company nor the Seller has knowledge of any development, occurrence, or condition which would adversely affect any of the Company's properties or which might curtail or interfere with the present or future use of such properties for the purposes for which they are now used.

3.13 *Environmental Compliance.* The Company is in full compliance with all applicable federal, state, and local laws, rules, and regulations relating to environmental regulation and to the disposal of waste products (including, but not limited to, those products defined as hazardous wastes under applicable federal and state laws). The Company does not lease, own, or operate a facility on, and has not leased, owned, or operated a facility on, any land or real property subject to any environmental contamination, violation, or requirement for clean up or any other environmental remediation.

3.14 *Tax Returns.* The Company has timely and correctly prepared and filed all tax returns, including federal and state income tax returns and sales tax returns, and the Company has paid all taxes due pursuant to such tax returns as well as all other taxes, including real and personal property taxes for which the Company is liable, except for certain property taxes which are accrued but not yet due as shown on Schedule 3.14. The Company has not filed for and is not now subject to any extension of time with respect to the filing of any tax return. The Company has provided to the Buyer true and correct copies of all federal and state income tax returns filed by it for the past three fiscal years. The Company is not aware of any actual or threatened tax audit. The Financial Statements reflect an adequate reserve, as of the dates thereof, for income taxes then due for the present tax year. The Company maintains all required payroll trust accounts, and the Company has timely paid all employee and employer withholding taxes into such trust accounts.

3.15 *Insurance.* The Company maintains adequate insurance with qualified insurance carriers with respect to liability and property loss or damage. A list of insurance policies showing coverage amounts, insurance carrier, and type of coverage is set forth on Schedule 3.15. Copies of all such policies have been provided to the Buyer.

3.16 *Complete Disclosure.* This Agreement and the agreements and instruments attached hereto and to be delivered at the time of Closing do not contain any untrue statement of a material fact by the Seller or the Company. This Agreement and such related agreements and instruments do not omit to state any material fact necessary in order to make the statements made herein or therein by the Company or the Seller, in light of the circumstances under which they are made, not misleading.

Article IV

REPRESENTATIONS AND WARRANTIES OF BUYER

The Buyer represents and warrants to the Company and to the Seller as follows:

4.1 *Organization and Qualification of the Buyer.* The Buyer is a corporation duly organized, validly existing, and in good standing under the laws of the State of [Name of State]. The Buyer is not required, by the nature of its assets or business, to qualify as a foreign corporation in any other state. The Buyer has full power to own all of its properties and to carry on its business as it is now being conducted.

4.2 *Corporate Authority.* The Buyer has the authority, pursuant to its articles of incorporation and bylaws, and pursuant to such additional action as is necessary by its officers, directors, and shareholders, to execute this Agreement and to consummate the transactions provided for herein.

4.3 *No Violation of Obligations.* The execution and delivery of this Agreement, and the consummation of the transactions provided for herein, will not violate any agreement or commitment made by the Buyer, or any requirement binding on the Buyer, including, without limitation, any lease, contract, loan agreement, promissory note, franchise agreement, court order, judgment, regulatory ruling, or any arbitration award.

4.4 *Financial Statements.* The financial statements previously delivered by the Buyer to the Seller are true and correct in all material respects. Such financial statements have been prepared in accordance with generally accepted accounting principles applied on a basis consistent with that of preceding years. The Seller has not experienced, will not experience through the time of Closing, and does not expect to experience thereafter, any material adverse change in the nature of its operations or business. Without limiting the foregoing, the Buyer has the ability to honor all of its obligations undertaken pursuant to this Agreement, specifically including the obligation to pay all amounts due pursuant to the Promissory Note in accordance with the terms thereof.

4.5 *Liabilities*. The Buyer has no liabilities, liquidated, actual or contingent, except as shown on the financial statements previously provided to the Seller and except for liabilities which have arisen in the ordinary course of Buyer's business from and after the date of the most recent financial statements so provided. Any liabilities arising after the data of such financial statements have arisen in the ordinary course of business of the Buyer and are similar as to kind and amount to the liabilities shown on such financial statements.

4.6 *Compliance with Law*. The Buyer is not in violation of any material law, regulation, rule, ordinance, or other governmental requirement relating to its properties or its business. The Buyer has no knowledge of any development, occurrence, or condition which would adversely affect any of the Buyer's properties or which might curtail or interfere with the present or future use of such properties for the purposes for which they are now used.

4.7 *Legal Proceedings*. There are no private or governmental proceedings pending, or to the knowledge of Buyer threatened, against the Buyer, including, without limitation, any investigation, audit, lawsuit, threatened lawsuit, arbitration, or other legal proceedings of any nature whatsoever.

4.8 *Liens*. Except as disclosed in the financial statements of the Buyer, the Buyer and the assets of the Buyer are not subject to any deed of trust, mortgage, security interest, or other lien or claim of any nature whatsoever.

4.9 *Securities Compliance*. The Buyer is a sophisticated purchaser which is either experienced in evaluating and acquiring businesses similar to the Company or which has had adequate advice from persons who have such experience. Buyer acknowledges that it has been provided with all information about the Company requested by Buyer, that Buyer, itself or through its advisors, has the expertise necessary to evaluate such information, that Buyer has been afforded opportunities to conduct its own investigation and to request additional information and that Buyer does not desire any further information or opportunity to investigate the Company. Buyer intends to hold all of the Company's stock for investment purposes and has no intent to resell or otherwise distribute any of such stock.

4.10 *Complete Disclosure*. This Agreement and the agreements and instruments related hereto do not contain any untrue statement of a material fact by the Buyer. This Agreement and such related agreements and instruments do not omit to state any material fact necessary in order to make the statements made herein or therein, in light of the circumstances under which they are made, not misleading.

Article V

INFORMATION AND CONFIDENTIALITY

5.1 *Provision of Information Relating to Company.* Prior to the execution of this Agreement, the Seller and the Company have made available to the Buyer information relating to the Company, including, without limitation, financial statements and records, depreciation schedules, lists of equipment, copies of contracts and agreements, and access to the properties, assets and operations of the Company. To the best knowledge of the Company and the Seller, all such information is substantially correct and complete. From and after the date of this Agreement and continuing through Closing, the Company and the Seller will continue to make available to the Buyer all information required hereunder or otherwise reasonably requested by the Buyer with respect to the Company.

5.2 *Confidentiality.* The Buyer acknowledges that all information with respect to the Company made available prior to and subsequent to the date of this Agreement and through the date of Closing is confidential. The Buyer shall use such information only for the purpose of evaluating the proposed transactions hereunder. In the event the transactions provided for in this Agreement fail to close for any reason whatsoever, the Buyer will promptly return all such information to the Seller, including any extracts, copies or analyses based thereon which were prepared by the Buyer. The Buyer will not use, nor will it permit any third party to use, any of such information in any manner which is competitive with or injurious to the Company.

5.3 *Provision of Information Relating to Buyer.* The Buyer has provided certain information to the Seller, including financial statements and other information relating to the ability of the Buyer to carry out his obligations hereunder. The Buyer represents and warrants that such information is complete and accurate, and the Seller agrees that all such information is to be treated as confidential and will be used only for the purpose of evaluating the Seller's decision to consummate the transactions provided for herein.

5.4 *Contacts with Third Parties.* The existence of this Agreement and the transactions provided for herein are confidential. Public announcements shall be made only pursuant to mutual agreement of the parties hereto. Prior to the time of any such public announcement, the Buyer shall not disclose to any third party that is contemplating the purchase of the Company, but the Seller agrees that it will at mutually agreeable times arrange for interviews by the Buyer, at which a representative of the Seller may be present, with key employees, suppliers, and customers of the Company. The Buyer agrees to conduct such interviews in such manner as to avoid any interference with the Company's relationships with such persons and subject to such reasonable constraints as are requested by the Seller.

Article VI

CONSULTING AND NONCOMPETITION AGREEMENTS

At the time of Closing, the Seller, individually, will enter into the following agreements:

6.1 *Consulting Agreement.* A consulting agreement in the form attached hereto as Exhibit D (the "Consulting Agreement") providing for substantially full-time consulting services to be rendered by the Seller to the Buyer and the Company for a period of 60 days after Closing and for part-time services to be rendered thereafter on a schedule mutually agreeable to the Buyer and the Seller.

6.2 *Noncompetition Covenant.* The Seller shall further enter into an agreement in the form attached hereto as Exhibit E (the "Noncompetition Covenant") whereby the Seller will agree not to compete with the business of the Company within a radius of 250 miles of the present principal place of business of the Company for a period of five years from and after the time of Closing.

Article VII

CONDITIONS TO CLOSING

The obligations of the parties to close the transactions provided for herein are subject to the following conditions, as well as to any other conditions expressed or implied in this Agreement.

7.1 *Seller's Conditions.* The obligations of the Seller and the Company are subject to the following conditions:

(a) All representations, warranties, covenants, and other agreements contained herein on the part of the Buyer will be true and correct at the time of Closing.

(b) The Seller will be satisfied, at his sole discretion, with the financial ability of the Buyer to honor its obligations pursuant to the Promissory Note.

(c) No lawsuit, governmental action, or other legal proceeding shall have been commenced which shall materially interfere with the ability of the parties to consummate the transactions provided for herein.

7.2 *Buyer's Conditions.* The obligations of the Buyer to complete the transactions provided for herein are subject to the following conditions:

(a) All representations, warranties, covenants, and other agreements contained herein on the part of the Seller and the Company will be true and correct at the time of Closing.

(b) No lawsuit, governmental action, or other legal proceeding shall have been commenced which shall materially interfere with the ability of the parties to consummate the transactions provided for herein.

(c) Buyer will have completed an investigation and examination of the Company, the results of which will be satisfactory to the Buyer in its sole discretion.

(d) The book value of the Company will be not less than the amount shown on the most recent balance sheet included in the Financial Statements.

(e) The Buyer will be reasonably satisfied as to the willingness of the key employees of the Company to continue working for the Company after the Closing hereunder.

Article VIII

CLOSING

The Closing of all transactions provided for herein will occur at the offices of legal counsel for the Buyer at 10:00 a.m. on [date] (the "Closing"). The transactions at Closing, when effective, will be deemed to be effective as of the opening of business on the day of Closing, except as otherwise specifically provided at the time of Closing. All actions to be taken at Closing will be considered to be taken simultaneously, and no document, agreement, or instrument will be considered to be delivered until all items which are to be delivered at the Closing have been executed and delivered. At the Closing, the following actions will occur:

8.1 *Certificates.* The Buyer, the Seller, and the Company will each, respectively, execute a certificate stating that all representations and warranties made by them respectively in this Agreement continue to be true as of the time of Closing.

8.2 *Company's Legal Opinion.* The Seller will deliver to the Buyer an opinion of Seller's and Company's legal counsel, in form reasonably satisfactory to the Buyer, opining favorably as to the matters set forth in Sections 3.1, 3.2, 3.3 and, to the best of such counsel's knowledge, to the matters in Section 3.4 of this Agreement.

8.3 *Endorsement of Stock Certificates.* The Seller will execute and deliver to the Buyer the stock certificate or certificates evidencing all ownership of all the stock of the Company which is now issued and outstanding, duly endorsed for transfer to the Buyer.

8.4 *Resignation of Seller.* The Seller shall resign as an officer, director, and all other positions with the Company.

8.5 *Election of New Officers and Directors.* The Buyer will cause the Company to elect new officers and directors designated by the Buyer.

8.6 *Issuance of New Stock Certificate.* The new officers and directors designated by the Buyer will cause a new stock certificate, evidencing ownership of all the shares of the stock which it surrendered, to be issued to the Buyer.

8.7 *Purchase Price.* The Buyer will pay the purchase price for the shares of stock purchased by delivery of $750,000 in cash or certified funds, by wire transfer, or in other form satisfactory to the Seller, and by execution and delivery of the Promissory Note.

8.8 *Security for Purchase Price.* As security for the payment of the deferred purchase price, the Buyer shall do the following:

(a) The directors of the Company, designated by the Seller, will cause the Company to guarantee the Promissory Note, by delivery of a duly authorized written guarantee in form satisfactory to the Seller.

(b) The Company will grant to the Seller a security interest in its furniture, fixtures, and equipment by executing and delivering the Company's Security Agreement and a Uniform Commercial Code financing statement fully executed in form suitable for recording.

(c) The Buyer will deliver to the Seller, endorsed in blank, the stock certificate or certificates evidencing ownership of all the stock purchased hereunder, and a fully executed Pledge Agreement.

8.9 *Consulting Agreement.* The Company, acting through the officers and directors appointed by the Buyer, shall execute the Consulting Agreement, and the Seller shall execute the Consulting Agreement.

8.10 *Noncompetition Covenant.* The Buyer and the Company, acting through the officers and directors appointed by the Buyer, shall execute the Noncompetition Covenant, and the Seller shall execute the Noncompetition Covenant.

8.11 *Noncompetition Payment.* The Buyer shall pay the Seller the sum of $250,000 in cash or certified funds, by wire transfer, or in other form satisfactory to the Seller as consideration for the Seller's noncompetition covenant.

8.12 *Other Acts.* The parties will execute any other documents reasonably required to carry out the intent of this Agreement.

Article IX

TERMINATION

This Agreement will terminate in accordance with the following provisions.

9.1 *Failure to Close.* If the purchase and sale provided for herein fails to close by the date provided in Article VIII above, then this Agreement shall terminate, unless the parties have, by mutual agreement, extended the time for Closing in writing. Termination shall not release any party of any liability for damages arising out of the breach, if any, of this Agreement, except as provided below.

9.2 *Failure of Condition.* If this Agreement terminates by reason of the failure of any condition provided for herein to be satisfied at the time of Closing, and if the failure to satisfy such condition occurs without material fault on the part of either party hereto, then this Agreement shall terminate without liability on the part of either party hereto, except that the confidentiality provisions set forth in Sections 5.2 and 5.3 shall remain in effect.

9.3 *Termination by Agreement.* If the parties hereto agree to terminate this Agreement, such termination shall be effective without liability to either party hereto.

Article X

MUTUAL INDEMNIFICATION

Each of the parties hereto agrees to indemnify and hold harmless each of the other parties against any loss resulting from a violation of this Agreement on the part of the indemnifying party. Such indemnification obligation shall include indemnification for any costs reasonably incurred by the indemnified party, including, without limitation, legal costs and reasonable attorneys fees. However, no right to indemnification shall arise hereunder unless the aggregate of all indemnified losses of any party hereto (net of any losses of the other party which are subject to indemnification) exceeds the sum of $25,000.

Article XI

POST-CLOSING OPERATIONS

From and after the time of Closing, the Buyer agrees as follows:

11.1   *Release of Seller.* The Buyer and the Company will utilize their best efforts to cause the Seller to be released from any guarantees or any other contingent obligations which the Seller may have with respect to the liabilities of the Company. Without limiting the generality of the foregoing, the Company will advise all lenders, lessors, and suppliers, at the time of renewing any existing leases, loans, lines of credit, or other obligations, that the Seller is no longer responsible for the obligations of the Company.

11.2 *Operations in Ordinary Course.* The Company shall continue to operate its business in the ordinary course, fulfilling all contracts and other obligations which have been properly disclosed hereunder and which are not yet completed as of the time of Closing. The Company will maintain in effect all insurance policies, or will establish substantially similar coverage, with respect to any liabilities of the Company for which the Seller may have personal responsibility.

11.3 *Reports.* For so long as any amount remains outstanding pursuant to the Promissory Note, the Company and the Buyer will cause copies of the Company's annual financial statements to be delivered to the Seller promptly after the preparation of such statements.

Article XII

GENERAL PROVISIONS

The following general provisions shall apply to this Agreement.

12.1 *Survival of Agreement.* This Agreement, and all terms, warranties, and provisions hereof will be true and correct as of the time of Closing and will survive the Closing for a period of three years.

12.2 *Notices.* All notices required or permitted hereunder or under any related agreement or instrument (unless such related agreement or instrument otherwise provides) will be deemed delivered when delivered personally or mailed, by certified mail, return receipt requested, or registered mail, to the respective party at the following addresses or to such other address as each respective party may in writing hereafter designate:

(a) To Seller:

_____

_____

_____

(b) To Buyer:

_____

_____

_____

(c) To Company:

_____

_____

_____

12.3 *Successors and Assigns*. This Agreement will be binding upon the parties hereto and their respective successors, personal representatives, heirs and assigns. However, no party hereto will have any right to assign any of its obligations pursuant to this Agreement, except with the prior written consent of all of the other parties.

12.4 *Merger*. This Agreement and the exhibits and other documents, agreements, and instruments related hereto, set forth the entire agreement of the parties with respect to the subject matter hereof and may not be amended or modified except in writing subscribed to by all such parties.

12.5 *Governing Law*. This Agreement is entered into in the State of [name of State], it will be performed within such state, and all issues arising hereunder shall be governed in all respects by the laws of such state.

12.6 *Obligations to Brokers*. No party hereto has incurred any obligation for the payment of any brokerage commission, finder's fee, or any other similar obligation relating to this Agreement or the consummation of the transactions provided for herein.

12.7 *Modification or Severance*. In the event that any provision of this Agreement is found by any court or other authority of competent jurisdiction to be illegal or unenforceable, such provision shall be severed or modified to the extent necessary to render it enforceable and as so severed or modified, this Agreement will remain in full force and effect.

12.8 *Captions*. The captions in this Agreement are included for convenience only and shall not in any way affect the interpretation of any of the provisions hereof.

IN WITNESS WHEREOF, the parties have read and entered into this Agreement as of the date above written.

Buyer:

By: _____

Seller:

Company:

By: _____

LIST OF EXHIBITS

Illustration of Assets Purchase Agreement

Table of Contents

XIII GENERAL PROVISIONS

Illustration of
Assets Purchase Agreement

This Assets Purchase Agreement is made and entered into as of _____ , 199__ , by and among Corporation A, a [Name of State] corporation (hereinafter referred as "Buyer"), John A. Seller (hereinafter referred to as the "Shareholder"), and Corporation B, a [Name of State] corporation (hereinafter called the "Seller").

Article I

PURCHASE AND SALE OF ASSETS

Subject to the terms and conditions of this Agreement set forth below, Seller agrees to sell, and Buyer agrees to purchase, all of the assets of the Seller and to assume certain specified liabilities of the Seller. The "Assets" to be acquired hereunder are all of the assets of the Seller shown on the financial statements of the Seller as of the date of closing, all assets arising in the ordinary course of business from and after the date of such balance sheet, and any and all other assets, owned by the Seller, including its files and records, intangible information, trademarks and trade names, previously expensed tools and supplies, and all other assets now located at the principal place of business of the Seller, except for those assets which have previously been identified by the Buyer and Seller as being the property of the Shareholder, which are to be retained by the Shareholder at the time of closing, which excluded assets are referred to herein as the "Excluded Assets."

Article II

PURCHASE PRICE AND NONCOMPETITION PAYMENT

The total consideration for the Assets and the noncompetition covenant of the Seller is the sum of $2,000,000, payable as set forth below, plus assumption of certain of Seller's liabilities as provided for in Article III below:

2.1 *Cash Payment.* At the time of Closing, the Buyer shall pay to the Seller the sum of $750,000 in certified funds, by wire transfer, or in other form satisfactory to the Seller.

2.2 *Noncompetition Payment.* The Buyer shall further pay the sum of $250,000 to the Shareholder, individually, at closing as consideration for the noncompetition covenant provided for in Section 7.2 below.

2.3 *Promissory Note.* The balance of the purchase price of $1,000,000 will be paid by the Buyer to the Seller by delivery of a promissory note in the form attached hereto as Exhibit A (the "Promissory Note"). The Promissory Note shall provide for the payment of $1,000,000 with interest at the rate of 8% per annum in equal monthly installments, amortizing principal and interest over a term of 10 years, with a balloon payment of all remaining principal and interest due 5 years after Closing.

2.4 *Security.* As security for the payment of the purchase price hereunder, the Buyer shall execute and deliver to the Seller a security agreement in the form attached hereto as Exhibit B (the "Security Agreement") providing to the Seller a senior security interest in all of the furniture, fixtures, and equipment purchased hereunder and a security interest subordinate only to the security interest of Buyer's lending bank in the accounts receivable, inventory, and other Assets acquired hereunder. The subordination agreement between the lending bank and the Seller shall be in the form of the subordination agreement attached hereto as Exhibit C (the "Subordination Agreement").

Article III

ASSUMPTION OF LIABILITIES

Subject to the terms and conditions of this Agreement, the Buyer agrees, as further consideration for the Assets to be acquired hereunder, to assume and pay in the ordinary course of business after closing, all of the liabilities of the Seller as shown on its most recent balance sheet included in the "Financial Statements" attached as Schedule 4.4 and all liabilities arising in the ordinary course of business from and after the date of such balance sheet, provided that such further liabilities shall be of similar kind and amount to those which have previously arisen in the ordinary course of the Seller's business.

Article IV

REPRESENTATIONS AND WARRANTIES OF THE SHAREHOLDER AND THE SELLER

The Shareholder and the Seller jointly and severally represent and warrant to the Buyer as follows:

4.1 *Organization and Good Standing.* The Seller is a corporation duly organized, validly existing, and in good standing under the laws of the State of [Name of State]. The Seller is not required, by the nature of its assets or business, to qualify as a foreign corporation in any other jurisdiction. The Seller has full power to own all of its properties and to carry on its business as it is now being conducted.

4.2 *Corporate Authority.* The Seller has the authority, pursuant to its articles of incorporation and bylaws, and pursuant to such additional action as is necessary by its officers, directors, and shareholders, to execute this Agreement and to consummate the transactions provided for herein. Without limiting the generality of the foregoing, the shareholders of the Seller will unanimously approve the transactions provided for herein prior to closing.

4.3 *No Violation of Obligations.* The execution and delivery of this Agreement, and the consummation of the transactions provided for herein, will not violate any agreement or commitment made by the Seller or the Shareholder, or any requirement binding on the Seller or the Shareholder, respectively, including, without limitation, any lease, contract, loan agreement, promissory note, franchise agreement, court order, judgment, regulatory ruling, or arbitration award.

4.4 *Financial Statements of the Seller.* The financial statements of the Seller attached hereto as Schedule 4.4 (the "Financial Statements") fairly present the financial position of the Seller as of the respective dates thereof and the results of the operations of the Seller for the periods indicated. All of the Financial Statements have been prepared in accordance with generally accepted accounting principles applied on a basis consistent with that of preceding years, but those Financial Statements which are internal and unaudited, have been prepared without certain year-end adjustments which are reflected in the audited statements. Neither the audited fiscal year-end Financial Statements nor the interim internal Financial Statements are, to the best knowledge of Seller and the Shareholder, misleading in any material respect.

4.5 *Assets.* The Seller has good and marketable title to all of the Assets. Except as disclosed in the Financial Statements of the Seller, the Assets are not subject to any deed of trust, mortgage, security interest, or other liens or claims of any nature whatsoever. All of the Assets are in satisfactory and operational condition, except as otherwise shown on Schedule 4.5. All inventory is shown on the Financial Statements at the lower of current fair market value or cost, and the accounts receivable shown thereon (net of bad debt reserves) are collectible in full in the ordinary course of business.

4.6 *Liabilities.* Except as shown on Schedule 4.6, the Seller has no liabilities, liquidated, actual, or contingent, except as shown on the Financial Statements and except for liabilities which have arisen in the ordinary course of Seller's business from and after the date of the most recent Financial Statement. Any liabilities arising after the date of the most recent Financial Statement have arisen in the ordinary course of business of the Seller and are substantially similar as to kind and amount to those shown on the Financial Statements. Schedule 4.6 specifically sets forth all accrued benefits due to employees, including sick leave and vacation rights, whether or not such liabilities are reflected on the Financial Statements.

4.7 *Operations Since the Financial Statements.* Since the date of the most recent Financial Statement, there has not been and there will not be through the date of Closing:

(a) Any change in the business, results of operations, assets, financial condition, or manner of conducting the business of the Seller, which has or may be reasonably expected to have a material adverse effect on such business, results of operations, assets, or financial condition;

(b) Any decrease in the net book value of the Seller shown on the most recent balance sheet included within the Financial Statements;

(c) Any damage, destruction, or loss (whether or not covered by insurance) which has or may reasonably be expected to have a material adverse effect upon any material asset or the business or operations of the Seller;

(d) Any declaration, setting aside, or payment of any dividend or other distribution with respect to the stock of the Seller;

(e) Any increase in the compensation payable or to become payable by the Seller to any of its officers, directors, employees, or agents;

(f) Any other distributions by the Seller of any nature whatsoever to or for the benefit of the Shareholder;

(g) Any issuance of shares of stock of the Seller, or any grant of any option to purchase, or other rights to acquire, stock of the Seller;

(h) Any employment, bonus, or deferred compensation agreement entered into between the Seller and any of its directors, officers, or other employees or consultants;

(i) Any entering into, amendment, or termination by the Seller of any material contract, franchise, permit, license, or other agreement; or

(j) Any indebtedness incurred by the Seller to borrow money, any commitment to borrow money, or any guarantee by the Seller of any third party obligations, or the imposition of any lien on the Seller's assets or the grant of any encumbrance by the Seller.

4.8 *Legal Proceedings.* There are no private or governmental proceedings pending, or to the knowledge of the Shareholder or Seller threatened, against the Seller, including, without limitation, any investigation, audit, lawsuit, threatened lawsuit, arbitration, or other legal proceedings of any nature whatsoever.

4.9 *Material Agreements.* The Seller is not a party to any employment agreement, equipment lease, real property lease, agreement for purchase or sale, franchise agreement, joint venture agreement, or any other contract, agreement, or other obligation, whether or not in writing (other than agreements which individually represent obligations on the part of the Seller of less than $5,000 and in the aggregate obligations of not more than $25,000), except for agreements which are terminable within 30 days by the Seller and any assignee of the Seller and except those agreements which are listed on Schedule 4.9 attached hereto. Copies of all agreements listed on Schedule 4.9 have been provided to the Buyer. None of such agreements is in default, nor is the Seller or the Shareholder aware of any claim or penalty against the Seller which has accrued or which will accrue as a result of the Closing hereunder or for any other reason under any of such agreements.

4.10 *Employees.* Attached hereto as Schedule 4.10 is a list of all the Seller's employees and the rate of compensation of each. None of such employees is a party to any employment agreement or other contract with the Seller, nor are any of such employees entitled to any fringe benefits or other compensation from the Seller except as reflected on Schedule 4.10 or separately reflected in a copy of the Seller's employment manual, a current copy of which has been delivered to the Buyer. None of the Seller's employees is subject to any collective bargaining agreement or other union agreement, nor is the Seller or the Shareholder aware of any effort to organize any of the work force of the Seller. No disputes or claims against the Seller exist on behalf of any of its employees, including, but not limited to, claims of employment discrimination, violation of wage and hour laws, or claims relating to past unpaid compensation. The Shareholder and the Seller believe that substantially all of the Seller's employees will accept employment with the buyer on terms substantially similar to the terms under which they are employed by the Seller.

4.11 *Compliance with Law.* The Seller is not in violation of any material law, regulation, rule, ordinance, or other governmental requirement relating to its properties or its business. Neither the Seller nor the Shareholder has knowledge of any development, occurrence, or condition which would adversely affect any of the Seller's properties or which might curtail or interfere with the present or future use of such properties for the purposes for which they are now used.

4.12 *Environmental Compliance.* The Seller is in full compliance with all applicable federal, state, and local laws, rules, and regulations relating to environmental regulation and to the disposal of waste products (including, but not limited to, those products defined as hazardous wastes under applicable federal and state laws). The Seller does not lease, own, or operate a facility on, and has not leased, owned, or operated a facility on, any land or real property subject to any environmental contamination, violation, or requirement for clean up or any other environmental remediation.

4.13 *Tax Returns.* The Shareholder has timely and correctly prepared and filed all tax returns, including federal and state income tax returns and sales tax returns, and the Seller has paid all taxes due pursuant to such tax returns as well as all other taxes, including real and personal property taxes for which the Seller is liable, except for certain property taxes which are accrued but not yet due, as shown on Schedule 4.13. The Seller has not filed for and is not now subject to any extension of time with respect to the filing of any tax return. The Seller has provided to the Buyer true and correct copies of all federal and state income tax returns filed by it for the past three fiscal years. The Seller is not aware of any actual or threatened tax audit. The Financial Statements reflect an adequate reserve, as of the date thereof, for income taxes now due for the present tax year. The Seller maintains all required payroll trust accounts, and the Seller has timely paid all employee and employer withholding taxes into such trust accounts.

4.14 *Insurance.* The Seller maintains adequate insurance with qualified insurance carriers with respect to liability and property loss or damage. A list of insurance policies showing coverage amounts, insurance carrier, and type of coverage is set forth on Schedule 4.14. Copies of all such policies have been provided to the Buyer.

4.15 *Complete Disclosure.* This Agreement and the agreements and instruments attached hereto and to be delivered at the time of Closing do not contain any untrue statement of a material fact by the Shareholder or the Seller. This Agreement and such related agreements and instruments do not omit to state any material fact necessary in order to make the statements made herein or therein by the Seller or the Shareholder, in light of the circumstances under which they are made, not misleading.

Article V

REPRESENTATIONS AND WARRANTIES OF BUYER

The Buyer represents and warrants to the Seller and to the Shareholder as follows:

5.1 *Organization and Qualification of the Buyer.* The Buyer is a corporation duly organized, validly existing, and in good standing under the laws of the state of [Name of State]. The Buyer is not required, by the nature of its assets or business, to qualify as a foreign corporation in any other state. The Buyer has full power to own all of its properties and to carry on its business as it is now being conducted.

5.2 *Corporate Authority.* The Buyer has the authority, pursuant to its articles of incorporation and bylaws, and pursuant to such additional action as is necessary by its officers, directors, and shareholders, to execute this Agreement and to consummate the transactions provided for herein.

5.3 *No Violation of Obligations.* The execution and delivery of this Agreement, and the consummation of the transactions provided for herein, will not violate any agreement or commitment made by the Buyer, or any requirement binding on the Buyer, including, without limitation, any lease, contract, loan agreement, promissory note, franchise agreement, court order, judgment, regulatory ruling, or any arbitration award.

5.4 *Financial Statements.* The financial statements previously delivered by the Buyer to the Seller are true and correct in all material respects. Such financial statements have been prepared in accordance with generally accepted accounting principles applied on a basis consistent with that of preceding years. The Buyer has not experienced, will not experience through the time of Closing, and does not expect to experience thereafter, any material adverse change in the nature of its operations or business. Without limiting the foregoing, the Buyer has the ability to honor all of its obligations undertaken pursuant to this Agreement, specifically including the obligation to pay all amounts due pursuant to the Promissory Note in accordance with the terms thereof.

5.5 *Liabilities.* The Buyer has no liabilities, liquidated, actual or contingent, except as shown on the financial statements previously provided to the Seller and except for liabilities which have arisen in the ordinary course of Buyer's business from and after the date of the most recent financial statements so provided. Any liabilities arising after the date of such financial statements have arisen in the ordinary course of business of the Buyer and are similar as to kind and amount to those shown on such financial statements.

5.6 *Compliance with Law.* The Buyer is not in violation of any material law, regulation, rule, ordinance, or other governmental requirement relating to its properties or its business. The Buyer has no knowledge of any development, occurrence, or condition which would adversely affect any of the Buyer's properties or which might curtail or interfere with the present or future use of such properties for the purposes for which they are now used.

5.7 *Legal Proceedings.* There are no private or governmental proceedings pending, or to the knowledge of Buyer threatened, against the Buyer, including, without limitation, any investigation, audit, lawsuit, threatened lawsuit, arbitration, or other legal proceedings of any nature whatsoever.

5.8 *Liens*. Except as disclosed in the financial statements of the Buyer, the Buyer and the assets of the Buyer are not subject to any deed of trust, mortgage, security interest, or other lien or claim of any nature whatsoever.

5.9 *Complete Disclosure*. This Agreement and the agreements and instruments related hereto do not contain any untrue statement of a material fact by the Buyer. This Agreement and such related agreements and instruments do not omit to state any material fact necessary in order to make the statements made herein or therein, in light of the circumstances under which they are made, not misleading.

Article VI

INFORMATION AND CONFIDENTIALITY

6.1 *Provision of Information Relating to Seller*. Prior to the execution of this Agreement, the Shareholder and the Seller have made available to the Buyer information relating to the Seller, including, without limitation, financial statements and records, depreciation schedules, lists of equipment, copies of contracts and agreements, and access to the properties, assets and operations of the Seller. To the best knowledge of the Seller and the Shareholder, all such information is substantially correct and complete. From and after the date of this Agreement and continuing through Closing, the Seller and the Shareholder will continue to make available to the Buyer all information required hereunder or otherwise reasonably requested by the Buyer with respect to the Seller.

6.2 *Confidentiality*. The Buyer acknowledges that all information with respect to the Seller made available prior to and subsequent to the date of this Agreement and through the date of Closing is confidential. The Buyer shall use such information only for the purpose of evaluating the proposed transactions hereunder. In the event the transactions provided for in this Agreement fail to close for any reason whatsoever, the Buyer will promptly return all such information to the Shareholder, including any extracts, copies or analyses based thereon which were prepared by the Buyer. The Buyer will not use, nor will it permit any third party to use, any of such information in any manner which is competitive with or injurious to the Seller.

6.3 *Provision of Information Relating to Buyer.* The Buyer has provided certain information to the Shareholder, including financial statements and other information relating to the ability of the Buyer to carry out his obligations hereunder. The Buyer represents and warrants that such information is complete and accurate, and the Shareholder and the Seller agree that all such information is to be treated as confidential and will be used only for the purpose of evaluating their decision to consummate the transactions provided for herein.

6.4 *Contacts with Third Parties.* The existence of this Agreement and the transactions provided for herein are confidential. Public announcements relating to this Agreement shall be made only pursuant to mutual agreement of the parties hereto. Prior to the time of any such public announcement, the Buyer shall not disclose to any third party that it is contemplating the purchase of the Assets, but the Seller agrees that it will at mutually agreeable times arrange for interviews by the Buyer, at which a representative of the Seller may be present, with key employees, suppliers, and customers of the Seller. The Buyer agrees to conduct such interviews in such manner as to avoid any interference with the Seller's relationships with such persons and otherwise subject to such reasonable constraints as are requested by the Shareholder.

Article VII

CONSULTING AND NONCOMPETITION AGREEMENTS

At the time of Closing, the Shareholder, individually, will enter into the following agreements:

7.1 *Consulting Agreement.* A consulting agreement in the form attached hereto as Exhibit D (the "Consulting Agreement") providing for substantially full-time consulting services to be rendered by the Shareholder to the Buyer for a period of 60 days after Closing and for part-time services to be rendered thereafter upon a schedule mutually agreeable to the Buyer and the Shareholder.

7.2 *Noncompetition Covenant.* The Shareholder (as well as the Seller) shall further enter into an agreement in the form attached hereto as Exhibit E (the "Noncompetition Covenant") whereby they will agree not to compete with the purchased business within a radius of 250 miles of the present principal place of business of the Seller for a period of five years from and after the time of Closing. The sum of $250,000 shall be paid at closing by the Buyer to the Shareholder in consideration of this noncompetition covenant.

Article VIII

CONDITIONS TO CLOSING

The obligations of the parties to close the transactions provided for herein are subject to the following conditions, as well as to any other conditions expressed or implied in this Agreement.

8.1 *Shareholder's and Seller's Conditions.* The obligations of the Shareholder and the Seller are subject to the following conditions:

(a) All representations, warranties, covenants, and other agreements contained herein on the part of the Buyer will be true and correct at the time of Closing.

(b) The Shareholder and the Seller will be reasonably satisfied with the financial ability of the Buyer to honor its obligations pursuant to the Promissory Note.

(c) No lawsuit, governmental action, or other legal proceeding shall have been commenced which shall materially interfere with the ability of the parties to consummate the transactions provided for herein.

8.2 *Buyer's Conditions.* The obligations of the Buyer to complete the transactions provided for herein are subject to the following conditions:

(a) All representations, warranties, covenants, and other agreements contained herein on the part of the Shareholder and the Seller will be true and correct at the time of Closing.

(b) No lawsuit, governmental action, or other legal proceeding shall have been commenced which shall materially interfere with the ability of the parties to consummate the transactions provided for herein.

(c) Buyer will have completed an investigation and examination of the Seller, the results of which will be satisfactory to the Buyer in its sole discretion.

(d) The book value of the Seller will be not less than the amount shown on the most recent balance sheet included in the Financial Statements.

(e) The Buyer will be reasonably satisfied as to the willingness of the key employees of the Seller to continue working for the Buyer after the Closing hereunder.

Article IX

CLOSING

The Closing of all transactions provided for herein will occur at the offices of legal counsel for the Buyer at 10:00 a.m. on [date] (the "Closing"). The transactions at Closing, when effective, will be deemed to be effective as of the opening of business on the day of Closing, except as otherwise specifically provided at the time of Closing. All actions to be taken at Closing will be considered to be taken simultaneously, and no document, agreement, or instrument will be considered to be delivered until all such items which are to be delivered at the Closing have been executed and delivered. At the Closing, the following actions will occur:

9.1 *Certificates.* The Buyer, the Shareholder, and the Seller will each, respectively, execute a certificate stating that all representations and warranties made by them respectively in this Agreement continue to be true as of the time of Closing.

9.2 *Seller's Legal Opinion.* The Shareholder will deliver to the Buyer an opinion of Shareholder's and Seller's legal counsel, in form reasonably satisfactory to the Buyer, opining favorably as to the matters set forth in Sections 4.1 and 4.2 and, to the best of such counsel's knowledge, to the matters in Section 4.3 of this Agreement.

9.3 *Assignment and Bill of Sale.* The Seller will execute and deliver to the Buyer an assignment and bill of sale, in form satisfactory to the Seller, transferring good and marketable title to all of the Assets to the Buyer free and clear of any liens or other adverse interests.

9.4 *Assignment of Intangibles and Contracts.* The Seller will execute such further assignments or other transfer documents as may be necessary to transfer all intangible Assets to the Buyer, including consents from third parties to the extent necessary to provide valid contract assignments. The Shareholder will confirm his prior transfer to the Seller of all information necessary to Seller's business.

9.5 *Assumption of Assumed Liabilities.* The Buyer will execute an assumption of liabilities, in form satisfactory to the Seller and the Shareholder, assuming and agreeing to pay all of the Assumed Liabilities in the ordinary course of the Buyer's business from and after the time of closing.

9.6 *Purchase Price.* The Buyer will pay the balance of the purchase price for the Assets by delivery of $750,000 in cash or certified funds, by wire transfer, or in other form satisfactory to the Seller, and by execution and delivery of the promissory note to the Seller.

9.7 *Security Agreement.* The Buyer shall execute and deliver the Security Agreement and shall execute and deliver a customary Uniform Commercial Code financing statement fully executed in form suitable for recording.

9.8 *Noncompetition Covenant.* The Seller and the Shareholder shall execute the Noncompetition Covenant.

9.9 *Noncompetition Payment.* The Buyer shall pay to the Shareholder the sum of $250,000 in cash or certified funds, by wire transfer, or in other form satisfactory to the Shareholder in consideration of the noncompetition covenant.

9.10 *Corporate Authorization.* The Buyer shall provide such corporate authorization as the Seller and the Shareholder may reasonably request for the purpose of verifying the validity of all instruments and security documents delivered at the time of closing by the Buyer.

9.11 *Tax Allocations.* The parties shall mutually agree to a schedule showing allocations of the purchase price to the various Assets, which allocations shall be consistent with Section 1060 of the Internal Revenue Code and the Regulations thereunder.

9.12 *Subordination Agreement.* The parties shall execute the Subordination Agreement in form satisfactory to Buyer's lending bank, in accordance with Section 2.4.

9.13 *Consulting Agreement.* The Shareholder and the Buyer shall execute the Consulting Agreement.

9.14 *Other Acts.* The parties will execute any other documents reasonably required to carry out the intent of this Agreement.

Article X

TERMINATION

This Agreement will terminate in accordance with the following provisions.

10.1 *Failure to Close.* If the purchase and sale provided for herein fails to close by the date provided in Article IX above, then this Agreement shall terminate, unless the parties have, by mutual agreement, extended the time for Closing in writing. Termination shall not release any party of any liability for damages arising out of the breach, if any, of this Agreement, except as provided below.

10.2 *Failure of Condition.* If this Agreement terminates by reason of the failure of any condition provided for herein to be satisfied at the time of Closing, and if the failure to satisfy such condition occurs without material fault on the part of either party hereto, then this Agreement shall terminate without liability on the part of either party hereto, except that the confidentiality provisions set forth in Sections 6.2 and 6.3 shall remain in effect.

10.3 *Termination by Agreement.* If the parties hereto agree to terminate this Agreement, such termination shall be effective without liability to either party hereto.

Article XI

MUTUAL INDEMNIFICATION

Each of the parties hereto agrees to indemnify and hold harmless each of the other parties against any loss resulting from a violation of this Agreement on the part of the indemnifying party. Such indemnification obligation shall include indemnification for any costs reasonably incurred by the indemnified party, including, without limitation, legal costs and reasonable attorneys fees. However, no right to indemnification shall arise hereunder unless the aggregate of all indemnified losses of any party hereto (net of any losses of the other party which are subject to indemnification) exceeds the sum of $25,000.

Article XII

POST-CLOSING OPERATIONS

From and after the time of Closing, the Buyer agrees as follows:

12.1 *Release of Shareholder.* The Buyer and the Seller will utilize their best efforts to cause the Shareholder to be released from any guarantees or any other contingent obligations which the Shareholder may have with respect to the liabilities of the Seller. Without limiting the generality of the foregoing, the Seller will advise all lenders, lessors, and suppliers, at the time of renewing any existing leases, loans, lines of credit, or other obligations, that the Shareholder is no longer responsible for the obligations of the acquired business.

12.2 *Operations in Ordinary Course.* The Buyer shall continue to operate the acquired business in the ordinary course, fulfilling all contracts and other obligations which have been properly disclosed hereunder and which are not yet completed as of the time of Closing. The Buyer will maintain in effect all insurance policies, or will establish substantially similar coverage, with respect to any liabilities of the Seller for which the Shareholder or the Seller may have responsibility.

12.3 *Reports.* For so long as any amount remains outstanding pursuant to the Promissory Note, the Buyer will cause copies of its annual financial statements to be delivered to the Shareholder promptly after the preparation of such statements.

Article XIII

GENERAL PROVISIONS

The following general provisions shall apply to this Agreement.

13.1 *Survival of Agreement.* This Agreement, and all terms, warranties, and provisions hereof will be true and correct as of the time of Closing and will survive the Closing for a period of three years.

13.2 *Notices.* All notices required or permitted hereunder or under any related agreement or instrument (unless such related agreement or instrument otherwise provides) will be deemed delivered when delivered personally or mailed, by certified mail, return receipt requested, or registered mail, to the respective party at the following addresses or to such other address as each respective party may in writing hereafter designate:

(a) To Shareholder:

_____

_____

_____

(b) To Buyer:

_____

_____

_____

(c) To Seller:

_____

_____

_____

13.3 *Successors and Assigns.* This Agreement will be binding upon the parties hereto and their respective successors, personal representatives, heirs and assigns. However, no party hereto will have any right to assign any of its obligations pursuant to this Agreement, except with the prior written consent of all of the other parties.

13.4 *Merger.* This Agreement and the exhibits and other documents, agreements, and instruments related hereto, set forth the entire agreement of the parties with respect to the subject matter hereof and may not be amended or modified except in writing subscribed to by all such parties.

13.5 *Governing Law.* This Agreement is entered into in the State of [name of State], it will be performed within such state, and all issues arising hereunder shall be governed in all respects by the laws of such state.

13.6 *Obligations to Brokers.* No party hereto has incurred any obligation for the payment of any brokerage commission, finder's fee, or any other similar obligation relating to this Agreement or the consummation of the transactions provided for herein.

13.7 *Modification or Severance.* In the event that any provision of this Agreement is found by any court or other authority of competent jurisdiction to be illegal or unenforceable, such provision shall be severed or modified to the extent necessary to render it enforceable and as so severed or modified, this Agreement will remain in full force and effect.

13.8 *Captions.* The captions in this Agreement are included for convenience only and shall not in any way affect the interpretation of any of the provisions hereof.

IN WITNESS WHEREOF, the parties have read and entered into this Agreement as of the date above written.

BUYER:

By: _____

SHAREHOLDER:

_____

SELLER:

By: _____

LIST OF EXHIBITS

Exhibit A   Promissory Note
Exhibit B   Pledge Agreement
Exhibit C   Subordination Agreement
Exhibit D   Consulting Agreement
Exhibit E   Noncompetition Covenant

Index